THE COLLECTED COURSES OF
THE ACADEMY OF EUROPEAN LAW

Volume XXX/3

Data at the Boundaries of European Law

THE COLLECTED COURSES OF THE ACADEMY OF EUROPEAN LAW

Edited by: Professor Neha Jain, Professor Claire Kilpatrick, Professor Sarah Nouwen, and Professor Joanne Scott

Assistant Editor: Joyce Davies

The Academy of European Law is housed at the European University Institute in Florence, Italy. The Academy holds annual advanced-level summer courses focusing on topical, cutting-edge issues in Human Rights Law and The Law of the European Union. The courses are taught by highly qualified scholars and practitioners in a highly interactive environment. General courses involve the examination of the field as a whole through a particular thematic, conceptual, or philosophical lens or look at a theme in the context of the overall body of law. Specialized courses bring together a number of speakers exploring a specific theme in depth. Together, they are published as monographs and edited volumes in the Collected Courses of the Academy of European Law series. The Collected Courses series has been published by Oxford University Press since 2000. The series contains publications on both foundational and pressing issues in human rights law and the law of the European Union.

OTHER TITLES IN THE SERIES INCLUDE:

Legal Mobilization for Human Rights
Edited by Gráinne de Búrca

Justifying Contract in Europe
Political Philosophies of European Contract Law
Martijn W. Hesselink

The UK's Withdrawal from the EU: A Legal Analysis
Michael Dougan

Reframing Human Rights in a Turbulent Era
Gráinne de Búrca

Contemporary Challenges to EU Legality
Edited by Claire Kilpatrick and Joanne Scott

New Legal Approaches to Studying the Court of Justice
Revisiting Law in Context
Edited by Claire Kilpatrick and Joanne Scott

EU Law Beyond EU Borders
The Extraterritorial Reach of EU Law
Edited by Marise Cremona and Joanne Scott

Data at the Boundaries of European Law

Edited by

DEIRDRE CURTIN
MARIAVITTORIA CATANZARITI

OXFORD
UNIVERSITY PRESS

OXFORD
UNIVERSITY PRESS

Great Clarendon Street, Oxford, OX2 6DP,
United Kingdom

Oxford University Press is a department of the University of Oxford.
It furthers the University's objective of excellence in research, scholarship,
and education by publishing worldwide. Oxford is a registered trade mark of
Oxford University Press in the UK and in certain other countries

First Edition published in 2023

Published in the United States of America by Oxford University Press
198 Madison Avenue, New York, NY 10016, United States of America

British Library Cataloguing in Publication Data

Data available

Library of Congress Control Number: 2022949286

ISBN 978–0–19–887419–5

DOI: 10.1093/oso/9780198874195.001.0001

Printed and bound by
CPI Group (UK) Ltd, Croydon, CR0 4YY

Contents

Notes on Contributors

Mariavittoria Catanzariti is currently Research Associate and former Jean Monnet Fellow at the Robert Schuman Centre for Advanced Studies (at the European University Institute), Adjunct Professor of Law and Ethics of Innovation and Sustainability at LUISS University, as well as Adjunct Professor of Regional Human Rights Systems at University of Padua. An attorney-at-law since 2010, she obtained a PhD in European Law in 2011 from Roma Tre University and the Italian qualification as Associate Professor in Legal Sociology in 2018. Her main research interests lie in the interaction of digital transformation and the information society with law. Her publications cover different legal areas such as privacy and data protection, law and technologies, human rights, and legal sociology.

Deirdre Curtin is Professor of European Law and Dean of Graduate Studies at the European University Institute, where she is also the Director of the Centre for Judicial Cooperation at the Robert Schuman Centre. Prior to joining the EUI, she held the Chair in European Law and Governance at the University of Amsterdam. She is an elected member of the Royal Netherlands Academy of Arts and Sciences (KNAW, 2003), of the Royal Irish Academy of Arts and Sciences (2020), and a laureate of the Spinoza prize (NWO, 2007) for research in the field of European law and governance. Her research interests are in the fields of European institutions and European administrative law with a particular interest in justice and home affairs, and data protection.

Marieke de Goede is Professor of the Politics of Security Cultures at the University of Amsterdam and Dean of the Faculty of Humanities. She has published widely on counter-terrorism and security practices in Europe, with specific attention to the role of financial data. She held a Consolidator Grant of the European Research Council (ERC) with the theme: FOLLOW: Following the Money from Transaction to Trial (www.projectfollow.org). De Goede is i.a. co-editor of *Secrecy and Methods in Security Research: A Guide to Qualitative Fieldwork* (2020) and co-editor of the special issue on 'The Politics of the List,' in *Environment and Planning D: Society and Space* (2016). De Goede is a Board member of the European International Studies Association and Honorary Professor at Durham University (UK).

Paul De Hert is Vice-Dean of the Faculty of Law and Criminology at the Vrije Universiteit Brussel (VUB), where he is Director of the research group on Human Rights (FRC) and former Director of the research group Law Science Technology and Society (LSTS) and of the Department of Interdisciplinary Studies of Law. He is also currently Associate Professor at the Tilburg Institute for Law, Technology, and Society (TILT).

Mireille Hildebrandt is a Research Professor of Interfacing Law and Technology at the Faculty of Law and Criminology of Vrije Universiteit Brussel (VUB) and Co-Director of the research group of Law Science Technology and Society (LSTS). She is also professor of law at the Science Faculty of Radboud University in Nijmegen in the department of computer science. She was awarded an ERC Advanced Grant on 'Counting as a Human Being in the Era of Computational Law' (2019–2024). She has published five scientific monographs, 23 edited volumes, and over 120 scientific articles. Her research is focused on the nexus of philosophy of law and philosophy of technology, enquiring into the implications of automated decision-making and artificial intelligence on the law and the rule of law.

Ida Koivisto is an Associate Professor of Public Law at the University of Helsinki. She specializes in administrative law, socio-legal studies, and transparency theory. Previously, she was a visiting professor in the Center for Ethics at the University of Toronto, professor of public law at the University of Tampere, Max Weber postdoctoral fellow at the European University Institute, and Global postdoctoral fellow at New York University. Her current research is focused on the digitalization of public administration and its legal and theoretical implications, in particular algorithmic transparency. She is the author of *The Transparency Paradox – Questioning an Ideal* (2022).

Niovi Vavoula is Senior Lecturer (Associate Professor) in Migration and Security at Queen Mary University of London. She was previously a post-doctoral Research Assistant at the same University and adjunct Professor at the London School of Economics and Political Science (2017-2018). Since 2014, she is Associate Editor of the *New Journal of European Criminal Law*, and a member of the ODYSSEUS Academic Network for Legal Studies on Immigration and Asylum in Europe, as well the European Criminal Law Academic Network. She has held visiting positions at Université Libre de Bruxelles (2014), George Washington University (2022 – Society of Legal Scholars grantee), and European University Institute (2022). She publishes in the areas of EU immigration law, criminal law, and data protection law and has acted as an expert consultant for the European Commission, the European Parliament, the Fundamental Rights Agency, and the European Council on Refugees and Exiles.

1

Data at the Boundaries of (European) Law: A First Cut

Mariavittoria Catanzariti and Deirdre Curtin

1. Introduction

In Europe, data-driven governance, both public and private, has taken root in myriad ways. Legislative responses echo and follow practice by both public and private actors, and grapple with the complex ways they intermingle both at the national level as well as that of the supranational European Union (EU) level. The EU has been itself 'mimetic' in certain legislative trajectories it has followed in the past decade and more.[1] In certain fields its stance is optimistic as to the role that data gathering, retention, and access can and should play in European governance. Banks play a role in combatting terrorist financing, airline carriers assist in tracking free movement, internet intermediaries in supporting law enforcement, and private companies receive support when combatting fraud. The extent to which Europe's governance has become data-driven is striking. The EU itself sees some of its data regulatory measures as truly world leading.[2] The most obvious example of this is in the field of data protection (GDPR) but more recent legislative initiatives place far reaching public obligations on private actors, for example, in the security field (TERREG), and also notably in the EU's draft regulation for artificial intelligence (the AI Act) as well as the Digital Services Act.[3] In these examples, a certain optimism is detected in the

[1] De Hert, Chapter 4, this volume.

[2] Kuner, 'The Internet and the Global Reach of EU Law', in M. Cremona and J. Scott (eds), *EU Law Beyond EU Borders: The Extraterritorial Reach of EU Law* (2019); A. Bradford, *The Brussels Effect: How the European Union Rules the World* (2020) 131; Greenleaf, 'The "Brussels Effect" of the EU's "AI Act" on Data Privacy Outside Europe', 171 *Privacy Laws & Business International Report* (2021) 1, at 3–7; Svantesson, 'Article 3. Territorial scope', in C. Kuner, L. A. Bygrave and C. Docksey (eds), *The EU General Data Protection Regulation (GDPR): A Commentary* (2019) 74.

[3] European Commission, 'Proposal for a Regulation of the European Parliament and of the Council laying down harmonised rules on Artificial Intelligence (Artificial Intelligence Act) and amending certain Union legislative acts', COM/2021/206 final; European Commission, 'Proposal for a Regulation of the European Parliament and of the Council on a Single Market For Digital Services (Digital Services Act) and amending Directive 2000/31/EC', COM/2020/825 final. On the role of private actors

Mariavittoria Catanzariti and Deirdre Curtin, *Data at the Boundaries of (European) Law: A First Cut* In: *Data at the Boundaries of European Law*. Edited by: Deirdre Curtin and Mariavittoria Catanzariti, Oxford University Press.
 DOI: 10.1093/oso/9780198874195.003.0001

underlying assumption that increased access to data will lead to better enforcement outcomes both at the European level and at the national level. It seems that data-driven Europe within and at the boundaries of European law has come squarely into its own.

The ambition (and practice) of the GDPR in particular is to be a regulatory model for the world.[4] While this effect should not be reduced to a unilateral exercise of EU power,[5] the fact remains that EU legislation in digital matters exerts direct and indirect influences on public and private actors around the world. Recent examples of this influence include the requirements that data controllers must observe when transferring data to non-EU jurisdictions not covered by an adequacy decision[6] and the frequent mention of the GDPR by legislators in various Latin American countries.[7] Institutional practice that has developed over many years in the field of EU external relations adopts individual country-specific adequacy rulings for third countries. This guarantees that third-country legislation/regulation is up to European standards and is required before data can be shared beyond the EU. This multiplication effect makes it very difficult for third countries to avoid negotiating arrangements that are basically EU law compliant. Ignoring or altering compliance brings with it the risk of the EU not agreeing to share data with them. This is at issue presently regarding the UK post Brexit, which announced its intention to move away from strict GDPR compliance (which it already adopted into its own legislation before its EU exit) for what it terms a more 'common-sense' approach. How this will fare in terms of the EU accepting its 'adequacy' will likely be a highly politicized and salient saga that could run over (many) years and will

in enforcing the AI Act, see Veale and Zuiderveen Borgesius, 'Demystifying the Draft EU Artificial Intelligence Act —Analysing the Good, the Bad, and the Unclear Elements of the Proposed Approach', 22 *Computer Law Review International* (2021) 97; Ebers, 'Standardizing AI—The Case of the European Commission's Proposal for an Artificial Intelligence Act', in L. A. Di Matteo, M. Cannarsa and C. Poncibò (eds), *The Cambridge Handbook of Artificial Intelligence: Global Perspectives on Law and Ethics* (2022). On the Digital Services Act as a mechanism for fostering the responsibility of private actors, see, e.g., Carvalho, Lima and Farinha, 'Introduction to the Digital Services Act, Content Moderation and Consumer Protection', 3 *Revista de Direito e Tecnologia* (2021) 71.

[4] Data protection law has been proposed as a paradigmatic instance of the global impact of EU law: Bradford (n. 2). This impact of EU law beyond the physical borders of the Union has implications for the promotion of EU fundamental values and to the definition of its legislative boundaries: Kuner (n. 2).

[5] Schwartz, 'Global Data Privacy: The EU Way', 94 *New York University Law Review* (2020) 771.

[6] See further, European Data Protection Board, 'Recommendations 01/2020 on Measures That Supplement Transfer Tools to Ensure Compliance with the EU Level of Protection of Personal Data' (2020).

[7] See for example, Bertoni, 'Convention 108 and the GDPR: Trends and Perspectives in Latin America', 40 *Computer Law & Security Review* (2021), 1.

have obvious implications also in the context of law enforcement and security data sharing as well as trade.[8]

Data sharing in the context of law enforcement and security by and to the EU is a subject about which considerably less has been written than on the GDPR (or only within highly specialized circles).[9] In substance it is a highly developed practice with its origins in soft law but more recently in some actual hard law. It is infused with optimism for the role of data and data interoperability in particular to thwart terrorism and assist in the arrest and prosecution of suspected criminals, not to speak of (illegal) immigrants. It is used both internally by the EU and its own institutions and agencies as well as by its Member States and externally with third countries under specific institutional arrangements (for example, by Europol with third countries).[10] Unlike the GDPR, it is a subject straddling the border of European law. Through specific regulations and international agreements (e.g. Terrorist Finance Tracking Programme (TFTP)) data sharing stands with one foot in European law, but with the other foot very much out in terms of how actual arrangements work in practice (non-regulatory interoperability—the so-called black box).

The debate on data within and beyond European law is also, given the nature of data, global, even if the solutions are often not global. Rather, they are national and increasingly supranational.[11] Part of what this book is about is

[8] Early signs of this politicization were seen when the European Parliament approved a resolution expressing a series of concerns about the then-forthcoming adequacy decision relating to the UK data protection regime: EP Resolution of 21 May 2021 on the adequate protection of personal data by the United Kingdom (2021/2594(RSP)). Since then, the British government has opened a public consultation on reforms to the UK data protection regime, with the stated goal of moving away from the general model of the GDPR: Department for Digital, Culture, Media & Sport, 'Data: A New Direction' (2021) Public Consultation.

[9] See for example, Galli, 'Interoperable Databases: New Cooperation Dynamics in the EU AFSJ?', 26 *European Public Law* (2020) 109; Purtova, 'Between the GDPR and the Police Directive: Navigating through the Maze of Information Sharing in Public–Private Partnerships', 8 *International Data Privacy Law* (2018) 52; Blasi Casagran, 'Fundamental Rights Implications of Interconnecting Migration and Policing Databases in the EU', 21 *Human Rights Law Review* (2021) 433; Dimitrova and Quintel, 'Technological Experimentation Without Adequate Safeguards? Interoperable EU Databases and Access to the Multiple Identity Detector by SIRENE Bureaux', in D. Hallinan, R. Leenes, and P. De Hert (eds), *Data Protection and Privacy: Data Protection and Artificial Intelligence* (2021) 217; V. Mitsegalis and N. Vavoula (eds), *Surveillance and Privacy in the Digital Age. European, Transatlantic and Global Perspectives* (2021).

[10] F. Coman-Kund, *European Union Agencies as Global Actors. A Legal Study of the European Aviation Safety Agency, Frontex and Europol* (2018), at 231–249.

[11] See, for example, Council of Europe's modernized Convention 108 has been proposed as a compromise solution for a global data protection regime: Mantelero, 'The Future of Data Protection: Gold Standard vs. Global Standard', 40 *Computer Law & Security Review* (2021) 1. While there is a considerable overlap between the parties to Convention 108 and the members of the EU, the convention has nevertheless managed to extend its reach beyond the Union and beyond Europe itself: Makulilo, 'African Accession to Council of Europe Privacy Convention 108', 41 *Datenschutz und Datensicherheit* (DuD) (2017) 364. Nevertheless, Greenleaf, 'How Far Can Convention 108+ 'Globalise'? Prospects for Asian Accessions', 40 *Computer Law & Security Review* (2021) 1, argues that there is a considerable number of countries that would not be able to meet the accession standards for Convention 108.

indeed the specifically European take on how to regulate the use of data in binding legislation. This will be enforced through national and supranational executive power as well as in the courts and by supervisory authorities. This is not just GDPR-related. In fact, the GDPR is not at the centre of what we—the authors of this volume—analyse, as this has been done very extensively elsewhere. The core of what we wish to uncover does not merely relate to data protection and/or privacy but to underlying systemic practices and the implications for law as we understand it in a non-digital context.

Making wider European institutional and code practices visible in and around the EU, but not exclusively so, can contribute to a much wider debate on several salient issues of substance and structure. In our introductory chapter to this book, we wish to consider more broadly what it means to speak of data at the borders or boundaries of the law in general and in Europe. This constitutes a red thread that informs some of the specific choices made in individual chapters throughout the book that we return to in our last paragraph. We will first dissect the meaning of the words 'boundary', 'border', 'law', and 'data' before moving on to analyse the more general approach of the EU not only regarding specific (draft) regulations but also to the role of law more generally in the European integration process. We then finish with an evaluation of data-led law in the EU system and ask the following questions. What has data-led law meant for individuals in terms of their rights? What has it meant for institutions in terms of their accountabilities? What are the challenges facing the EU in this regard in the coming five or ten years? What are the more general global challenges in this regard?

2. Data from Boundaries to Borders

The idea of boundaries is inherent to legal rationality. The law in fact distinguishes an inside from an outside to define itself. It generally aims to shape a locked system in the sense that it limits itself with regard to other social systems and self-defines its scope and the remit of its relevance. Only the law says what the law is. The concept of boundary is thus quintessential to the concept of law. Boundaries of the law can be of various types and forms. The law not only asserts its authority with respect to what is non-law, but also within itself across

Consequently, it seems somewhat unlikely that Convention 108 will become a global standard in the near future.

different areas.[12] It constantly differentiates its functioning, rationales, and by-products in various modalities. Boundaries of the law lie in between the law and what the law excludes from itself or lie beyond its remit. Boundaries have a normative meaning, as they describe the way of being of the law in its positioning towards other relevant fields, such as politics, ethics, technology, and economy. They are not fixed and can change over time on different grounds as a measure of asserting authority or re-establishing order.[13] An obvious example is the legal concept of territory as the physical area where a specific legal order is established; another is the tension between deterritorialization and re-territorialization of legal spaces in times of crises, for example, the migration crisis or the securitization of Europe.[14] A logical starting point to define a boundary for the law is the use of language and the way definitions are built up. The law defines its own vocabulary. It is self-standing and autonomous. In terms of semantics, the fact that the law should be informed by the context that it aims to rule determines its own legal definition of the context as well as its own meaning or translation of reality into its own language.

This book mainly deals with a type of boundary that has profoundly shaped a new way of lawmaking: automation combined with personal data. In other words, this refers to the way algorithms make use of personal data to classify individuals, predict their behaviour, and make decisions about them.[15] It seeks to explore different layers of decision making using personal data—national, supranational, transnational—that are woven together with data-driven techniques and have differential impacts upon legal relationships and governance. In this data-driven field, the boundary of law and technologies is narrow and permeable, such that technology may replace the law. First, as one of our contributors, Hildebrandt (Chapter 2) has reminded us (in *Law for Computer Scientists and Other Folk*), legal design is not enough to ensure a legal disciplinary domain.[16]

The awareness that technological determinism may impair individual freedom of choice and information—e.g. the need to preserve human agency—makes urgent the integration of legal protection by design in human rights

[12] N. Luhmann, *The Differentiation of Society* (1982) 122.

[13] G. Popescu, *Bordering and Ordering the Twenty-first Century: Understanding Borders* (2011).

[14] See further: M. Fichera, *The Foundations of the EU as a Polity* (2018) at 132, 154; V. Squire, *Europe's Migration Crisis. Border Deaths and Human Dignity* (2020), at 15–42; J. Martín Ramírez, 'The Refugee Issue in the Frame of the European Security: A Realistic Approach', in J. Martín Ramírez and J. Biziewski (eds), *Security and Defense in Europe* (2020) 47.

[15] G. Sartor and F. Lagioia, *The Impact of the General Data Protection Regulation on Artificial Intelligence* (2020), https://www.europarl.europa.eu/RegData/etudes/STUD/2020/641530/EPRS_STU(2020)641530_EN.pdf (last visited 9 February 2022).

[16] M. Hildebrandt, *Law for Computer Scientists and Other Folk* (2020), at 267–270.

protection with research on and the architecture of data-driven systems.[17] Second, many areas where automation is applied and are currently not covered by the law in fact produce legal effects. Article 22(1) GDPR for example is explicit in its reach over decisions that produce 'legal effects concerning [the data subject] or similarly significantly affects him or her'.[18] As De Hert correctly points out in Chapter 4 this results in a lack of creativity: 'Is human intervention and the prohibition to use sensitive data all provided for by this provision that is needed to regulate profiling well?' It is then clear enough that data accuracy cannot be the exhaustive response to the lack of interpretability of an automated process, as explained by Hildebrandt: 'we should not buy into the narrative that proprietary software may be more opaque but will nevertheless be more accurate'.[19]

The transformation of human as well as of global relationships into data lies unquestionably at the crossroads of salient challenges for law and society.[20] Data may affect the legal dynamics in at least three ways: as the specific object of regulation; as a source of the law; and finally, as informing the functioning of legal patterns (not formally included in an actual law). These cases are examples of data-driven law but to varying degrees and in different ways. The first case specifically refers to regulatory models of data flows and data governance;[21] the second case relies on forms of personalized laws or tailored contracts targeting certain subjects;[22] and the third case is instead related to data-driven legal design combined with AI applications that are used in diverse areas of the law, such as predictive policing, insurance, and public administration.[23]

[17] See further on this distinction, ibid. 270–277 and 302–315.

[18] On the meaning of 'similarly significant' in the GDPR, see Bygrave, 'Article 22. Automated Individual Decision-Making, Including Profiling', in C. Kuner, L. A. Bygrave, and C. Docksey (eds), *The EU General Data Protection Regulation (GDPR): A Commentary* (2020) 522.

[19] Hildebrandt, Chapter 2, this volume.

[20] S. Zuboff, *The Age of Surveillance Capitalism. The Fight for a Human Future at the New Frontier of Power* (2019).

[21] The most relevant instruments for this volume's discussions are the GDPR (Regulation (EU) 2016/179, OJ 2016 L 119/1), the Law Enforcement Directive (LED: Directive (EU) 2016/680, OJ 2016 L 119/89), the Regulation on the free flow of non-personal data (Regulation (EU) 2018/1807, OJ 2018 L 303/59), the Open Data Directive (Directive (EU) 2019/1024, OJ 2019 L 172/56), and the Network and Information Security Directive (Directive (EU) 2016/1148, OJ 2016 L 194/1). To these we can add several ongoing legislative procedures: the Data Governance Act (Commission, 'Proposal for a Regulation of the European Parliament and of the Council on European data governance', COM/2020/767 final), recently adopted as Regulation (EU) 868/2022 of the European Parliament and of the Council of 30 May 2022 on European data governance and amending Regulation (EU) 2018/1724 (hereinafter, Data Governance Act); the Digital Services Act (European Commission, COM/2020/825 final); and the AI Act (European Commission, COM/2021/206 final).

[22] Casey and Niblett, 'A Framework for the New Personalization of Law', 86 *University of Chicago Law Review* (2019) 333, at 335.

[23] K. Yeung and M. Lodge (eds), *Algorithmic Regulation* (2019).

The processing of huge amounts of data increasingly shapes the morphology of regulatory instruments. At the same time, algorithm-based regulation, and algorithmic personalization of legal rules (so-called granular norms) are instead one of the key portals through which data disruptively enters and modifies legal rationality. The collection of data inevitably acts as a new source for the law. What is at stake is not only the autonomy of the law in managing 'datafied' relationships and phenomena, but also the certainty of the law in its general applicability *erga omnes* and not only in relation to targeted/profiled subjects.

In terms of defining data in an operational fashion, a European perspective arguably adds value. The EU regulatory quest for a data strategy recently led to the very first definition of the term 'data' in a legal instrument. Both the Data Governance Act and the Data Act define data as 'any digital representation of acts, facts or information or any compilation of such acts, facts or information, including in the form of sound, visual or audiovisual recording'.[24] The relevance of the digitalization itself represents the threshold of the law seeking to incorporate data into its domain. Data first of all sets the boundaries of the law, before a binary approach follows with data either personal or non-personal in nature. In recent years the regulatory tendency was indeed quite the opposite. Data protection reform, including the GDPR and its sister Law Enforcement Directive,[25] represent a truly monumental set of rules seeking to harmonize data privacy laws across Member States. Conversely, the Regulation on the free flow of non-personal data was merely a residual piece of legislation applicable only to data that is non-personal. As a result, the processing of non-personal data is not subject to the obligations imposed on data controllers by the GDPR and its offspring. This is a clear example of how the processes of differentiation within the law precisely aim to identify certain relevant patterns that are made different by other patterns according to how they are matched with their specific normative consequences.[26] This has been, for example, the approach to data regulation across Europe, modelled with the GDPR as the foundation. The GDPR has been constructed around the definition of personal data, but as a result, the related legal regime has also affected that of non-personal data as

[24] Article 1(1) Data Governance Act (n. 21) and Article 2(1) Data Act (Commission, 'Proposal for a Regulation of the European Parliament and of the Council on harmonized rules on fair access to and use of data (Data Act), COM/2022/68 final).

[25] See n. 21.

[26] Luhmann (n. 12), at 229. Specifically, on the issue of the European integration, see De Witte, 'Variable Geometry and Differentiation as Structural Features of the EU Legal Order', in B. De Witte, A. Ott, and E. Vos (eds), *Between Flexibility and Disintegration. The Trajectory of Differentiation in EU Law* (2017) 9.

the result of differentiation. All that exceeds the definition of personal data included in the GDPR is non-personal data,[27] but quite often data is disruptive with respect to legal definitions.[28]

One problematic issue is that the differentiation of the law is not a single act but a never-ending process, and specifically in the case of GDPR, the attempt at uniformity across Europe has encountered national specificities and legal traditions. It has also created legal frictions in the sense that it is obvious that 'personal data' inherently presents a different relevance in different legal contexts—law enforcement, intelligence sharing, fundamental rights protection. The use of a predefined legal definition risks being based on assumed facts and patterns that continue to change and are constantly differentiated by the law with respect to other social systems. In this sense, Paul De Hert recalls Teubner, arguing that 'Attempts to intervene in subsystems, even with translation, are not necessarily successful because of the resistance of these subsystems to "code" that is not theirs'.[29] This may in particular be the case when it comes machine-learning technologies that are used to process data. This compels the law to be an effective tool for the identification of new legal objects when previous differentiation processes—as in the case of personal/non-personal data—have exhausted some of their effects or are no longer adequate to represent regulatory needs.

Data shapes the boundaries of the law into a variable geometry.[30] At the same time, data is disruptive of any idea of boundaries since its very nature can blur the threshold between what is inside and what is outside the law. Sometimes, however, data moves this threshold across disciplines, territories, policy actions, humans, and machines. It is extremely hard to describe the precise geographical route of data in motion, as data is to be found in many formats and

[27] Article 1 of the Regulation (EU) 2018/1807 on the free flow of non-personal data in the EU, OJ 2018 L 303/59.

[28] One of the thorny points in the separation between personal and non-personal data appears when it comes to pseudonymization and anonymization. Before the GDPR, it was common to see actors (both technical and legal) mentioning pseudonymization as a form of anonymization, and Article 4(5) GDPR seems to be a direct response to this form of dodging, as pointed out by Tosoni, 'Article 4(5). Pseudonymisation', in C. Kuner, L. A. Bygrave, and C. Docksey (eds), *The EU General Data Protection Regulation (GDPR): A Commentary* (2020) 132. Furthermore, anonymization itself is not a stable concept, as what counts as truly anonymized data depends on the risks associated with re-identification in a given moment of time, which are themselves dependent on the technical possibilities for data deanonymization: Almada, Maranhão, and Sartor, 'Article 4 Para. 5. Pseudonymisation', in I. Spiecker gen. Döhmann, *et al.* (eds), *European General Data Protection Regulation* (2022); Finck and Pallas, 'They Who Must Not Be Identified—Distinguishing Personal from Non-Personal Data under the GDPR', 10 *International Data Privacy Law* (2020) 11.

[29] De Hert, Chapter 4, this volume.

[30] Daskal, 'The Un-territoriality of Data', 125 *Yale Law Journal* (2015) 326; Daskal, 'The Overlapping Web of Data, Territoriality and Sovereignty', in P. S. Bermann (ed.), *The Oxford Handbook of Global Legal Pluralism* (2020) 955.

in many different places. Data is shared across territories and among actors, all beyond specific nation states. In fact, the intangible character of data renders the boundaries of the law more permeable and porous to data flows in various ways. If we consider the physical boundaries of the law, data alters them because it is not based on any territorial linkage with a physical place.[31] Data is also ubiquitous in the sense that it can be used by multiple actors while being accessed everywhere irrespective of where it is located. In the context of interconnected networks, this assumption questions the traditional understanding of the association between sovereignty, jurisdiction, and territory, according to which sovereign powers have jurisdictional claims over a territory.[32] If we instead look at the way in which data reshapes the disciplinary boundaries of the law, data constantly shifts the public–private divide. Governments systematically access private sector data through their cooperation and this creates issues, for example, in terms of reuse of data for purposes other than those initially foreseen at the time of collection. The purpose limitation principle is one of the absolutely core principles of data protection according to which data can be collected for specified, explicit, and legitimate purposes but cannot be processed in a manner that is incompatible with the original purpose for which it was collected. How is that to be implemented in practice when widespread sharing, also by private actors, takes place across territorial limits?

Our contention is that the sharing of data among public actors but also with or by private actors should be regulated by specific agreements, even if this almost inevitably implies that the boundaries of legal categories traditionally belonging to specific areas of the law—such as public law, private law, international law—fade or become fuzzy. Moreover, the interaction of massive data flows with machine-learning techniques inevitably produces hybrid outcomes. Legal rationality quite often struggles to set up its own boundaries with respect to data-driven solutions that are efficient, non-time consuming, and quick to respond. Legal predictions are in fact the result of calculations applied to past data to anticipate probable legal outcomes, as Hildebrandt reminds us time and again,[33] including in her chapter in this book.

The development of AI in the field of public administration offers new opportunities to implement the principle of good administration and the

[31] J. Branch, *The Cartographic State. Maps, Territory, and the Origins of Sovereignty* (2014).

[32] C. Ryngaert, *Jurisdiction in International Law* (2015); Besson, 'Sovereignty', in *Max Planck Encyclopedias of International Law*, https://opil.ouplaw.com/view/10.1093/law:epil/9780199231690/law-9780199231690-e1472?prd=EPIL, (last visited 18 December 2021).

[33] Hildebrandt, 'Law as Computation in the Era of Artificial Legal Intelligence: Speaking Law to the Power of Statistics', 68 *University of Toronto Law Journal* (2018) 12.

functioning of public services. This should be coupled with a system of safeguards which ensure the fulfilment of fundamental rights' protection as well as specific requirements regarding the principle of good administration in terms of citizen participation, and transparency and accountability of the adopted AI-based applications. In the area of law enforcement, it is the private sector that remains at the forefront of enforcement. In this respect, automated decision-making appears to have the potential not only to enhance the operational efficiency of law enforcement and criminal justice authorities, but also to undermine fundamental rights affected by criminal procedures. The risk that a shift from post-crime policing to proactive measures based on algorithmic predictions could for instance potentially produce disparate treatment should be carefully addressed. Moreover, predictive crime solutions raise the question of their legitimacy, where AI solutions may affect the right to be presumed innocent until proved guilty.[34]

Law enforcement and policing is obviously not the only field where AI technologies have been successfully applied. AI applications have been widely deployed in different areas of the law, including insurance law, where the calculating capability of algorithms aims to prospectively target probabilities of events and certain individual propensities to experience those events in the future. This field offers relevant examples that come from behavioural policy pricing, customer experience, and coverage personalization, as well as customized claims settlement. The first is based on ubiquitous Internet of Things sensors that provide personalized data to pricing platforms, allowing, for example, safer drivers to pay less for auto insurance (usage-based insurance) and healthier people to pay less for health insurance. The second is based on mechanisms that include chat-boxes pulling on customers' geographic and social data to personalize interactions and customize events and needs (on demand-insurance). The third relies on interfaces and online adjusters that make it easier to settle and pay claims following an accident and decrease the probability of fraud. These examples are emblematic given the risk of discriminatory practices, also in terms of indirect discrimination. Here too, the biased design of AI applications may negatively impact individuals and groups.

In the long run, data-driven solutions may, however, determine convergent solutions regardless of the different surrounding legal cultures and different areas of the law. One of the most relevant examples is the National Security

[34] Mantelero and Vaciago, 'The 'Dark Side' of Big Data: Private and Public Interaction in Social Surveillance, How data collections by private entities affect governmental social control and how the EU reform on data protection responds', 14(6) *Computational Law Review International* (2013) 161.

Agency mass-surveillance scandal that saw different countries systematically violating data privacy using bulk data collection.[35] These examples link to the concerns expressed by the AI Act in different areas. The use of AI systems by law enforcement authorities can be 'characterised by a significant degree of power imbalance and may lead to surveillance'.[36] AI systems used in migration, asylum, and border control management may 'affect people who are often in [a] particularly vulnerable position and who are dependent on the outcome of the actions of the competent public authorities'.[37] In the field of employment, worker management, and access to self-employment aimed at the recruitment and selection of persons, promotion, termination or task allocation, monitoring or evaluation of persons in work-related contractual relationships, the use of AI 'may appreciably impact future career prospects and livelihoods of these persons'.[38] It is worth noting that the AI Act has identified those practices of AI that shall be prohibited.[39] Among these practices, those that are particularly relevant are those related to AI systems that: deploy 'subliminal techniques beyond a person's consciousness in order to materially distort a person's behaviour';[40] exploit any of the vulnerabilities of a social group in order to distort their behaviour;[41] are based on the evaluation of social behaviour (social scoring) or on predictions of personal or personality characteristics aimed at assessing the trustworthiness of individuals, leading to a detrimental or unfavourable treatment;[42] the real-time remote biometric identification systems in publicly accessible spaces for law enforcement purposes unless under certain limited conditions.[43] These practices are considered unacceptable because they contravene EU values and fundamental rights.

The levelling functioning of data-driven technologies, if one can call it that, makes it hard to compare the results of specific legal choices as well as those of specific legal institutions and transplants. Legal design alone cannot set up a boundary between law and technology because they are quite radically out of kilter timewise. The time of the law is almost invariably much slower than the time of technology.[44] To be subject to effective regulation, the time of the law

[35] F. Cate and J. Dempsey, *Bulk Collection. Systematic Government Access to Private-Sector Data* (2017).

[36] AI Act, Recital 38.

[37] Ibid. Recital 39.

[38] Ibid. Recital 36.

[39] Ibid. Article 5(1).

[40] Ibid. Article 5(1)(a).

[41] Ibid. Article 5(1)(b).

[42] Ibid. Article 5(1)(c).

[43] Ibid. Article 5(1)(d).

[44] However, this is not always the case, as there are situations in which technology must itself catch up with legal change, for example, when it comes to the adoption of a new legal framework such as the one

and the time of technology as a specific data-driven object of the law should be synchronized in a manner consonant with legal legitimacy. Algorithms make it possible to calculate in advance the compliance of technological performance with the law. For the law it is more complex. Only what is authorized and thus legitimate is allowed although being not necessarily possible, depending upon the personal obedience to legal rules.[45] This difference is irreducible and inevitably creates a temporal gap between the legal and the technological performance that is only addressed by what Lessig ambivalently names the *code*.[46]

The examples discussed above not only address issues of definition but also show how data increasingly pushes the boundaries of the law by creating bridges with changing contexts of relevance. Data is in fact becoming the common currency through which to measure and exchange heterogeneous values, various contexts, and different interests in the sense that it transforms experiences and facts and creates relationships that need to be regulated. This inevitably implies a blurring of possible uses for data flows that also shapes the way in which the law shall face its boundaries. According to a specific legal rationale, a certain use of data may be impeded or allowed by the law and this informs the architecture surrounding the possible consequences. Often, a certain type of data use depends on the available infrastructure and data accessibility. From a linguistic perspective, this means that the law shall increasingly incorporate descriptive tools for defining reality in its own terms, but at the same time the law risks losing its own specificity while enriching its vocabulary.

Data can in and of itself act as a boundary in the sense of constituting an overarching metaphor of the real world: the daily life connections.[47] The law needs to find new strategies to interact with other domains of knowledge, especially when it is not sufficiently clear where information comes from, as is the case with big data. To the extent that the law is capable of incorporating data into legal patterns, it guarantees itself a long life as an autonomous and independent system. Of course, the threshold between autonomy and dependency

provided by the GDPR. While technological artefacts are indeed more malleable than legal institutions, the latter are not inert actors, and the former often take some time to adjust to new circumstances, especially in the case of large-scale systems with many elements that must be updated. For further analysis of the relation between the temporal regimes of law and technology, see Bennett Moses and Zalnieriute, 'Law and Technology in the Dimension of Time', in S. Ranchordás and Y. Roznai (eds), *Time, Law, and Change: An Interdisciplinary Study* (2020).

[45] Hart, *The Concept of Law* (1961).
[46] Lessig, *Code and Other Laws of Cyberspace* (1999), 89–90.
[47] Floridi, *The Onlife Manifesto. Being Human in a Hyperconnected Era* (2014).

is very narrow and the challenge faced by the law is to ensure its autonomy while being informed and receptive towards the external environment.[48]

3. Digital Borders and Enforcement of the Law

The boundaries of the law—the dividing line between law and non-law—may at some point overlap with the concept of borders—in the sense of the outer edge of the law. This happens in particular when the scope of application of the law is at stake or when the law aims to control the flows of goods and persons. It has been put like this: 'a boundary is not merely a line but a line in a borderland. The borderland may or may not be a barrier'.[49] The main stages in the history of a boundary are the following: the political decision on the allocation of a territory; the delimitation of a boundary in a treaty; the demarcation of the boundary on the ground; the administration of a boundary.[50] The semantic shift from boundaries to borders is also inherent in the foundation of the law.[51] To build itself, the law needs to build its physical limit where one sovereignty ends, and another begins. This represents the core of each sovereign power and requires the exercise of an authority provided by law on a tangible space limited and separated from other spaces. In Carens's words, 'the power to admit or exclude aliens is inherent in sovereignty and essential for any political community'.[52]

Policies on borders are almost always a metaphor of changing times, as we are daily reminded in our newspapers no matter where we are located in the world. It was a clear metaphor during the so-called global war on terrorism and more recently with the refugee crisis, in particular in Europe but also on an ongoing basis in the US. In each crisis, borders come back strongly and play a salient role in making the relevant public authority visible. The EU recently, for example, decided to reopen borders to vaccinated travellers in the form of an app, the Green Pass, thus superseding the temporary reintroduction of internal border control during the pandemic.[53] In the EU, external borders have

[48] Luhmann, *Law as a Social System* (2004).

[49] S. B. Jones, *Boundary Making. A Handbook for Statesmen, Treaty Editors and Boundary Commissioners* (1971) 6.

[50] Ibid. 4.

[51] J. Hagen, *Borders and Boundaries* (2018); Johnson and Post, 'Law and Borders: The Rise of the Law in Cyberspace', 48(5) *Stanford Law Review* (1996) 1367; A. Riccardi and T. Natoli (eds), *Borders, Legal Spaces and Territories in Contemporary International Law* (2019).

[52] Carens, 'Aliens and Citizens. The Case for Open Borders', 49 *Revue of Politics* (1987) 251.

[53] EU Digital Covid Certificate to revive travel in Europe, https://www.etiasvisa.com/etias-news/digital-covid-certificate, (last visited 18 September 2021).

been instrumentalized to enhance security and control, although they do not belong within any notion of European sovereign power as such. Although the external borders are the borders of the countries of the EU and countries that are not members of the EU, the balance struck by the Schengen Agreement on border management has revealed failures. It underlines yet again the age-old fact that the absence of internal border controls for persons in Europe was never coupled with a common policy on asylum, immigration, and external borders.

The boundaries of the law always show their ambivalence on borders. In the case of the EU, this is significant if we consider that the external borders of the EU coincide with the borders of some Member States (for example, Ireland and its border with Northern Ireland, still part of the UK). Strengthening and upgrading the mandates of the EU agencies such as the new Frontex (European Border and Cost Guard Agency), eu-Lisa, European Union Agency for Asylum, and Europol, and also the reinforcement of EU Schengen rules has represented an alternative answer to the lack of internal borders by securing the external borders. The management of external borders, as shared competence provided by Article 77 Treaty on the Functioning of the European Union (TFEU), is in fact the bedrock of a type of composite border management with shared responsibilities. In particular, the administration of borders is the object of multiple forms of delegation from the European Commission and EU agencies in the Area of Freedom, Security and Justice (hereafter: AFSJ).[54]

Recently, AFSJ agencies expanded their operational functions in supporting Member States with new transboundary issues, such as border management, asylum, and migration.[55] The hotspot approach is a clear example of their horizontal cooperation in securing Union standards in the face of the migration crisis. It has also shown how influential AFSJ agencies are in assisting Member States in their national sovereign prerogatives. Examples showing how these agencies determine policies of border administration[56] include Frontex's power to determine the nationality of migrants and its capacity to monitor Member States,[57] Europol's support in the exchange of information

[54] Dehousse, 'The Politics of Delegation in the European Union', in D. Ritleng (ed.), *Independence and Legitimacy in the Institutional System of the European Union* (2016) 57; Hofman, Rowe, and Türk, 'Delegation and the European Union Constitutional Framework', in *Administrative Law and Policy of the European Union* (2011), 222; M. Simoncini, *Administrative Regulation Beyond the Non-Delegation Doctrine: a Study on EU Agencies* (2018), 14, 177.

[55] Nicolosi and Fernandez-Rojo, 'Out of Control? The Case of the European Asylum Support Office', in M. Scholten and A. Brenninkmejer (eds), *Controlling EU Agencies. The Rule of Law in a Multi-jurisdictional Legal Order* (2020) 177.

[56] J. Wagner, *Border Management in Transformation: Transnational Threats and Security Policies of European States* (2021), 209, 227.

[57] Coman-Kund (n. 10), at 163, 167.

and coordination of police operational activities of data extraction related to migrants' transboundary smuggling, and EASO's power to undertake vulnerability assessments in the context of asylum applications. These examples show how flexible the concept of external borders can be and how national authorities can be influenced by EU institutional actors in very sensitive policy areas representing the core of national sovereignty.[58] Indeed, the dynamics of control of the in-between autonomy and interdependence of these agencies, should be carefully considered, taking into account the interaction among multiple executives at national and EU level. It must be borne in mind, after all, that procedural rules should be functional to the tasks that EU agencies pursue and are tied to the interests at stake as well as the inevitable limits.

The Union when imposing these limits must strike a balance between the necessary unity while respecting diversity in the Union.[59] In substantive terms, national authorities are bound to comply with the Union law they implement. This basic tenet of legality follows from the binding nature of Union law underpinned by the principle of supremacy. In procedural terms, national autonomy is limited by primary Union law, including the Charter of Fundamental Rights, Union legislation, and case law of the Union courts. Such limitations are intended to ensure the effective application of Union law but are often the result of precepts of the rule of law as formulated by the Union. But Union law can also impact on the organizational autonomy of national administrations, where, for example, Union legislation requires the independence of national regulatory authorities in the application of Union law. Where representatives of the Member States are integrated within the Union's institutional structure, as is the case of comitology and agencies, they exercise their mandate as part of Union bodies, even though they remain otherwise part of their national organizational structure. This classic dual role may lead to a conflict of interest, but it is an essential aspect of composite administration.[60]

The legal consequences of the integration of national administrations into European administration vary according to the degree of integration in specific policy fields. The national authorities enjoy a certain degree of autonomy when they implement Union law, which is of course limited by the requirements of

[58] D. Fernandez-Rojo, *EU Migration Agencies. The Operation and Cooperation of Frontex, EASO and Europol* (2021) 218.

[59] Article 4(2) TEU.

[60] Schmidt-Aßmann, 'Introduction: European Composite Administration and the role of European Administrative Law', in O. Jansen and B. Schöndorf-Haubold (eds), *The European Composite Administration* (2011); Hofmann and Türk, 'The Development of Integrated Administration in the EU and its Consequences', 13(2) *European Law Journal* (2017) 253; R. Schütze, *From Dual to Cooperative Federalism* (2009).

Union law to ensure uniformity and effectiveness of Union law. This aspect is even more visible in the AFSJ, where the initial intergovernmental origins have included incremental operational and implementation tasks that are not precisely limited by national or EU legal instruments.[61] The case of Europol is illustrative in the way it has engaged in shaping borders through sharing information. The principle of originator control, which requires recipients to obtain the originator's authorization to share data—informs in a tailored way the relationships of Europol with other actors. For example, the European Parliament can be prevented by national authorities from accessing information processed by Europol, resulting in a lack of scrutiny of relevant information.[62] Member States can indicate restrictions on the access and use of information they provide to Europol,[63] and they may have direct access only to certain information stored by Europol.[64] Europol shall further establish its own rules for the protection of classified or non-classified information[65] with obvious implications for originator control (see further Catanzariti and Curtin, Chapter 5, in this volume).

The autonomous data protection framework applying specifically to Europol is also a relevant example of the shared powers that data sharing implies. It shows the tension underlying the model of composite administration in the EU. In fact, the responsibility for the legality of a data transfer lies with: (a) the Member State which provides the personal data to Europol; (b) Europol in the case of personal data provided by it to Member States, third countries, or international organizations (also directly with private persons under the new Commission's amendment proposal). In the context of information sharing, this seems to be far from actual practice. It implies that different layers of administration intertwine with one another also with regard to competences and responsibilities. In terms of data protection obligations, the first controller should be held responsible by virtue of legal status, without a clear distinction of duties. This architecture seems to reflect a double movement increasing formal accountability and at the same time increasing informal autonomy.[66] This relies on a complex interplay between them. Europol's action

[61] Fernandez-Rojo (n. 58) 217.

[62] Article 52 of the Europol Regulation: Regulation (EU) 2016/794, OJ 2016 L 135/53.

[63] Article 19 of the Europol Regulation.

[64] Article 20 of the Europol Regulation. Member States have direct access to information provided for cross-checking to identify connection between information and convicted/suspected persons, and indirect access to information provided for operational analysis.

[65] Article 67 of the Europol Regulation.

[66] Busuioc, Curtin, and Groenler, 'Agency Growth Between Autonomy and Accountability: The European Police Office as a 'Living Institution', 18(6) *Journal of European Public Policy* (2011) 846, at 860.

and its shared competences among different intergovernmental and supranational layers are based on fragmented legal regimes which exist alongside de facto practices of information sharing. The latter plays a crucial role in setting boundaries between competent authorities and expanding or otherwise borders among states.

The amended Europol Regulation weakens the European Data Protection Supervisor (EDPS) supervisory powers.[67] The reform also seeks to enable Europol to register information alerts in the Schengen Information System (SIS).[68] This is arguably paradigmatic of how boundaries of the law and of legal borders may overlap in the field of information sharing.[69] Europol's access to interoperable information systems in the area of security, migration, and external borders management goes in practice far beyond its mandate. The result is that the broader purpose of the so-called integrated border management at external EU borders—which clearly exceeds the mandate of Europol—in practice means control of relevant related information. The proposal for the amendment of the SIS Regulation enabling Europol to enter alerts in the SIS illustrates the trend to increasing the access of Europol to non-law enforcement data[70] and this incremental power of Europol is highlighted in this and related ways in the contribution by Curtin and de Goede in this book (Chapter 6). At the same time, control of information shifts those boundaries of the law that are established between legal areas (law enforcement, intelligence, migration, borders, security), competences, and jurisdictions.[71] Rules on access to data

[67] As put by Regulation (EU) 2022/991 of the European Parliament and of the Council of 8 June 2022 amending Regulation (EU) 2016/794, as regards Europol's cooperation with private parties, the processing of personal data by Europol in support of criminal investigations, and Europol's role in research and innovation, OJ 2022 L 169/1 and Regulation (EU) 2018/1725 of the European Parliament and of the Council of 23 October 2018 on the protection of natural persons with regard to the processing of personal data by the Union institutions, bodies, offices and agencies and on the free movement of such data, and repealing Regulation (EC) No 45/2001 and Decision No 1247/2002/EC, OJ 2018 L 295/39. See N. Vavoula and V. Mitsilegas, *Strengthening Europol's Mandate. A Legal Assessment of the Commission's Proposal to Amend the Europol Regulation* (2021), 62. On 3 January 2022, the EDPS issued an order to Europol to delete data concerning individuals with no established link to a criminal activity (Data Subject Categorisation), https://edps.europa.eu/system/files/2022-01/22-01-10-edps-decision-europol_en.pdf (last visited 4 November 2022).

[68] Regulation (EU) 2022/1190 of the European Parliament and of the Council of 6 July 2022 amending Regulation (EU) 2018/1862 as regards the entry of information alerts into the Schengen Information System (SIS) on third-country nationals in the interest of the Union, OJ 2022 L 185/1.

[69] See Bossong and Carrapico, 'The Multidimensional Nature and Dynamic Transformation of European Borders and Internal Security', in R. Bossong and H. Carrapico (eds.) *EU Borders and Shifting Internal Security* (2016) 1–21; for an overview on issues related to digital borders and effective protection see E. Brouwer, *Digital Borders and Real Rights. Effective Remedies for Third-Country Nationals in the Schengen Information Systems* (2008), 47 ff., 71 ff.

[70] See the proposed amendments to the Schengen Information System (SIS) regulation: European Commission, Communication COM/2020/791 final.

[71] Jeandesboz, 'Justifying Control: EU Border Security and the Shifting Boundary of Political Arrangement', in R. Bosson and H. Carrapico (eds.) *EU Borders and Shifting Internal Security* (2016) 221–238.

held by Europol and on access by Europol to data provided by third parties are sometimes set up by national authorities, sometimes by Europol, and are often blurred together. This means that information sharing is increasingly becoming a field that includes new paths of shared administration mechanisms but not always effective and adapted accountability mechanisms.[72]

4. Digital Autonomy and European Regulation

Borders are a site for global experimentation using advanced AI technologies.[73] EU initiatives on AI for borders use four categories of AI applications: (1) biometric identification (automated fingerprint and face recognition); (2) emotion detection; (3) algorithmic risk assessment; and (4) AI tools for migration monitoring, analysis, and forecasting.[74] There have been various initiatives on so-called smart borders. These are borders based on the capability to collect and process data and exchange information. The capability of technology to move external borders outside the Union or create digital borders is a way in which the law artificially aligns political and legal boundaries with borders.[75]

In conceptual terms, one might say that data and borders are incompatible, as data is borderless. This means that data, in and of itself, cannot be limited by physical frontiers. Data flows through spaces and across borders, regardless of boundaries of any type. Irrespective of the fact that data evades borders, the law tries to pin it down in various ways. Within the EU, there is a striking and ever-increasing attention to data governance over the course of the past decade. The free circulation of persons and goods has been enabled by data flows in many areas of the law. Conversely, the use of borders as a tool to exercise sovereign powers linked to data can take very different forms. Data enhances the polarity of borders. Although the ubiquitous nature of data that can be accessed and used anywhere makes different spaces replicable or at least closer to each other, at the same time its fragmented character divides, creates frictions, and produces a perception of reality on demand. Data can offer different

[72] See, further, Chapter 6 by Curtin and de Goede in this volume.

[73] M. Longo, *The Politics of Borders: Sovereignty, Security, and the Citizen After 9/11* (2018) 204–228; Akhmetiva and Harris, 'Politics of technology: the use of artificial intelligence by US and Canadian immigration agencies and their impacts on human rights', in E.E. Korkmaz (ed.) *Digital Identity, Virtual Borders and Social Media: A Panacea for Migration Governance?* (2021).

[74] C. Dumbrava, 'Artificial Intelligence at EU Borders: Overview of Applications and Key Issues' (2021), https://www.europarl.europa.eu/RegData/etudes/IDAN/2021/690706/EPRSIDA(2021)690706EN.pdf, (last visited 10 September 2021).

[75] Brkan and Korkmaz, 'Big Data for Whose Sake? Governing Migration Through Artificial Intelligence', 8 *Humanities and Social Science Communications* (2021) 241.

representations of facts depending on how it is aggregated and matched. These facts when filtered through impersonal automated decisions can or cannot be relevant to affect legal or political choices regarding borders. Like all bureaucratic forms based on impersonal law that are applicable regardless of specific situations, algorithms apply indiscriminately and may produce equal results (and possibly related coercive effects) for different personal situations.[76]

Data protection has in fact been used by the EU in order to get around territorial borders. The right to dereferencing (e.g. the removal of links related to personal information) is apparently only for data located within the EU.[77] At the same time, it has also been granted to individuals vis-à-vis companies established outside the EU and against which EU data protection law is applied.[78] With regard to law enforcement access to data more globally, warrants have been issued by public authorities to service providers to release data irrespective of their location storage.[79] As for the global protection of human rights, transatlantic mass-surveillance programmes of individuals have been criticized as being in violation of the right to respect private life under the European Convention of Human Rights.[80] As for the global reach of the European Charter of Fundamental Rights, the Safe Harbor Agreement,[81] and its successor, the Privacy Shield,[82] were declared invalid under EU law for violating Max Schrems' fundamental right to data protection after his data were transferred and physically relocated in the United States.

Data protection law has in fact become an area of the law where the EU has exploited the cross-border potential of data to expand its extraterritorial reach and to limit the interference as well as the impact of other regulatory models in the EU. This has been very clear in the case law of the Court of Justice of the European Union (CJEU), which invalidated international agreements for non-compliance with EU law[83] but also when the Court held that the use of European data by third countries could have implied a violation of EU law.[84]

[76] Visentin, 'Il potere razionale degli algoritmi tra burocrazia e nuovi idealtipi', XX(4) *The Lab's Quarterly* (2018) 47, at 57, 58.

[77] Case C-507/17, *Google LLC, successor in law to Google Inc v Commission nationale de l'informatique et des libertés (CNIL)* (EU:C:2019:772).

[78] Case C-131/12, *Google Spain SL and Google Inc v Agencia Española de Protección de Datos (AEPD) and Mario Costeja González* (EU:C:2014:317).

[79] *United States v Microsoft Corp.*, 584 U.S., 138 S. Ct. 1186 (2018).

[80] ECtHR, *Big Brother Watch and Others v the United Kingdom*, Appl. nos. 58170/13, 62322/14 and 24969/15, Grand Chamber Judgment of 25 May 2021.

[81] Case C-362/14, *Maximillian Schrems v Data Protection Commissioner* (EU:C:2015:650).

[82] Case C-311/18, *Data Protection Commissioner v Facebook Ireland Limited and Maximillian Schrems* (EU:C:2020:559).

[83] See cases *Schrems I* (n. 81) and *Schrems II* (n 82).

[84] Joined Cases C-293/12 and C-594/12, *Digital Rights Ireland Ltd v Minister for Communications, Marine and Natural Resources and Others and Kärntner Landesregierung and Others* (EU:C:2014:238), para. 68.

GDPR is a much-quoted example of standard-setting law projecting EU law all over the world, even in countries where the cultural premises of data protection are completely different from those in Europe, such as China,[85] Australia,[86] and Canada.[87] The GDPR embraced a functional approach, seeking to expand EU borders based on individual freedoms and fundamental rights protection and striking a balance with economic liberties. According to this approach, established in Article 3 GDPR, EU data protection law applies in three scenarios: in the context of the activities of a company in the Union regardless of whether the data processing takes place in the Union; upon the offering of goods and services to data subjects in the EU or the monitoring of their behaviour; if the company is not located in the Union, but in a place where domestic law applies by virtue of public international law. In even more explicit terms, the AI Act has a much broader scope than the GDPR, as it basically also applies to providers and users of AI systems that are located in a third country 'where the output produced by the system is used in the Union'.[88] This general formulation considerably expands the scope of EU law all over the world. This tendency shows a specific institutional choice to promote the relevant EU rules all over the world as a model of lawmaking which other countries have to abide with if they wish to enter the European market and more generally have a legal relationship involving data with the EU.

The recent past saw the adoption of elaborate European data protection rules with quite a complex institutional architecture; the present sees the reality of data sharing and the wish to further enhance and regulate such processes. The EU in fact undertook a project to create a strong framework of protection for personal data that focuses on the individual rights of data subjects and ideally should lay down the conditions for the free data flow across sectors, data access, and data reuse for multiple purposes, enhancing business-to-government data sharing in the public interest. In this context of increased demand for data processing in the public and private sectors, recent initiatives have sought to

[85] China's major data protection laws, including the Personal Information Protection Law (PIPL) (effective from November 2021) and the Data Security Law (DSL) (effective from September 2021), are currently in a transitional moment, moving away from a sectorial approach and towards a systemic view of data protection: Pernot-Leplay, 'China's Approach on Data Privacy Law: A Third Way Between the U.S. and the E.U.?', 8 *The Penn State Journal of Law & International Affairs* (2020) 49, at 62–84. While this regime differs in some substantial points from the EU data protection regime, notably in the limits to state power, the PIPL provides a comprehensive regulation with some similarities to the GDPR.

[86] For an overview of the differences between Australian and EU data protection systems, see Watts and Casanovas, 'Privacy and Data Protection in Australia: A Critical Overview', *W3C Workshop on Privacy and Linked Data* (2018).

[87] On the Canadian data protection system, see Scassa, 'Data Protection and the Internet: Canada', in D. Moura Vicente and S. de Vasconcelos Casimiro (eds), *Data Protection in the Internet* (2020).

[88] Article 2(c) AI Act.

ensure that the EU can ensure its sovereignty over the conditions of processing of personal data, both in terms of the effective application of the EU data protection framework beyond European borders and, in some cases, of encouraging processing within EU borders.

The EU finds itself now at the crossroads of several different regulatory choices which in general terms can be said to reflect its own digital sovereignty defined in terms of a European take on digital autonomy.[89] The EU aims to avoid digital dependence on third countries but in order to pursue this objective, it identifies and makes recognizable the cultural model it wishes to promote. This model is basically grounded on data protection, trustworthy standards for data sharing of privately held data by other companies and governments, and of public sector data by businesses.[90] At the same time, data has reinforced the desire for sovereignty of the EU, on the assumption that by linking sovereignty to its 'digital' vision it can consolidate its existing position. By contrast, justifying it legally would have been hard, as the term 'sovereignty' never appears in the Treaty on European Union (TEU) or in the TFEU.[91] In reality, the capacity of Europe to manage huge flows of data is greatly limited by foreign digital infrastructures. The latter's operational rules in fact determine the effective power of the EU to control data flows. The real challenge for Europe is to avoid undue dependence on foreign digital infrastructures. As pointed out by Celeste 'the main rationale behind digital sovereignty claims in the EU lies in the desire to preserve European core values, rights and principles' while exerting full control over data including storage, processing, and access.[92] This is part of a broader phenomenon mostly triggered by data protection law, as also observed by De Hert in Chapter 4. He points to how European data protection, as an EU policy area, is not an independent goal in itself, but is to be seen as part of larger agenda of the Digital Single Market, a strategy aiming to open up digital opportunities for people and business and enhance Europe's position as a world leader in the digital economy.

[89] L. O'Dowd, J. Anderson, and T. W. Wilson, *New Borders for a Changing Europe. Cross-Border Cooperation and Governance* (2003).

[90] European Commission, 'A European Strategy for Data', COM/2020/66 final.

[91] Christakis, *European Digital Sovereignty. Successfully Navigating Between the 'Brussels Effect' and Europe's quest for Strategic Autonomy*, https://cesice.univ-grenoble-alpes.fr/actualites/2020-12-15/european-digital-sovereignty-successfully-navigating-between-brussels-effect-and-europe-s-quest, 8, (last visited 16 July 2021). See also Avbelj, 'A Sovereign Europe as a Future of Sovereignty?', 5(1) *European Papers* (2020) 299.

[92] Celeste, 'Digital Sovereignty in the EU: Challenges and Future Perspectives', in F. Fabbrini, E. Celeste, and J. Quinn (eds), *Data Protection Beyond Borders: Transatlantic Perspectives on Extraterritoriality and Sovereignty* (2021) 211.

In seeking digital autonomy, the EU aims to avoid resorting to protectionist practices of data governance in a sort of imitation game. After all cross-border data control practices determine the risk of retaliation by other states.[93] For example, the adoption of the CLOUD Act (Clarifying Lawful Overseas Use of Data Act) in the US—an Act that enables public authorities to compel private intermediaries to hand over data regardless its location, even outside the US—might be read as a reaction to European activism towards the expansion of the scope of the European Charter of Fundamental Rights and the GDPR beyond the Atlantic.[94] It created a conflict of jurisdiction with the GDPR since US requests for data located in Europe that are lawful under US law cannot now be blocked. Understanding this process under the lenses of the law and its boundaries sheds light on the steps needed to lead to an autonomous data infrastructure compatible with EU regulatory trends. It is also a good example of how physical borders matter in an interconnected world, notwithstanding the original optimism regarding the role of the internet.

5. A New Regulatory Compass for the EU

A digital single market of data flowing across and through the EU aims to ensure technical competitiveness and the autonomy of relevant infrastructures. To develop this goal, fundamental rights and property rights need protection but at the same time trust among actors who share data also needs to be built. The ambition is to create a framework in which the principles enshrined in data protection law can be reconciled with the interests of individuals and businesses to access digital goods and services and maximize the growth potential of the digital economy. The new model of the European data strategy is based on a set of legal instruments with twin aims. First, to improve specific regulatory segments for online marketplaces, social networks, content-sharing platforms, app stores, and online travel and accommodation platforms in order to develop a single market for data, avoiding platforms as gatekeepers to the internal market (Digital Services Act and Digital Markets Act). Second, to make public sector data available for reuse in situations in which this data is subject to the rights of others, such as personal data, data protected by intellectual property rights, or data that contains trade secrets or other commercially sensitive information (Digital Governance Act, hereinafter 'DGA'). This ambitious

[93] Ibid. 61.
[94] See cases *Schrems I* (n. 81), *Schrems II* (n.82), and *Digital Rights Ireland* (n.84).

initiative is intended to enhance access to data for individuals, businesses, and administrations. It takes for granted the *acquis* of the GDPR as a building block upon which a new set of regulatory tools can be built, regardless of any possible misalignments.[95] Once data is protected, the idea is that it should also be managed during its whole lifecycle. The EU has bet on a model of data management based on the 'recycling' by private entities of data initially stored by public authorities. In particular, the DGA has four main pillars: (1) making public sector data available for reuse; (2) sharing of data among businesses, against remuneration in any form; (3) allowing personal data to be used with the help of a 'personal data-sharing intermediary', designed to help individuals exercise their rights under the GDPR; (4) allowing data use on altruistic grounds. This regulatory instrument seeks to overcome the public–private divide providing a cooperative framework between private- and public-sector data that is supplied as part of the execution of public tasks, with the exception of data protected for reasons of national security.

The AI Act functions as a type of *passe-partout* crosscutting these various new regulatory strands and aims to address critical issues of the data-driven market. It provides a further body of rules, formulated under the legal basis of Article 114 TFEU, to ensure the establishment and the promotion of the internal market and, specifically, of lawful, safe, and the trustworthy use of AI systems. Data represents the drive of a broad legislative process that aims to provide a consistent legal toolkit to address the challenges of the blurring of many existing boundaries between data and the law: which data can be shared, which data can be used by AI systems, which data needs specific safeguards. Data control is in fact the most effective way to enhance security, both at a substantive level and at the technical organizational level. Several regulatory instruments have recently tried to implement the multifaceted goal of security in different regulatory segments: protection of networks and information systems; interoperability of information systems in the field of police and judicial cooperation, asylum, migration, visa, and borders; processing of special categories of data by police (biometric verification and identification); European integrated border control. In the field of security management, information sharing is of particular relevance in the context of mechanisms of composite administration. However, it is never clear, particularly in the field of law enforcement, whether personal data belongs to data subjects or authorities, be they domestic, European, or foreign. Moreover, when personal data

[95] The compatibility of definitions like 'data holder' in the DGA and 'data user' in the GDPR is not clear, nor is the distinction between data belonging to physical persons or legal persons.

processing is enhanced by the use of AI systems, it is not always easy to put a clear line of demarcation between law enforcement purposes, on the one hand, and border management, asylum, and migration purposes, on the other hand.[96] For example, the AI Act does not generally allow the use of 'real-time' remote biometric identification systems in publicly accessible spaces for the purpose of law enforcement, unless specific conditions are met,[97] but it broadly applies to AI systems used for border control management, migration, and asylum.[98] In practice, the boundary between law enforcement and migration, borders, and asylum is not clear enough.[99] The new institutional framework of interoperable information systems in effect overturns the purpose limitation principle, one of the boundaries of data protection law, according to which data should be processed only for specified, explicit, and legitimate purposes and

[96] Daskal, 'Law Enforcement Access to Data Across Borders: The Evolving Security and Rights Issues', 8 *Journal of National Security Law & Policy* (2016) 473.

[97] Article 5 1(d) and Recital 38 AI Act.

[98] Pursuant to Recital 39 AI Act (n. 37), these systems are for example polygraphs and similar tools or to detect the emotional state of a natural person or those intended to be used for assessing certain risks posed by natural persons entering the territory of a Member State or applying for visa or asylum; for verifying the authenticity of the relevant documents of natural persons; for assisting competent public authorities for the examination of applications for asylum, visa and residence permits and associated complaints with regard to the objective to establish the eligibility of the natural persons applying for a status.

[99] Annex III of AI Act specifies that both law enforcement and migration, border and asylum are high-risk AI systems and differentiates them as follows: Law enforcement AI systems includes (a) AI systems intended to be used by law enforcement authorities for making individual risk assessments of natural persons in order to assess the risk of a natural person for offending or reoffending or the risk for potential victims of criminal offences; (b) AI systems intended to be used by law enforcement authorities as polygraphs and similar tools or to detect the emotional state of a natural person; (c) AI systems intended to be used by law enforcement authorities to detect deep fakes as referred to in Article 52(3); (d) AI systems intended to be used by law enforcement authorities for evaluation of the reliability of evidence in the course of investigation or prosecution of criminal offences; (e) AI systems intended to be used by law enforcement authorities for predicting the occurrence or reoccurrence of an actual or potential criminal offence based on profiling of natural persons as referred to in Article 3(4) of Directive (EU) 2016/680 or assessing personality traits and characteristics or past criminal behaviour of natural persons or groups; (f) AI systems intended to be used by law enforcement authorities for profiling of natural persons as referred to in Article 3(4) of Directive (EU) 2016/680 in the course of detection, investigation or prosecution of criminal offences; (g) AI systems intended to be used for crime analytics regarding natural persons, allowing law enforcement authorities to search complex related and unrelated large data sets available in different data sources or in different data formats in order to identify unknown patterns or discover hidden relationships in the data. Migration, asylum and border control management AI systems include (a) AI systems intended to be used by competent public authorities as polygraphs and similar tools or to detect the emotional state of a natural person; (b) AI systems intended to be used by competent public authorities to assess a risk, including a security risk, a risk of irregular immigration, or a health risk, posed by a natural person who intends to enter or has entered into the territory of a Member State; (c) AI systems intended to be used by competent public authorities for the verification of the authenticity of travel documents and supporting documentation of natural persons and detect non-authentic documents by checking their security features; (d) AI systems intended to assist competent public authorities for the examination of applications for asylum, visa and residence permits and associated complaints with regard to the eligibility of the natural persons applying for a status.

not for further purposes incompatible with the original ones.[100] Although the law constantly sets up boundaries among the activities that fall (or do not fall) within its specific field of application, the ability of data to blur these boundaries is magnified by the way technologies make it possible to use data.

Finally, international negotiations on cross-border access to electronic evidence, necessary to track down dangerous criminals and terrorists, are currently ongoing, and the proposal on e-evidence is at the final stage of public consultation.[101] It is significant that in the field of law enforcement, the Law Enforcement Directive does not allow—unlike the GDPR—the recognition of any judgment of a court or tribunal and any decision of an administrative authority of a third country requiring a controller or processor to transfer or disclose personal data to be recognized or enforceable in any manner. This is irrespective of whether or not it is based on an international agreement, such as a mutual legal assistance treaty, in force between the requesting third country and the Union or a Member State. This illustrates how physical boundaries among the EU and third countries are resistant to data processing for law enforcement purposes that imply exchange of information among third countries. Law enforcement data sharing often happens at an informal level which is quite often at the boundaries of the law.[102]

6. Data-Driven Law as Performance and Practice: European Intermezzos

As has been recalled many times, the GDPR can still be considered a type of modern-day foundation stone that spawned, or has been mimicked in, various other regulations.[103] The GDPR has seen a growth in practice (and eventually

[100] Article 5 GDPR. See Vavoula, 'Databases for Non-EU nationals and the Right to Private Life: Towards a System of Generalized Surveillance of Movement?', in F. Bignami (ed.), *EU Law in Populist Times: Crises and Prospects* (2020) 227, at 227–266, 231–232; Brouwer, 'A Point of No Return in Purpose Limitation? Interoperability and the Blurring of Migration and Crime', *Un-Owned Personal Data Blog Forum*, https://migrationpolicycentre.eu/point-no-return-migration-and-crime/, (last visited 10 September 2021); Bunyan, 'The point of no return', *Statewatch Analysis* (updated July 2018), https://www.statewatch.org/media/documents/analyses/no-332-eu-interop-morphs-into-central-database-revised.pdf, (last visited 10 September 2021).

[101] European Commission, *E-evidence — cross-border access to electronic evidence* (2021), https://ec.europa.eu/info/policies/justice-and-fundamental-rights/criminal-justice/e-evidence-cross-border-access-electronic-evidenceen (last visited 17 December 2021).

[102] Aguinaldo and De Hert, 'European Law Enforcement and EU Data Companies: A Decade of Cooperation Free from Law', in E. Celeste, F. Fabbrini, and J. Quinn, *Data Protection Beyond Borders: Transatlantic Perspectives on Extraterritoriality and Sovereignty* (2020) 157; Daskal, 'The Opening Salvo. The CLOUD Act, the e-evidence Proposals, the EU-US Discussions Regarding Law Enforcement Access to Data Across Borders', in F. Bignami (ed.), *EU Law in Populist Times* (2020) 319.

[103] See De Hert, Chapter 4, this volume.

also in regulation) alongside it, bordering it as it were, in particular in the field of law enforcement and (national) security.[104] The thrust of the book is deliberately not Eurocentric but rather aims to give voice to scholars based in Europe to reflect on problems of principle in terms of law and its boundaries as relating to data systems in their various aspects. This is at times Europe focused if the object is an evaluation of regulatory instruments, which some consider potentially world leading, and at times the object is a much broader and more general remit. What is arguably distinctive about this collection of chapters by a number of leading legal scholars—and one political scientist—in Europe is that its focus is not on the GDPR when it comes to data and issues of access, use, and sharing (as opposed to processing). Rather the focus across all chapters is on data access, use, and sharing essentially by public authorities (although private actors inevitably intersect with this). It is also on the institutional choices that make Europe an international actor and a competitive interlocutor in the area of data-driven governance. Given that the backdrop is data and that the market on data is global with so many data providers or data intermediaries located outside Europe and also subject to other jurisdictions in law and otherwise, this book covers both more general issues on which there are substantial theoretical and legal debates globally[105] as well as more specific issues that either are already grounded in specific EU regulations[106]—or may well be.

A more specifically European take on more general issues is of value and we hope will contribute to various ongoing debates around the globe and be of interest not only to scholars, lawyers, and political scientists who study data-driven processes but also those working on the meaning and substance of much broader issues in the modern world, such as transparency, accountability, the role of public authorities, and territorial issues that go beyond borders and jurisdictional questions. The other way in which the authors of this volume give a European perspective is by not only all being European, employed at European universities but, more importantly, even when speaking to general theoretical or wider conceptual themes, we all use European examples where appropriate.

Mireille Hildebrandt in Chapter 2, which opens the collection after this introductory chapter, reasons at a general level on the boundaries between text-driven modern law and computational law with specific attention to the case of legal judgments and machine learning technologies to predict legal judgments.

[104] See Curtin and de Goede, Chapter 6, as well as Catanzariti and Curtin, Chapter 5, this volume.

[105] See for example the Compulaw Project. Governance of Computational Entities Through an Integrated Legal and Technical Framework (ERC Advanced Grant), https://site.unibo.it/compulaw/en, last visited on 11 February 2022.

[106] De Hert, Chapter 4, this volume.

She conducts boundary work between modern positive law and technological determinism. She explores the differences between the *performativity* of legal norms (based on positivity, multi-interpretability, and contestability) and the *performance* of predictive legal technologies, arguing that the latter is disruptive of the way of existence of the law 'as we know it': 'If legal practice were to adopt these kinds of technologies, it may end up disrespecting the boundary between a law that addresses people as human agents and a law that treats them as subject to a statistical, machinic logic.' Hildebrandt argues that the 'affordances' of data-driven modern law cannot be integrally transposed into the use of predictions as a new way to establish the law, because human anticipation and machine anticipation are profoundly different. Text-driven anticipation has a qualitative probability that relies on 'doing things with words'. It is constituted by the performative effect while data-driven prediction, based on mathematical assumptions, has a quantitative probability and its effect is caused by the fulfilment of the conditions. Turning legal anticipation into data-driven prediction has a clear impact in terms of effects on legal protection 'that is *part of* law's instrumentality', in the sense that it allows individuals to 'contest claims of validity regarding both legal norms and legally relevant facts'. Legal protection by design and legality by design are not equivalent, but the gap between the two can be filled by human oversight, as now provided by the terms of the draft AI Regulation.

This is certainly also the case for understanding transparency more conceptually as it relates to automated practices. In Chapter 3, Ida Koivisto digs deeply into the value of transparency as well as some aspects of its conceptualization in the digital context. She questions whether the promise of transparency in the GDPR is in fact a normative rationale, or only an umbrella concept or a more general interpretative concept. She argues that the line between secrecy of automated processes and transparency is very thin, especially when it is not clear what the principle of transparency should protect: readability of data, explanation of processes, or fair procedures. Koivisto correctly warns about the tautology of transparency, which is 'performative in nature' and may turn to a simplistic meaning of being able to see a transparent object, the inner functioning of machines, and not instead a 'meaningful information of the logic involved'. This means that transparency is performative as far as it makes visible only a transparent object that can be seen and into which we can see inside, but it keeps secret what lies behind it. She perceptively notes that 'seeing inside the black box does not necessarily lead to understanding, and understanding does not necessarily lead to control or other type of action'. Therefore, explainability seems to be the most accountable declination of the principle of transparency, understood as 'description of logics to justification'.

Moving to the more specific phenomenon of GDPR mimesis, according to Paul De Hert in Chapter 4, this is present in various EU legislative instruments, in particular the Network and Information Security Directive, the EU regulations on drones,[107] and the DGA as well as the AI Act. He argues that the GDPR has formulated a type of EU model for technology regulation, a kind of *acquis*, but without an adequate or full integration of the principles enshrined in the GDPR. Among the factors that have increased mimesis among different measures are the institutional tendencies to adopt very general measures—what De Hert calls 'open texture' and EU-wide agencification. These factors are exemplified by general rules often included into regulations seeking to harmonize national laws and ex post uniformized by legally binding decision of the Luxembourg Court or in case of political disagreement by the action of EU agencies, that act as 'epistemic communities ... with shared knowledge, culture, and values'. Arguably, lack of creative legal thinking by those drafting legislation as well as path dependency with previous legislative choices and the coexistence of regulatory spaces have played a crucial role in the repeated spread of the norms of the GDPR without looking to the bigger picture of what these repeated steps means in terms of overall EU integration.

An example of the lack of integration of the GDPR in other contexts of data processing that are not represented by a few distinct legislative measures is the interoperability of information systems used for migration, asylum, and borders. The analysis of data originalism conducted by Mariavittoria Catanzariti and Deirdre Curtin arguably offers a new conceptualization of personal data sharing. It reflects upon the original status of data—personal and thus non-appropriable by any authority or individuals—but also on the role of data originators, namely those authorities who originate data and share them first. The authors argue that although originators can set up specific rules for data sharing, the original status of personal data as non-appropriable entities is not to be undermined. This in practical terms implies attaching broad data protection safeguards plus specific rules set up by data originators for data sharing among users that have access to interoperable data. It is an odyssey in many ways to untangle and deconstruct interoperability not only conceptually but

[107] Directive (EU) 2016/1148 of the European Parliament and of the Council of 6 July 2016 concerning measures for a high common level of security of network and information systems across the Union, OJ 2016 L 194/1; Commission Implementing Regulation (EU) 2019/947 of 24 May 2019 on the rules and procedures for the operation of unmanned aircraft, OJ 2019 L 152/45; and Commission Delegated Regulation (EU) 2019/945 of 12 March 2019 on unmanned aircraft systems and on third-country operators of unmanned aircraft systems, OJ 2019 L 152/1.

also in terms of its possible legal neighbours and peers. The authors believe that such detailed analysis is not only essential in and of itself for a better conceptual and legal understanding but also in the process reveals the political lurking in the shadows.

A final contribution by Deirdre Curtin and Marieke de Goede explores the byzantine complexity of what is now known generically as interoperability, which breathes technical configurations and exchanges rather than legal analysis and its positioning in accountability terms. The authors reveal how data-led security, represented by policies and practices of security integration through the building and connecting of databases, is a concept that involves a cross-border dimension but also different levels of decision making. Both of these factors are reflected in different and multiple purposes of data processing that are hardly integrated at all. To approach the boundaries of what we know (and do not know) through data, this chapter investigates the role of accountability in a data-driven security explored throughout various case studies, such as tracking terrorist financing, targeting terrorist online content, and interoperability. In the opinion of the authors, data-led security should be coupled with mechanisms of logged-in accountability that prevent *ad hoc* or in any event limited forms of oversight. The practice of 'logging' is then inspected through the scrutiny of the adequacy or inadequacy of its standardized format that often leaves accountability mechanisms simply not connected to the actual data analysis in practice.

The common thread of these six chapters is the intrinsic tension between the transformations taking place as a result of data flows affecting individuals, institutions, legal regimes, and practices, and the reality of the bounded nature of the law when faced with the use and sharing of data. The responses have tackled specific areas of relevance where they criss-cross key issues of democratic legitimacy, the process of European integration, and the evolving digital European strategy. Our aim as editors has been to raise the wider issues and to make a contribution to the more global debate on the basis of a more granular and sectoral understanding of the way that European law and institutional practice is taking shape and maybe occasionally leading in terms of specific choices that are being made. Our purpose is certainly not to push a 'Brussels effect' or its equivalent, but rather to dig deeper into the lesser-known areas of data that can, for one reason or another, be said to be at the boundary or borders of law. The 'intermezzos' in this book are however part of a much wider performance that takes place and is influenced globally and not only in Europe.

2

Boundary Work between Computational 'Law' and 'Law-as-We-Know-it'

*Mireille Hildebrandt**

1. Introduction

Though some may still be dreaming of law *as* literature or of law *as* logic,[1] the legal services market is currently swamped by the advertorial lure of big data analytics, promising cheap and easy solutions to many of the inefficiencies and to the ineffectiveness of professional legal advice and decision making. Big law firms are investing in the development, purchase, and deployment of data-driven artificial intelligence (AI) systems,[2] facing the challenges of big tech companies as new competitors for control over legal knowledge.[3] The old(er) paradigm of 'legal knowledge management' is traded for a belief in opaque systems whose advocates pledge new types of transparency and unprecedented speed when searching, analysing, summarizing, and building upon big data in law.[4] Such data consists of documentation in the realm of evidence

* The author acknowledges that the research done for this chapter has benefited from the funding by the European Research Council under the HORIZON2020 Excellence of Science programme ERC-2017-ADG No 788734.

[1] Though scepticism against law as logic has been around for some time, e.g. Kennedy, 'The Disenchantment of Logically Formal Legal Rationality, or Max Weber's Sociology in the Genealogy of the Contemporary Mode of Western Legal Thought', 555 *Hastings Law Journal* (2004) 1031. A more interesting perspective may have been that of J. White, *Justice as Translation: An Essay in Cultural and Legal Criticism* (1990). This is not to claim that logic plays no role in legal reasoning, on the contrary, I would say it constrains the decision space by requiring a justification that reads like a syllogism, where the major is a valid legal norm. For such justification, however, logic is just one condition.

[2] Henderson, 'From Big Law to Lean Law', 38 *International Review of Law and Economics* (2014) 5; R. Susskind, *The End of Lawyers? Rethinking the Nature of Legal Services* (2010). Note that many legal scholars who advocate legal tech have a background in 'old school' law and economics. For new inroads see 5(1) *Critical Analysis of Law* (2018), the special issue on 'new economic analysis of law', https://cal.library.utoronto.ca/index.php/cal/issue/view/1977 (last visited 6 April 2022).

[3] Though this may be more a challenge for big publishers and 'legaltech' start-ups than 'traditional' big tech (Stevenson and Wagoner, 'Bargaining in the Shadow of Big Data', 67(4) *Florida Law Review* (2015), 1337–1400.

[4] An in-depth survey of previous and current legal analytics: K. Ashley, *Artificial Intelligence and Legal Analytics: New Tools for Law Practice in the Digital Age* (2017).

Mireille Hildebrandt, *Boundary Work between Computational 'Law' and 'Law-as-We-Know-it'* In: *Data at the Boundaries of European Law*. Edited by: Deirdre Curtin and Mariavittoria Catanzariti, Oxford University Press. © Mireille Hildebrandt 2023.
DOI: 10.1093/oso/9780198874195.003.0002

(e-disclosure), and of text corpora in the realm of case law and legislation to detect patterns in legal reasoning (legal search and argumentation mining), or of various types of data in the realm of case law and regulation to predict the outcome of future cases (prediction of judgment).[5] Based on the idea that machine-readable access to legally relevant data will bring unprecedented foresight to both lawyers and their clients, some authors even herald 'data-driven law' or computational law as the new *path of the law*.[6] In other words, predictive legal technologies may transform the way that law-as-we-know-it exists, disrupting the *mode of existence* of modern positive law. Such disruption is a concern because it may transform or diminish both the legal protection and the instrumentality offered by law and the rule of law. In point of fact, it may turn law into administration when crossing the boundaries between legal judgment and data-driven calculation, and between legal argumentation and the statistics of natural language processing.

In the second part of this chapter, I will enquire into the lure of data-driven law, starting with a discussion of predictive legal technologies (based on machine learning) and their mathematical assumptions, zooming in on a specific type (called natural language processing or NLP), followed by a more in-depth discussion of predictive software applied to the judgments of the European Court of Human Rights (ECtHR). The second part should thus provide the reader with a first taste of what these data-driven AI systems afford as 'legal' technologies. The term 'AI systems' aligns with the definition in the proposed EU AI Act,[7] which defines such systems in terms of software that can 'for a given set of human-defined objectives, generate outputs such as content, predictions, recommendations, or decisions influencing the environments they interact with', based on a variety of techniques, notably machine learning.[8] I will refer to the latter as 'data-driven AI systems', while also using the terms 'legal technologies' or computational 'law' as these are terms of the trade in the relevant domain of scholarly research.

The third part is dedicated to an in-depth enquiry into the *affordances* of text-driven law, to better understand what enabled modern law's mode of existence and what we stand to lose if law comes to depend on data-driven technologies. This will involve an analysis of 'natural language and speech',

[5] M. Livermore and D. Rockmore (eds), *Law as Data: Computation, Text, & the Future of Legal Analysis* (2019).

[6] Alarie, 'The Path of the Law: Towards Legal Singularity', 66(4) *University of Toronto Law Journal* (2016) 443.

[7] European Commission, Communication COM/2021/206 final.

[8] Article 3(1) and Annex I of the proposed AI Act.

highlighting the implications of the shift from oral to written speech acts, while paying keen attention to the notion of a 'speech act' as key to a proper understanding of the force of law. This feeds into a discussion of 'structure and action' to mark the multi-interpretability of human action, the contestability this implies, and how this relates to the concepts of legal certainty and the rule of law. I then clarify how the text-driven nature of modern law enabled some of the core tenets of the rule of law, notably its positivity (the notion of legal effect) and contestability (based on the multi-interpretability of text and human action) and argue that both are dependent on the performativity of legal decisions. This will allow me to address the difference between the *performativity* of legal norms and the *performance* of predictive legal technologies. If legal practice were to adopt these kinds of technologies, it could end up disrespecting the boundary between a law that addresses people as human agents and a law that treats them as subject to a statistical, machinic logic.

The fourth part will draw some pertinent conclusions and advocate the notion of *legal protection by design* as a means to ensure that legal protection is preserved or reinvented in the era of computational 'law', with various pointers to the proposed EU AI Act. This will require a new type of boundary work on the cusp of law, computer science, and engineering.

2. The Lure of Data-Driven 'Law'

A. A Tasting of Predictive Legal Technologies

1. Anticipation as the Heart of the Law

In this chapter the focus will be on technologies used to predict the outcome of a court case, or prediction of judgment (PoJ).[9] This may remind us of Oliver Wendell Holmes's seminal work on *The Path of the Law*, where he wrote that:[10] 'The prophecies of what the courts will do in fact, and nothing more pretentious, are what I mean by the law.' Though I often hear people quoting Holmes as saying that 'law is what the courts say', he instead situated the law in the *anticipation* of court decisions, tasking lawyers with the role of providing those subject to the law with a reasonably predictable path of the law.

[9] See for a focus on the use of AI systems for 'legal search' (such as e.g. Westlaw Edge) Hildebrandt, 'A Philosophy of Technology for Computational Law', in D. Mangan and C. Easton(eds) *The Philosophical Foundations of Information Technology Law* (forthcoming 2022), draft available at https://doi.org/10.31228/osf.io/7eykj (last accessed 18 November 2020).

[10] Holmes, 'The Path of the Law', 110(5) *Harvard Law Review* (1997) 991.

This anticipation may assuage but cannot resolve the fundamental uncertainty about 'what the courts will do in fact'. Instead, it prepares the road for 'legal certainty' by helping those subject to law to estimate the legal consequences of their actions, such as a legal obligation to pay compensation, to perform a contractual obligation, a duty to refrain from interference with another's property, or punishability due to a violation of the criminal law. Interestingly, Holmes speaks of what the courts do rather than what they say; he seems on par with Austin's *How to Do Things with Words*,[11] to which I will return below.

Legal scholars trained in the assumptions of 'law and economics' often claim that the success of predictive technologies asserts Holmes' prophetic foresight about the direction of the law,[12] as he also claimed that: '[f]or the rational study of the law the blackletter man may be the man of the present, but the man of the future is the man of statistics and the master of economics.'[13] One could surmise that the combination of machine learning (a modulation of statistics) and nudge theory (a modulation of behavioural economics) may one day qualify as the new hermeneutics of legal professionals.[14] Instead of engaging in the close reading of legal texts to argue their case, lawyers may soon be asked to outsource their 'reading' to sophisticated software systems. The claim is that these systems are capable of anticipating what a court would decide, based on the processing of incredible amounts of legally relevant data. If it is true that law must be situated in such anticipation, their predictions could be framed as the new way to establish positive law. This is why some scholars speak of 'computational law'.[15] Though I believe that data-driven AI systems could be deployed to establish positive law (meaning their output would have legal effect), it is crucial to gain a proper understanding of the difference that makes a difference[16] between human and machine anticipation, as such difference denotes the boundary between human and machinic agency.

In this part (2) of the chapter I will investigate software capable of what has been coined as 'distant reading' by way of NLP,[17] which is a specific type of machine learning (ML). This will be done below, in section B, discussing the mathematics of ML, in section C, exploring the nature of meaning in NLP,

[11] J. Austin, *How to Do Things with Words* (1975).

[12] I. Ayres, *Super Crunchers: Why Thinking-by-Numbers Is the New Way to Be Smart* (2007).

[13] Holmes (n. 10), at 1001.

[14] Yeung, '"Hypernudge": Big Data as a Mode of Regulation by Design', 20(1) *Information, Communication & Society* (2017) 118.

[15] Genesereth, 'Computational Law. The Cop in the Backseat', White Paper (2015), http://logic.stanford.edu/complaw/complaw.html (last visited 6 April 2022).

[16] G. Bateson, *Steps to an Ecology of Mind* (1972) defined information as 'the difference that makes a difference'.

[17] F. Moretti, *Graphs, Maps, Trees. Abstract Models for a Literary History* (2005).

and in section D, taking the example of using NLP to predict judgments of the ECtHR. First, however, under 2 of this section (A), I will look into predictive technologies that are not even concerned with content, while nevertheless claiming to reliably predict the outcome of court cases.

2. Using Machine Learning Technologies to Predict Legal Judgments

To highlight that a PoJ is not necessarily concerned with substance (content),[18] I will briefly discuss PoJ based on sensor and behavioural data. This should warn us against the trap of thinking that data-driven AI systems perceive, reason, and cognize as we do, just because they manage to arrive at similar conclusions.

In their article 'Emotional Arousal Predicts Voting on the U.S. Supreme Court',[19] Dietrich, Enos, and Sen discussed their use of 'vocal pitch data' (sensor data) of justices during oral arguments in the US Supreme Court (SC) to predict what they term the 'voting behaviour' of the justices. They summarize their findings in stating that the 'results show that the higher emotional arousal or excitement directed at an attorney compared to his or her opponent, the less likely that attorney is to win the Justice's vote ($p < 0.001$)'. Interestingly, the predictive value of their experiment was 1.79 per cent higher than the famous algorithm developed by Katz, Bommarito II, and Blackman in 2014,[20] suggesting that emotional inferences based on vocal pitch were more predictive than the 95 variables used by Katz, Bommarito II, and Blackman.

Three years later Katz, Bommarito II, and Blackman published their latest findings in a seminal article,[21] claiming their algorithm provides for predictions that generalize beyond the data on which it was trained, is consistent across time and across different justices, and notably also generalizes to future cases (this is called 'out of sample' testing in ML-speak). The so-called accuracy of their predictions is said to be 70.2 per cent for the outcome of the case and 71.9 per cent for the voting behaviour of individual justices.[22] This links back

[18] In ML terms, substance is called 'content'. ML thinks in terms of content and metadata, as we (lawyers) think in terms of substance and procedure (which is not to say that metadata is equivalent to procedure). In relation to PoJ we have content data (texts of judgments), sensor data (e.g. voice pitch of judges), behavioural data (e.g. voting behaviour of judges), and metadata (e.g. date, case-number, court, judges, outcome). Note that the categories are debatable and may overlap.

[19] Dietrich, Enos, and Sen, 'Emotional Arousal Predicts Voting on the U.S. Supreme Court', 27(2) *Political Analysis* (2019) 237.

[20] Katz, Bommarito II, and Blackman, 'Predicting the Behavior of the Supreme Court of the United States: A General Approach', *ArXiv:1407.6333 [Physics]* (2014) http://arxiv.org/abs/1407.6333 (last visited 6 April 2022).

[21] Katz, Bommarito II, and Blackman, 'A General Approach for Predicting the Behavior of the Supreme Court of the United States', 12(4) *PLOS One* 12 (2017) e0174698.

[22] Accuracy is a technical term in ML, where it refers to the ratio between the number of correct predictions and the total number of predictions (G. James *et al.*, *An Introduction to Statistical Learning: with*

to the fact that—in line with the limits of predictive technologies—they had to seek out questions that allow for discrete answers:[23]

> While many questions could be evaluated, the Court's decisions offer at least two discrete prediction questions: 1) will the Court as a whole affirm or reverse the status quo judgment and 2) will each individual Justice vote to affirm or reverse the status quo judgment?

Though a lawyer may find these the least interesting and the least informative questions, for a machine that is at its best when crunching numbers this is a wonderful chance to show how it can outperform human experts, distracted as they may be by the substance (content) of the case law.

Katz, Bommarito II, and Blackman trained their algorithm on the Supreme Court Database (SCDB), containing the machine-readable text of all court cases decided by the SC, where 240 metadata were added (as relevant variables), such as:[24]

> chronological variables, case background variables, justice-specific variables, and outcome variables. Many of these variables are categorical, taking on hundreds of possible values; for example, the ISSUE variable can take 384 distinct values. These SCDB variables form the basis for both our features and outcome variables.

To train an algorithm, a 'machine readable task' must be developed. This is done in terms of a so-called 'target variable', in this case a variable that refers to the outcome of the case (reversal or affirmation of the verdict that is appealed). The *outcome variable* must be correlated with relevant *input variables*. All this goes back to the need to develop a type of questions that can be formalized to enable number crunching, instead of questions that require acuity in terms of ambiguous concepts with an open texture. Next, a subset of the available variables is selected as potentially relevant *features*, enriched with additional

Applications in R (2021), at section 2.2). Other metrics are precision, which refers to the ratio between true positives and the sum of true and false positives, and recall, which refers to the ratio between true positives and the sum of true positives and false negatives (James *et al.* (n. 22) 152). Especially where the real-world implications of a positive or negative prediction matter, it becomes very important to know precision and recall. To seriously assess the reliability of a predictive system all three metrics must be provided.

23 Katz, Bommarito II, and Blackman (n. 21), at 2.
24 Ibid., at 4.

features that were 'engineered' by the authors, e.g. those that relate to the circuit courts whose decisions are appealed, those related to whether or not oral arguments were heard, and those specifying the historical reversal rate (per Justice).

After thus curating and enriching the *training data*, a model is constructed to detect potentially relevant correlations between the *feature set* and the *target variable*. The model used here is a so called 'random forest classifier', i.e. a set of *statistical learners* (trees) that correlate features with the target variable and then take the average over the set (the forest).[25] Please note that the term 'statistical learners' refers to the use of mathematical functions that best 'capture' the correlation. In ML this set is usually called the *hypothesis space*. Whereas lawyers may think hypotheses are statements such as 'if intent is not proven conviction is not likely', in data-driven legal technologies a hypothesis is a *mathematical function* that depicts a very precise mathematical relationship between a specific combination of input variables (with different weights) and a specified target variable.

As indicated above, the results of thus training the algorithm are presented in terms of the accuracy of the model: in 70.2 per cent of cases the model correctly predicted the outcome, which depends on the voting of all the justices, and in 71.9 per cent of cases the model correctly predicted the votes of the individual justices. The model does not *explain* why justices voted in one way or another (a correlation is not a cause), nor does it *justify* the decision of the SC (it does not engage in legal reasoning). The only thing it does is predict binary decisions made by the SC and by individual justices, based on the statistical relationships within the training data.

To argue why this is interesting at all, Katz, Bommarito II, and Blackman compare the accuracy of their predictions with the predictive force of other models, which is called comparing against a *baseline* or *null model*.[26] One such model would be to flip a coin, though that does not sound very impressive as it refers to a random distribution of outcomes. According to the authors, the legal community agrees that the best bet is to predict reversal, because—statistically—this is what the SC more often decided during the previous 35 terms: 57 per cent of justices voted reverse, and 63 per cent of SC decisions were reverse.[27] Interestingly, this baseline does not hold if one goes further back in

[25] Taking the average over the set reduces potential *overfitting*, which refers to developing a model that is highly accurate on the training data but not on new data (meaning it does not generalize). See James *et al.* (n. 22) 22.

[26] A baseline is any model that one hopes to outperform, e.g. the most frequent output variable, a random outcome, the median of the training set, or simply another ML model you want to outperform: James *et al.* (n. 22) 86. A null model is based on the assumption that the features one wishes to test do not influence the target variable: James *et al.* (n. 22) 79.

[27] Katz, Bommarito II, and Blackman (n. 21) 9.

time, whereas their own model does hold sway. After adding some constraints, they come up with three baseline models[28] and conclude that their predictions 'outperform' the most relevant one by 5 per cent.[29]

Though this may sound like a minor advantage, they point out that: 'Indeed, with respect to markets, given judicial decisions can impact publicly traded companies . . . even modest gains in prediction can produce significant financial rewards.'[30] This raises the question of the aim of this type of legal technology. Is the lure of their accuracy connected with the intent to use the measure they provide as a target (for financial gain)? In that case we may be in for some very unwelcome dynamics, taking into account the so-called Goodhart effect that 'predicts' that: '[w]hen a measure becomes a target, it ceases to be a good measure.'[31] This can be due to attempts to game the measures, but just as well because human beings are always in the process of anticipating the consequences of their actions. Both those using the measure as a target (an insurance company anticipating whether they will win a case) and those being targeted (judges with access to predictions of their voting behaviour) will probably change their actions in view of the predictions (this is also referred to as automation bias).[32] Even if those changes are incremental in the first instance, they may have far reaching consequences in the long run, as legal practice crosses the boundary between legal assessment and computational prediction.

B. The Mathematical Assumptions of Machine Learning

1. Learning as a Machine

In his textbook on ML, Tom Mitchell describes ML as drawing on 'ideas from a diverse set of disciplines, including artificial intelligence, probability and statistics, computational complexity, information theory, psychology and neurobiology, control theory, and philosophy'.[33] For a machine to learn, a well-defined learning problem must be articulated, because computing systems can only operate when given formalized *machine-readable tasks*:[34]

[28] P. Cilliers, *Complexity and Postmodernism: Understanding Complex Systems* (1998).
[29] Katz, Bommarito II, and Blackman (n. 21) 14.
[30] Ibid.
[31] Strathern, '"Improving Ratings": Audit in the British University System', 5(3) *European Review* (1997) 305.
[32] Strauß, 'Deep Automation Bias: How to Tackle a Wicked Problem of AI?', 5(2) *Big Data and Cognitive Computing* (2021) 18.
[33] T. Mitchell, *Machine Learning* (1997) 17.
[34] Ibid.

> A well-defined learning problem requires a well-specified task, performance metric, and source of training experience.
>
> Designing a machine learning approach involves a number of design choices, including choosing the type of training experience, the target function to be learned, a representation for this target function.

This implies a number of design decisions, including the making of a number of assumptions that may or may not be valid. Many of these decisions relate to issues on the nexus of logic and statistics, where grotesque mistakes can be made.[35] In ML these mistakes are difficult to assess because they are hidden in the design process. The most blatant and hazardous, though also inevitable and reasonable, assumption concerns *the distribution of training data and future data*:[36]

> We shall see that most current theory of machine learning rests on the crucial assumption that the distribution of training examples is identical to the distribution of test examples. Despite our need to make this assumption in order to obtain theoretical results, it is important to keep in mind that this assumption must often be violated in practice.

In other words: ML cannot do anything but scale the past; contrary to what some may believe, it cannot predict the future unless the future is the same as the past. For PoJ this has many implications, because deploying these technologies to decide cases would not just scale the past but thereby also freeze the future.[37]

2. No Machine Learning without Mathematical Assumptions

This links up with another—even more fundamental—assumption of ML, which is that of an underlying mathematical reality that 'maps' human intercourse. Without that assumption ML makes no sense. It is the ground on which all ML research design stands, and therewith the point of departure for all ML applications.[38] Though one can be agnostic about whether such mapping implies either causality between the mathematics and the real world, or

[35] Gigerenzer, 'Statistical Rituals: The Replication Delusion and How We Got There', 1(2) *Advances in Methods and Practices in Psychological Science* (2018) 198; Yarkoni, 'The Generalizability Crisis', 45 *Behavioral and Brain Sciences* (2022) e1.

[36] Mitchell (n. 33) 6.

[37] Hildebrandt, 'Code-Driven Law: Freezing the Future and Scaling the Past', in C. Markou and S. Deakin (eds), *Is Law Computable? Critical Perspectives on Law and Artificial Intelligence* (2020).

[38] McQuillan, 'Data Science as Machinic Neoplatonism', 31(2) *Philosophy & Technology* (2018) 253.

neo-Platonic realism, it remains an assumption that requires critical attention. Legal technologies that employ ML techniques, or have been built using ML techniques, depend on this assumption and require keen attention to its implications. For instance, the *limits* that are inherent in mathematical and computational inquiry should be foregrounded when trusting predictive software, taking into account that such limits may impact the *reliability* of these techniques, especially if there are no institutional checks and balances to detect and counter unsubstantiated claims regarding the functionality and validity of their outputs.

I believe that reducing the problem of ML applications to their black box nature or to the potential bias they may create or reinforce distracts attention from the range of trade-offs that are inherent in any ML *research design*. Whereas lawyers and computer scientists are exploring explainable AI on the one hand,[39] and seeking ways to ensure fair computing on the other,[40] the more fundamental question about what kind of questions these systems can actually address is hardly touched upon. For lawyers, however, this is crucial. If the assumption that legal practice reflects a deeper, mathematical reality is incorrect, we need to acknowledge that data-driven legal technologies address questions that may not be relevant for legal practice. The latter is concerned with meaning and judgment rather than statistics and calculation.

C. Natural Language Processing as 'Distant Reading'

1. Distant Reading of Legal Text

Having discussed several examples of PoJ technologies based on voice pitch, prior voting behaviours, and other metadata, we will now focus on the more obvious legal ML technology, namely NLP. Though NLP is again about detecting mathematical patterns in data, the relevant data here is legal text; the mathematics concerns the content, not the metadata.[41]

In 2000, literary historian Franco Moretti explained how computational techniques can be used to map and mine an immensely large corpus of texts

[39] Kaminski, 'The Right to Explanation, Explained', 34(1) *Berkeley Technology Law Journal* (2019) 189; Chouldechova and Roth, 'The Frontiers of Fairness in Machine Learning', *ArXiv:1810.08810* (2018), http://arxiv.org/abs/1810.08810 (last visited 18 December 2021); Powles, 'The Seductive Diversion of "Solving" Bias in Artificial Intelligence', *Medium* (2018), https://medium.com/s/story/the-seductive-diversion-of-solving-bias-in-artificial-intelligence-890df5e5ef53 (last visited 18 December 2021).

[40] Chouldechova and Roth (n. 39).

[41] Note that the distinction between content and metadata is itself a new way of understanding legal text.

for potentially relevant patterns. His book was called *Distant Reading*,[42] and it has captured the imagination of those versed in what has been called the 'digital humanities', by uncovering heretofore unknown patterns within and without the literary canon. To give just one example we can quote Clement on her findings after distant reading the infamously arduous novel *The Makings of Americans* by Gertrude Stein:[43]

> The particular reading difficulties engendered by the complicated patterns of repetition in *The Making of Americans* by Gertrude Stein make it almost impossible to read this text in a traditional, linear manner. However, by visualizing certain patterns and looking at the text 'from a distance' through textual analytics and visualizations, we are enabled to make readings that were formerly inhibited. Initial analysis on Making within the MONK (metadata offer new knowledge) project (http://www.monkproject.org/) has yielded evidence which suggests that the text is intricately and purposefully structured. Using text mining to retrieve repetitive patterns and treating each as a single object makes it possible to visualize and compare the three dimensions upon which these repetitions co-occur—by length, frequency, and location—in a single view. Certainly, reading *The Making of Americans* in a traditional way appears to have yielded limited material for scholarly work, but reading the text differently, as an object of pairings or as parts of combinations, ultimately works in contrast to the supposition that the text is only meaningful to the extent that it defeats making meaning. A distant view of the text's structure allows us to read the text as an object that becomes, as it continues to turn in on itself with a centrifugal force, a whole history without beginning or ending.

Just as legal scholarship concerns the exegesis of a corpus of legal texts, the humanities have been known for their methodological rigour in 'close reading' and philological inquiry, supposedly thus uncovering the meaning of literary and other texts. Computational distant reading confronts us with an entirely different perspective on our ability to map and navigate complex textual

[42] F. Moretti, *Distant Reading* (2013); Schulz, 'What Is Distant Reading?', *New York Times* (2011), https://www.nytimes.com/2011/06/26/books/review/the-mechanic-muse-what-is-distant-reading.html (last visited 18 December 2021); Jänicke *et al.*, 'On Close and Distant Reading in Digital Humanities: A Survey and Future Challenges', *Eurographics Conference on Visualization (EuroVis) - STARs* (2015).

[43] Clement, '"A Thing Not Beginning and Not Ending": Using Digital Tools to Distant-Read Gertrude Stein's *The Making of Americans*', 23(3) *Literary and Linguistic Computing* (2008) 361 (the quotation is the full extract).

sources. This has heralded a new era of purportedly enhanced comprehension of textual corpora, raising a number of interesting questions about the extent to which these computational X-rays are capable of grasping a deeper, novel, more relevant or merely different meaning of text. Especially where the sheer volume precludes close reading by any individual human scholar. When investigating 'the meaning and mining of legal text' in a chapter of a Berry's *Understanding Digital Humanities*, I referred to the relevance of previous work by Moretti and Clement:[44] 'Rather than painstakingly reading one's way into a mass of individual cases to see how codes and statutes are interpreted, helped by legal treatises on the relevant legal doctrine, the developers of the inference machines discussed above hope that they will at some point provide a more immediate oversight regarding whatever may be the factual and legal issues at stake.'

2. Caveats when Engaging with Distant Reading of Legal Text

Eight years later, Livermore and Rockmore, in their *Law as Data*, again refer to Moretti, suggesting that 'the potential utility of distant reading for many different types of legal scholarship is great',[45] quoting a number of studies that employ a variety of NLP methodologies to actually mine legal text. Their overview, however, does not address the new kind of questions that are raised by NLP and does not provide the caveats lawyers should take into account when outsourcing the 'reading' of legal text. Clearly, the output of the computational methodologies presents us with a new kind of 'text', consisting of trees, graphs, and scattergrams, based on the latest approaches in NLP, such as the 'fantastic' bi-directional encoder representations from transformers (BERT),[46] which has revolutionized both search and machine translation. This will require what I have called a 'new hermeneutics', capable of sustaining legal certainty in the face of oftentimes inscrutable claims about the reliability and relevance of NLP's output for the law. Based on the work of Sculley and Pasanek,[47] I articulated five caveats for legal scholars that still seem highly relevant:[48]

[44] Hildebrandt, 'The Meaning and Mining of Legal Texts', in D. Berry (ed.), *Understanding Digital Humanities: The Computational Turn and New Technology* (2011) 153. Referring to Moretti (n. 17); Clement *et al.*, 'How Not to Read a Million Books' (2008), https://web.archive.org/web/20110810212513/http://www3.isrl.illinois.edu/~unsworth/hownot2read.html (last visited 18 December 2021).

[45] Livermore and Rockford, 'Distant Reading the Law', in M. Livermore and D. Rockford (eds), *Law as Data: Computation, Text, and the Future of Legal Analysis* (2019) 19.

[46] Devlin *et al.*, 'BERT: Pre-Training of Deep Bidirectional Transformers for Language Understanding', *Proceedings of NAACL-HLT 2019* (2019) 4171.

[47] Sculley and Pasanek, 'Meaning and Mining: The Impact of Implicit Assumptions in Data Mining for the Humanities', 23(4) *Literary and Linguistic Computing* (2008) 409.

[48] Hildebrandt (n. 44) 155.

First, the collaborative effort of computer engineers and lawyers who sit down together to mine legal data bases should focus on making their assumptions about the scope, function and meaning of the relevant legal texts explicit.

Second, they should use multiple representations and methodologies, thus providing for a plurality of mining strategies that will most probably result in destabilising any monopoly on the interpretation of the legal domain.

Third, all trials should be reported instead of 'cherry-picking' those results that confirm the experimenters' bias. As they suggest, at some point failed experiments can reveal more than supposedly successful ones. This is particularly important in a legal setting, because the legal framework of constitutional democracy should prevent individual outliers and minority positions from being overruled by dominant frames of interpretation.

Fourth, in a legal setting the public interest requires transparency about the data and the methods used to make the data-mining operations verifiable by other joint ventures of lawyers and software engineers.

This connects to their fifth recommendation, regarding the peer review of the methodologies used. The historical artifact of a legal system that is relatively autonomous in regard to both morality and politics, and safeguarded by an independent judiciary has been nourished by an active class of legal scholars, and practitioners willing to test and contest the claimed truth of mainstream legal doctrine. Only a similarly detailed and agonistic scrutiny of the results of data-mining operations can sustain the fragile negotiations of the rule of law.

Since writing this, I have also developed the notion of agonistic ML,[49] to refer to ways and means to ensure both the *testing* and the *contesting* of truth claims made 'on behalf of' ML applications. More recently I added a plea to introduce a pertinent requirement of preregistration of ML research design by developers and producers of ML systems, in combination with strict liability for damage caused by the deployment of such systems, where such liability should target those who put these systems on the market (as they stand to profit).[50] Though it may not be obvious whether the use of NLP as a legal technology has caused damage, it seems crucial that technologies capable of influencing or even determining legal advice and legal decision making must obey the highest standards in terms of testability and contestability to thus ensure their reliability. In

[49] Hildebrandt, 'Privacy as Protection of the Incomputable Self: From Agnostic to Agonistic Machine Learning', 20(1) *Theoretical Inquiries in Law* (2019).

[50] Hildebrandt, 'Preregistration of Machine Learning Research Design. Against P-Hacking', in E. Bayamlioglu *et al.* (eds), *Being Profiled: Cogitas Ergo Sum* (2018).

the proposed AI Act, these kinds of requirements have been integrated as legal obligations for providers of high-risk AI systems, and the proposal qualifies AI systems deployed by the judiciary as high risk.[51] It seems pivotal, however, that all data-driven legal technologies deployed in legal practice should all be qualified as high risk, due to their impact on the fundamental rights of those involved in a legal dispute, whether on the side of law firms, public prosecutor, judiciary, or even in the realm of legal insurance or legal dispute resolution by commercial parties.

D. The Case of Predicting the European Court of Human Rights

1. Using Supervised NLP for PoJ

Having explained the affordances of AI systems that aim to predict the outcome of court cases, highlighting the need to verify and falsify the claims made regarding the behaviour of these technologies, I will now discuss a European example of PoJ. Other than the previous examples, in section A, the predictions are based on NLP instead of sensor data (such as vocal pitch) or behavioural metadata (such as voting behaviour of individual judges). This should give us a clear example of the 'distant reading' of legal text.

In 2016 Aletras *et al.* published the findings of their application of NLP on judgments of the ECtHR.[52] After training an algorithm on the published texts of judgments relating to a limited set of articles of the ECHR, they concluded that their algorithm managed to correctly predict a binary outcome (violation or no violation) with 79 per cent accuracy. Based on their findings, they also suggest that their algorithm confirmed that it is the facts of the case rather than issues of law that decide the outcome, thus supposedly validating core tenets of legal realism. In other work I have explained that these conclusions are brittle, based on a number of assumptions, most of which do not fly.[53] The most problematic assumptions were that (1) the text of published judgments is proper proxy for the underlying briefs and evidence, and that (2) the rendering of the

[51] Chapter 2 of Title 3 of the proposed AI Act stipulates the requirements for high-risk systems. Annex III point 8 defines AI systems in the area of 'Administration of justice and democratic processes' as high risk, though for now only 'AI systems intended to assist a judicial authority in researching and interpreting facts and the law and in applying the law to a concrete set of facts'.

[52] Aletras *et al.*, 'Predicting Judicial Decisions of the European Court of Human Rights: A Natural Language Processing Perspective', 2 *PeerJ Computer Science* (2016) e93.

[53] Hildebrandt, 'Algorithmic Regulation and the Rule of Law', 376 *Philosophical Transactions of the Royal Society A* (2018).

facts as related in the Court's judgment is an independent variable. The first assumption is problematic because many relevant data are missing (e.g. sections on law in cases deemed inadmissible by the Court). One could say that mistaking the published judgment for the relevant data demonstrates the 'survival bias' or the 'low hanging fruit bias'.[54] The second assumption is clearly incorrect as any lawyer knows that the Court will formulate the facts such that they are well attuned to the verdict (as the authors actually acknowledged). Though in ML it is necessary to make a number of assumptions to enable the computational research design, it is not a good idea to draw real life conclusions based on the outcome.[55]

2. Using Unsupervised NLP for PoJ

In 2019 Chalkidis, Androutsopoulos, and Aletras published new research into the use of NLP on legal text, this time based on the employment of so-called neural nets. They speak of 'legal judgment prediction', which they define as 'the task of automatically predicting the outcome of a court case, given a text describing the case's facts'. The paper 'sells' the idea of modelling PoJ by claiming that '[s]uch models may assist legal practitioners and citizens, while reducing legal costs and improving access to justice.' They add that '[l]awyers and judges can use them to estimate the likelihood of winning a case and come to more consistent and informed judgments, respectively.'[56] This again implies that the research aims for people to use the *measure* that is the outcome of the research as a *target* for cost reduction, for 'better' judgments, and for better access to justice. These types of claims are questionable, more fit for consultants than scientists, and highly problematic in view of the Goodhart effect referred to above. Obviously, the ability to predict the outcome of cases, when based on statistical correlations, will not necessarily result in better judgments. The authors seem to be aware of this, in their conclusions, to which I will return after recounting their research.

The research presented in 2019 differs from that in 2016. First, the dataset is extended from 600 to 11,500 cases. Second, the binary prediction (violation/no violation) is no longer limited to a restricted set of articles but concerns

[54] On the 'cognitive' biases of ML systems, see Geckoboard, 'Data fallacies', https://www.geckoboard.com/best-practice/statistical-fallacies/ (last visited 18 December 2021).

[55] Computer scientists actually warn against this, see notably Medvedeva, Wieling, and Vols, 'The Danger of Reverse-Engineering of Automated Judicial Decision-Making Systems', *ArXiv:2012.10301* (2020) http://arxiv.org/abs/2012.10301 (last visited 6 April 2022).

[56] Chalkidis, Androutsopoulos, and Aletras, 'Neural Legal Judgment Prediction in English', *Proceedings of the 57th Annual Meeting of the Association for Computational Linguistics* (2019) all quotes from p. 4317.

violations of any article (including those in the Protocols of the Convention). Third, the prediction not only concerns whether or not the Court decided that a violation had taken place, but also whether the case is important on a scale of 1–4 (the scores were provided by the Court). Fourth, the methodology differs substantially from that used in 2016, as the authors tested four types of 'neural models', including a modulation of the famous BERT model that involves highly complex and layered processing of word sequences, taking into account the way potentially relevant wordings are embedded in sentences and textural corpora. Using the modulated BERT model, the accuracy for the binary violation task is now 82 per cent, more than 10 per cent higher than that of the previous research.

3. The Accuracy–Reliability Trade-off

As often in the case of neural networks, high accuracy combines with a lack of interpretability.[57] Whereas the previous research allowed one to detect which features correlated with the target variable, the neural nets operate as a black box and hide potentially relevant features, their interrelations, and their weightings. As the authors assert in the conclusions, the model does not provide an explanation for its predictions.[58] Instead of speaking of an explanation, however, they speak of a justification, pointing out that judges will need a 'justification' for the model's predictions. In the legal sense, an explanation of how the system reached its conclusion does not provide a justification, which must be based on the available legal reasons, not on statistical correlations. Chalkidis, Androutsopoulos, and Aletras plan 'to expand the scope of this study by exploring the automated analysis of additional resources (e.g., relevant case law, dockets, prior judgments) that could be then utilized in a multi-input fashion to further improve performance and justify system decisions'.[59] Once again, what they call 'a justification' of system decisions is not a justification in the legal sense, but the verification of a causal influence of specified input features on the system's output variable (violation or no violation). The law is, however, not about the causality between specific arguments and their conclusion, which would entail a category mistake.[60] The law

[57] The accuracy-interpretability trade-off suggests that though one cannot explain the outcome, in the case of neural networks it is nevertheless highly accurate. This is, however, not necessarily the case, and the lack of interpretability makes it hard to check, see notably Caruana *et al.*, 'Intelligible Models for HealthCare: Predicting Pneumonia Risk and Hospital 30-Day Readmission', in *Proceedings of the 21th ACM SIGKDD International Conference on Knowledge Discovery and Data Mining* (2015) 1721.

[58] Chalkidis, Androutsopoulos, and Aletras (n. 56) 4321, also referring to Jain and Wallace, 'Attention Is Not Explanation', *Proceedings of NAACL-HLT 2019* (2019) 3543.

[59] Chalkidis, Androutsopoulos, and Aletras (n. 56) 4321.

[60] G. Ryle, *The Concept of Mind* (1949).

requires that a legal decision (the attribution of legal effect, such as 'these facts qualify as a violation') is based on the fulfilment of specified legal conditions, which in turn requires a reflective equilibrium between qualifying the facts in terms of the relevant legal norm and the relevant legal norm in terms of the facts.[61] Other than this type of predictive NLP systems assume, the facts are not given. As the French say: *les faits sont faits* (the facts are made).[62] Not in the sense of 'made up', but in the sense that what counts as the criminal offence of murder depends on the double focus of looking at the facts from the perspective of the criminal law and looking at the criminal law from the perspective of the facts. There is a feedback loop between how we read the facts and how we read the law, which marks the difference between *logical consistency* and what Dworkin called the *integrity of the law*.[63] Consistency would freeze both the law and our understanding of the facts, whereas integrity leaves room for the multi-interpretability of both, while still requiring a decision—grounded in the shared experience of being human in a shared jurisdiction. This 'shared world' dimension is connected with empathy and common sense, tacit knowledge, and the need to anticipate the institutional world we navigate.[64] This dimension, however, is not shared by the NLP systems that cannot but restrict themselves to text *as data*. In short, these systems have a very poor grasp of the world that grounds the ECtHR, which is also the world the Court must decide upon in its verdicts. Taking these predictions seriously as if they were law or legally relevant would stretch the boundaries of modern positive law into the territory of machinic calculation, shifting the focus of legal judgment from meaning to computation.

3. Text-driven Law: What We Stand to Lose

A. Language and Speech

1. The Nature of Text-driven Law

In light of the statistical underpinnings of ML, as discussed in part 2, let me return to Holmes' prophecy. A prophecy implies uncertainty. It may refer to

[61] J. Rawls, *A Theory of Justice* (2005).

[62] See also B. Shapiro, *A Culture of Fact: England, 1550–1720* (2003).

[63] R. Dworkin, *Law's Empire* (1991); de Graaf, 'Dworkin's Constructive Interpretation as a Method of Legal Research', 12 *Law and Method* (2015).

[64] Hildebrandt, 'The Artificial Intelligence of European Union Law', 21(1) *German Law Journal* (2020) 74.

an educated guess or to trained intuition, while an ML expert may associate a prophecy with feedforward, backpropagation, or reinforcement mechanisms. A guess can be explained by way of the underlying psychology, or by way of the sociological patterns that prevail in a particular society. It can also be explained with the help of model interpretability, if the prophecy was provided by an NLP prediction algorithm. In the context of the law, however, the validation of the prophecy must be developed in the space of interpretation and argumentation; it is not a matter of explanation (in the causal or motivational sense) but of justification. One can understand law and the rule of law as an institution that restricts the decision space of judges: whatever their inclination, the law constrains the kind of reasons they can provide and therewith the set of decisions they can take. That is where the naïve interpretation of legal realism fails; it is not 'the facts' as given parameters that decide the case, because courts are not free to decide in whatever way suits them. Even the fabrication of the facts is bound by the law of evidence. Their construction must be reliable, and their truth claims must be verifiable as well as falsifiable, though the extent to which this is the case will depend on the legal domain.[65]

In this part I address the question of whether the anticipation of legal decision-making by the courts that is core to positive law, implies that PoJs by ML applications should be qualified as law.[66] If they were to qualify as law, we would have to attribute legal effect to the output of prediction machines. If not, they might instead count as public administration[67] or technological management,[68] and in that case, they must be brought under the rule of law—implementing checks and balances such as the right level of transparency, to achieve their contestability. This makes the question of whether or not PoJ qualifies as law of prime importance. To approach this question I will investigate the nature of text-driven law, its affordances, and how they align with

[65] In private law the autonomy of the parties may reduce the role of the court in establishing the facts of the case, to the extent that the parties agree. In criminal law the court may have a duty to establish the material truth, even if it differs from what prosecutor and defence agree upon (especially in civil law jurisdictions).

[66] See also Kerr's argument that Holmes focused on prediction to enable protection of those subject to law rather than enabling protection of either the state or other big players against individuals. Kerr, 'Prediction, Pre-Emption, Presumption: The Path of Law After the Computational Turn', in M. Hildebrandt and K. de Vries (eds), *Privacy, Due Process and the Computational Turn: The Philosophy of Law Meets the Philosophy of Technology* (2013), 91.

[67] Hildebrandt (n. 53).

[68] Brownsword, 'Technological Management and the Rule of Law', 8(1) *Law, Innovation and Technology* (2016) 100, https://doi.org/10.1080/17579961.2016.1161891 (last visited 6 April 2022).

the rule of law as a system of checks and balances that counters the law of the jungle.[69] To come to terms with the shift from current law to data-driven 'law' we need to re-assess the nature of modern positive law *as text-driven law*, embodied in a specific technology, i.e. the printing press. Precisely because the textual nature of contemporary law seems obvious, we may overlook the critical affordances of text-driven infrastructures, taking for granted what may be on the verge of a major transformation.

To investigate the assumptions implied by law's dependence on text and their implications, I will employ the work of Paul Ricoeur,[70] a Continental (French) philosopher in the traditions of phenomenology and hermeneutics, who integrated relevant parts of analytical philosophy in his work, more notably speech act theory. His writings on interpretation align with historical and anthropological research into the relationship between speech, writing, and printing press on the one hand, and the size, structure, and organization of society on the other.[71] The latter research has a much broader scope than traditional speech act theory, notably where it pays keen attention to the move from orality to script (as speech act theory largely overlooks the difference between spoken and written speech acts).[72] Don Ihde, the founding father of philosophy of technology in the empirical tradition, has worked extensively with Ricoeur's work, demonstrating its relevance for understanding the constitutive nature of information and communication infrastructures.[73] After investigating 'natural language and speech' in this section A, to highlight the nature of oral and written speech acts, I will discuss 'structure and action' to mark the nature of meaningful action (section B), followed by conclusions about the nature of text-driven law and the rule of law (section C).

[69] M. Hildebrandt, *Smart Technologies and the End(s) of Law. Novel Entanglements of Law and Technology* (2015) ch. 8; Hildebrandt, 'Law As an Affordance: The Devil Is in the Vanishing Point(s)', 4(1) *Critical Analysis of Law* (2017).

[70] Ricoeur, 'The Model of the Text: Meaningful Action Considered as a Text', 5(1) *New Literary History* (1973) 91; Austin (n. 11); J. Searle, *Speech Acts: An Essay in the Philosophy of Language* (2011); N. MacCormick and O. Weinberger, *An Institutional Theory of Law: New Approaches to Legal Positivism* (1986).

[71] W. Ong, *Orality and Literacy: The Technologizing of the Word* (1982); J. Goody, *The Logic of Writing and the Organization of Society* (1986); E. Eisenstein, *The Printing Revolution in Early Modern Europe* (2005).

[72] Hildebrandt, 'Text-Driven Jurisdiction in Cyberspace', in M. O'Flynn *et al.*, *The Transformation of Criminal Jurisdiction: Extraterritoriality and Enforcement* (forthcoming 2023), preprint available at https://doi.org/10.31219/osf.io/jgs9n (last visited 6 April 2022).

[73] D. Ihde, *Technology and the Lifeworld: From Garden to Earth* (1990); Hildebrandt, *Smart Technologies* (n. 69).

2. Language System and Language Usage

In line with linguistic theory, more precisely semiology, Ricoeur distinguishes between *langue* (language system or code) and *parole* (speech, discourse, or language usage):[74]

> [Speech] is always realized temporally and in a present, whereas the language system is virtual and outside of time. Whereas language lacks a subject (in the sense that the question 'Who is speaking?' does not apply at its level), [speech] refers to its speaker by means of a complex set of indicators such as the personal pronouns. We will say that the 'instance of speech' is self-referential.

Though language is virtual in the sense of providing myriad possibilities to express oneself without being itself an expression,[75] I would not qualify it as outside of time. Language is both the *condition of possibility for* and *the result of* speech, meaning it is necessarily in constant flux, helping us to navigate a changing environment. What Ricoeur rightly points out is that language is not something we invent as individuals, instead, we are 'thrown into' a language that enables us to speak while constraining what we can say, and how. In that sense language is 'given' and outside of time. With 'outside of time' Ricoeur refers to the intralinguistic meaning of a term that is restricted to the other terms it refers to. If we ask for the meaning of a term, the answer will be given by the use of other terms, thus creating a web of meaning. However, to navigate the real world, we need to simultaneously grasp the extralinguistic meaning of a term. That is, its reference to our material and institutional environment. Speech, therefore, is an event that brings together the intra- and extralinguistic meaning, thus producing a 'world', which depends on an interpretive community to make sense. As Cantwell Smith argues in his *The Promise of Artificial Intelligence*,[76] current approaches to AI do not allow computational systems to perceive, cognise or navigate the world outside the code and the data, thus limiting its 'experience' to intra'linguistic' meaning. In other words, the code and the data that inform current AI systems may register or represent the real world but they do not encounter or interact directly with a world of real objects.

If we apply Ricoeur's distinction between language and speech to the law, we can affirm that just like in the case of speech, a legal decision is always realized temporally and in a present, whereas just like in the case of

[74] Ricoeur (n. 70) 92. The translation I quote uses 'discourse' for 'parole'; I prefer to use 'speech'.

[75] Virtuality and actuality are used here in a sense similar to that introduced by Deleuze and Guatari, as elaborated by P. Lévy, *Becoming Virtual. Reality in the Digital Age* (1998).

[76] B. Cantwell Smith, *The Promise of Artificial Intelligence: Reckoning and Judgment* (2019).

language, the legal system is virtual and to some extent given. It is 'outside of time' in the sense that its intrasystematic coherence remains within the bounds of the legal system, as legal concepts are explained in terms of other legal concepts. The legal system lacks a subject (in the sense that the question 'Who is speaking?' does not apply at the level of the system), whereas a legal decision refers to its speaker by means of a complex set of indicators, such as the personal pronouns. We can therefore say that the 'instance of legal decisions' is self-referential: the decision maker may be a legislature, a court, public administration, a corporation, a natural person, or any other legal subject. A legal decision thus refers to an extrasystematic reality (the life world) that is configured by the intrasystematic web of references (terms, rules, and principles) which decides both the meaning of the law and its application.[77]

Ricoeur finds that:[78]

> Whereas language is only the condition for communication, for which it provides the codes, it is in [speech] that all messages are exchanged. In this sense, [speech] alone has not only a world, but an *other*—another person, an interlocutor to whom it is addressed.

We can once more apply this to the law, by confirming that a legal decision is always about something. It refers to a world that it claims to order and decide. And, whereas the legal system is only the condition for legal effect, for which it provides the codes, it is in legal decision making that legal effect is attributed. In this sense, a legal decision creates not only a world and has an author, but also addresses an *other*—another person, an interlocutor. The legislature addresses those under its jurisdiction; courts address the parties, the lower court, the public prosecutor, or the defendant; a party to a contract addresses the other party; the owner who transfers property addresses all others that should refrain from interference with that property. The problem with, for instance, NLP or distant reading of legal text, is that computing systems only have access to the intrasystematic web of legal references; it remains stuck in the sterile environment of formalized objects and relations without a clue as to the life world it supposedly represents and predicts.

[77] The concept of the 'life world' has a long history in phenomenology and hermeneutics, and it is close to Wittgenstein's concept of 'forms of life'. See, e.g., Ihde (n. 73).

[78] Ricoeur (n. 70) 92.

3. From Speaking to Writing

Speech (language usage) is a matter of speaking or writing. Ricoeur developed some incisive insights into the consequences of moving from speaking to writing, by distinguishing three types of distantiation: (1) a distantiation of meaning, because the author cannot control the meaning of their inscription; (2) a distantiation from the ostensive reference, because the reader may no longer share the same space and time as the author, moving from a shared situation to a shared world; and (3) a distantiation from the interlocutor, meaning that the author addresses a potentially unlimited audience. This triple distantiation implies that the meaning of a text cannot be defined by the intention of the author. This nicely ties in with the difference between the German *Verstehen*, in the sense of understanding a *speaker's intent*, and the German *Auslegung*, in the sense of understanding the *meaning of the text*. An oral speech act enables those addressed to check directly with the author, whether they got them right; it also enables the author to exercise some control over their audience, by telling them when they misunderstand. In written speech the author may not be present or even dead, and the lapse in time or the distance in space may require that the reader makes up their own mind about the meaning of the text. Ricoeur explains that the shift from spoken to written speech therefore necessitates the emancipation of the text from the tutelage of the author, instantiating the *autonomous meaning of the text*—based on a reflective equilibrium between the author's intent, the reader's response, and the way the text has been embedded in the contemporary context of the reader. This accords with the idea of an 'autonomous law' that is not under the control of the legislature, as its meaning is ultimately decided by the court, taking into account that its interpretation must make sense to those under its jurisdiction, while also respecting the *telos* of the law in the wider context of the legal system. As Dworkin argued,[79] this is directly connected with the difference between rules and principles and the nature of discretion as bound by the *implied philosophy of the law*. The rise of an autonomous law and the *rule of law* as opposed to the *rule by law* (which is a rule by humans) can thus be traced to the affordances of the printing press that reinforced and extended the triple distantiation described above, which basically forced the rise of an autonomous, positive law that can no longer be controlled by the arbitrary will of an undivided sovereign (who would rule, as a human, *by law*, ignoring the rule *of law* to which a sovereign would have to submit).

[79] Dworkin (n. 63).

4. Speech Act Theory and Institutional Facts

Having thus clarified the difference between positive law and legal decision making, we can now explore their relationship by moving into speech act theory. Invoking Austin,[80] Ricoeur distinguishes between three different types of speech, highlighting the fact that speaking is acting: (1) *locutionary acts* that equate with propositional acts, for instance, describing that you 'are getting married'; (2) *illocutionary acts* or *performative speech acts*, for instance, declaring you 'husband and wife', meaning that from that moment onwards you will be qualified as 'husband and wife'; and (3) *perlocutionary acts* that are meant to exert influence, for instance, urging you 'to get married'. Clearly, legal decisions have illocutionary force, because they generate 'legal effect'. They are performative speech acts (as in, 'I declare you "husband and wife"'), *legal decisions do what they say*. The importance of this simple statement can hardly be overstated. Legal decision making does not *cause* legal effect; it *constitutes* such effect. Mistaking the illocutionary act for a perlocutionary act means mistaking the *instrumentality* of law (its ability to constitute institutional facts) for a utilitarian or behaviourist *instrumentalism* (the ability to nudge or force people into certain behaviours). *Institutional facts* are facts that result from a performative speech act and they are usually opposed to brute facts.[81] A stone or a pregnancy may be considered as 'brute facts', whereas a marriage, a university, money, or the rule of law are 'institutional facts'—they depend on a 'language game' that qualifies specific 'things' as such,[82] while this qualification or 'counting as' defines the institution.

The performative effect of oral or written speech acts cannot be achieved by way of computer code, even when such code is said to 'outperform' human experts. Computer code has different affordances, and 'doing things with words' is not one of them. This—obviously—does not mean that computer code is not capable of forcing or luring people into specific behaviours. On the contrary, many automated decision systems are very good in doing just that. They remain, however, in the realm of perlocutionary acts,[83] which means that the effect they have is causal rather than constitutive, they generate a rule of machines instead of a rule of law. If data-driven regulation were to become law, we

[80] Austin (n. 11).

[81] J. Searle, *The Construction of Social Reality* (1995). Even more interesting, building on e.g. Wittgenstein, without however employing the terminology of speech act theory, P. Winch, *The Idea of a Social Science* (1958).

[82] The concept of language games was instituted by L. Wittgenstein and G. Anscombe, *Philosophical Investigations: The German Text, with a Revised English Translation* (2003) vol. 3.

[83] Note that the difference, as made by Austin (n. 11), is notoriously confusing. My notion of performativity also builds on the work of Judith Butler, as e.g. in her, *Giving an Account of Oneself* (2005), which better grounds the concept in continental philosophy.

would end up with a rule by machines by humans, even though we should not overestimate the control that those in charge of the machines have over their own invention. We should also be reminded of the difference between *rule of law* and *rule by law* (by humans), raising the question of whether and if so, how such a *rule by machines* could evolve into *a rule of law*.

B. Structure and Action

1. From Text to Action

Ricoeur then moves into the issue of meaningful action, as a sequel to his discussion of the meaning of text. As discussed above, the meaning of text derives from the interplay between a given language system (structure) and the speech it enables (action). This means that text (as a type of speech) is understood as an action, whose meaning depends both on the language system (the structure) and on how it is used (the action). Simultaneously, the distantiation between author, text, and reader requires an iterant act of interpretation on the side of the readers, who are, however, constrained by both the language system and the way others use it. In other words, though the meaning of a specific speech act requires interpretation, there are constraints that consolidate and stabilize meaning, to allow people to actually understand each other.

When speaking of action, Ricoeur notes that for the same reason, the meaning of an action requires what he calls fixation. It must be stabilized, to be recognizable as a specific type of action. For instance, the gesture of 'thumbs up' has meaning, but this meaning is not *caused* by the physical behaviour of keeping your thumb up. Just like speech acts, actions such as 'thumbs up' require a certain 'autonomization of action', such that similar behaviour invites similar interpretation, and recognition as being of a certain type, with a specific meaning that qualifies the gesture as an encouragement or approval. For *behaviour* to count as a certain type of *action* it has to fit with sedimented mutual expectations, the behaviour must be 'legible' as such an action. The implication is that human action is 'an open work',[84] its meaning is underdetermined, and just like with the interpretation of words, human action is multi-interpretable. This also means that the author of the action (the actor) cannot define the meaning of their action all by themselves. If a person puts up their middle finger, they cannot claim that it was their intention to give a 'thumbs up' and therefore others are wrong to interpret the gesture as a sign of contempt or aggression.

[84] Ricoeur (n. 70), at 103.

The objective meaning of an action is something other than the subjective intention of the author, and it may be construed in various ways, depending on the habits of the interpretive community that must be navigated. The problems of the right understanding cannot, therefore, be solved by a simple return to the alleged intention of the actor, it must be situated in the context, the culture, or the institutional environment of those affected by the act. Problems arise when the context, culture, and institutional environment of those affected are not shared with the actor, who could perhaps not foresee the consequences of their behaviour.

2. Anticipation and Validation

This generates a dialectic of anticipation and validation, since it is always possible to relate the same gesture in different ways to, for instance, different types of gestures that play out as cornerstones of a specific context. For instance, putting up one's little finger may either be interpreted as a reference to the thumbs up, or to the middle finger. Actions must be understood based on the 'plurivocity' that is inherent in their context, culture, or institutional environment, which is not the same as saying that they are 'polysemous'. They may indeed have different meanings (just like words, such as 'pupil'), but what Ricoeur is after here is the fact that the meaning of an action is interwoven with the context in which it was taken, and that shifts in meaning within other parts of that context may result in a different meaning for the action itself. Ricoeur suggest that:[85]

> To show that an interpretation is more probable in the light of what is known is something other than showing that a conclusion is true. In this sense, validation is not verification. Validation is an argumentative discipline comparable to the juridical procedures of legal interpretation. It is a logic of uncertainty and of qualitative probability.

This is in turn connected with the fact that though there is often more than one way to give meaning to an action, this does not imply that all possible interpretations are equally valid. Acknowledging that author's intent does not suffice does not imply that it does not matter or that anything goes. Presenting or claiming that a certain action must be read in one way rather than another, however, opens the floor for contestation; the interpretation that is put forward

[85] Ibid. 107.

will have to be defended and argued if an attempt is made to defeat it. Ricoeur reiterates his reference to the law:[86]

> Only in the tribunal is there a moment when the procedures of appeal are exhausted. But it is so only because the decision of the judge is implemented by the force of public power. Neither in literary criticism nor in the social sciences is there such a last word. Or, if there is any, we call that violence.

The force of public power is part of what lawyers call the 'positivity' of the law.[87] It is part of the monopoly of violence that makes positive law possible, including the protection it offers against the arbitrary powers of a sovereign. Despite this aspect of violence that is inherent in legal decision making, legal effect and the force of law ultimately depend on *the performative effect of meaningful action*, which should not be confused with either physical causality or subjective motivation.

This, in turn, has many implications for the operations of data-driven 'law'. Distant reading offers a mathematical (probabilistic) compression of legal text, but the patterns do not represent causality. They map, for instance, conceptual overlap and the way speech acts are coordinated, whereas these mathematical patterns do not engage in speech acts themselves. They are about something (law), but they are not that something (law).[88] The anticipation that situates law entails what Ricoeur calls a 'qualitative probability',[89] not the quantitative probability of number crunching machines.

C. Text-Driven Law

1. The Nature of Legal Effect

Modern positive law is a system of interrelated legal norms. Such norms basically attribute a specified legal consequence whenever specified legal conditions apply. This legal consequence is not 'caused' by the fulfilment of the conditions but is constituted by the performative effect of their 'being the case'.[90]

86 Ibid. 110.

87 Radbruch, 'Legal Philosophy', in K. Wilk (transl.), *The Legal Philosophies of Lask, Radbruch and Dabin* (2014) 44.

88 Hildebrandt, 'Law as Information in the Era of Data-Driven Agency', 79(1) *The Modern Law Review* (2016) 1.

89 Ricoeur (n. 70) 107; Aldous, 'Probability, Uncertainty and Unpredictability', *Probability and the Real World*, https://www.stat.berkeley.edu/~aldous/Real-World/phil_uncertainty.html (last visited 18 December 2021).

90 Which is itself a qualification that qualifies as a speech act, *les faits sont faits*.

The normativity of positive law depends on: (1) the performative nature of written and unwritten law;[91] (2) the mutuality between primary and secondary rules;[92] (3) the state's monopoly of violence;[93] which in turn depends on (4) international law that institutes internal and external sovereignty, which depend on each other.[94] This implies that positive law is not merely a matter of brute force (monopoly of violence), and/or mechanical application, because brute force, here, depends on the performativity of international law, while mechanical application hinges on the performative nature of the written and unwritten speech acts that 'make' the law.[95]

The fact that 'mechanical application' hinges on the performative nature of (un)written speech acts can be explained by the insights gained from the previous sections. If objective meaning is something other than the subjective intentions of either the author or the reader, it may be construed in various ways. This generates a dialectic of anticipation and validation, as it is always possible to relate the same content in different ways to other content within the same context.[96] Such—fundamentally text-driven—*multi-interpretability* is what 'makes' modern positive law. It implies a type of contestability that requires argumentation, as neither logic nor brute force would do. Logic can be used to test the soundness of argumentation but cannot decide which of several sound arguments must be chosen; brute force can enforce but not legitimate. The argumentative nature of current law is an affordance of its textual embodiment and defines the kind of certainty it offers. As Waldron has argued,[97] legal certainty is not only about providing foresight, trust, and stability but simultaneously about the need to argue for whatever legal decision is be taken, acknowledging that both the applicability and the application of the relevant legal norm can always be contested. To make this merry-go-round between contestation and consolidation work in practice, an institutionalized system of checks and balances is required. For instance, by establishing and sustaining independent courts. These courts will have room for discretion though not for arbitrary decision making—as they need to stay within the decision space offered by written law, precedent, and—paradoxically—also by future case law.

[91] MacCormick and Weinberger (n. 70).

[92] H. L. A. Hart, *The Concept of Law* (1994) ch. V.

[93] H. Berman, *Law and Revolution. The Formation of the Western Legal Tradition* (1983).

[94] Waldron, 'The Rule of International Law', 30(1) *Harvard Journal of Law & Public Policy* (2006) 15.

[95] B. Latour, *The Making of Law: An Ethnography of the Conseil d'Etat* (2009).

[96] This is one of the crucial insights of Wittgenstein, who concludes that at some point a decision must be made, see Wittgenstein and Anscombe (n. 82) para. 217.

[97] Waldron, 'The Rule of Law and the importance of procedure', 50 *Nomos* (2011) 3.

2. Legal Decision Making as Performative Speech Acts

To demonstrate the importance of thinking in terms of *performatives*—decisions with a performative effect—I will inquire into the *Google Spain v Costeja* decision of the Court of Justice of the EU (CJEU).[98] One of the questions raised was whether a search engine must be qualified as a controller in the sense of the (then applicable) Data Protection Directive,[99] which defined (just like the current General Data Protection Regulation (GDPR)) a data controller as the entity that determines the purpose and the means of the processing of personal data. The Advocate General (AG) recounts the following:[100]

> The internet search engine service provider merely supplying an information location tool does not exercise control over personal data included on third-party web pages. The service provider is not 'aware' of the existence of personal data in any other sense than as a statistical fact web pages are likely to include personal data. In the course of processing of the source web pages for the purposes of crawling, analysing and indexing, personal data does not manifest itself as such in any particular way.

The AG finds that a search engine cannot be qualified as a controller:[101]

> An opposite opinion would entail internet search engines being incompatible with EU law, a conclusion I would find absurd.

This was not at all a controversial position. The idea that a search algorithm is a neutral tool that provides an objective listing of relevant search results, that is not 'controlled' by the search engine provider may seem naïve but has its attractions (similar to those that would qualify the predictions of legal technologies as objective outputs). The hidden nature of the algorithm probably contributes to its technocratic aura, distracting attention from the choices made when designing the search engine and the invisible trade-offs involved (in the case of PoJ algorithms the use of terms such as 'accuracy' invites a similar trust in the neutrality of the software). Though, just checking the paper published by Brin and Page in 1997,[102] would already clarify that even at that time it was apparent

[98] Case C-131/12, *Google Spain SL and Google Inc. v Agencia Española de Protección de Datos (AEPD) and Mario Costeja González* (EU:C:2014:317) ('*the right to be forgotten*').

[99] Directive 95/46/EC, OJ 1995 L 281/31, now replaced by the GDPR: Regulation (EU) 2016/679, OJ 2016 L 119/1.

[100] Opinion of Advocate General Jääskinen (EU:C:2013:424) on Case C-131/12 (n. 98), para. 84.

[101] Ibid. para. 90.

[102] Brin and Page, 'The Anatomy of a Large-Scale Hypertextual Web Search Engine', 30 *Computer Networks and ISDN Systems* (1998) 107, at 109 and notably Appendix A.

that commercializing the service would 'corrupt' its employment. The authors of the PageRank algorithm, who are now running the Google company, observed in 1997, when still at Stanford University:[103]

> At the same time, search engines have migrated from the academic domain to the commercial. Up until now most search engine development has gone on at companies with little publication of technical details. This causes search engine technology to remain largely a black art and to be advertising oriented (see Appendix A in the full version). With Google, we have a strong goal to push more development and understanding into the academic realm.

And, in '8. Annex A, Advertising and Mixed Motives' they explain in salient detail why they:[104]

> ... expect that advertising funded search engines will be inherently biased towards the advertisers and away from the needs of the consumers.

It would be interesting to see whether developers of legal technologies have similar insights. Let us note the straightforward decision of the Court, deciding without further ado in a way that is diametrically opposed to the opinion of the AG:[105]

> It is the search engine operator which determines the purposes and means of that activity and thus of the processing of personal data that it itself carries out within the framework of that activity and which must, consequently, be regarded as the 'controller' in respect of that processing pursuant to Article 2(d).

And, despite the fact that the AG had advised that:[106]

> The rights to rectification, erasure and blocking of data provided in Article 12(b) of the Directive concern data, the processing of which does not comply with the provisions of the Directive, in particular because of the incomplete or inaccurate nature of the data.

The CJEU decided that:[107]

[103] Ibid. at sec. 1.3.2.
[104] Ibid. at Annex A.
[105] Case C-131/12 (n. 98), para. 33.
[106] AG Opinion on Case C-131/12 (n. 100), para. 104.
[107] Case C-131/12 (n. 98), para. 92–94.

> 92. As regards Article 12(b) of Directive 95/46, the application of which is subject to the condition that the processing of personal data be incompatible with the directive, it should be recalled that, as has been noted in paragraph 72 of the present judgment, such incompatibility may result not only from the fact that such data are inaccurate but, in particular, also from the fact that they are inadequate, irrelevant or excessive in relation to the purposes of the processing, that they are not kept up to date, or that they are kept for longer than is necessary unless they are required to be kept for historical, statistical or scientific purposes.
>
> 93. It follows from those requirements, laid down in Article 6(1)(c) to (e) of Directive 95/46, that even initially lawful processing of accurate data may, in the course of time, become incompatible with the directive where those data are no longer necessary in the light of the purposes for which they were collected or processed. That is so in particular where they appear to be inadequate, irrelevant or no longer relevant, or excessive in relation to those purposes and in the light of the time that has elapsed.
>
> 94. Therefore, if it is found, following a request by the data subject pursuant to Article 12(b) of Directive 95/46, that the inclusion in the list of results displayed following a search made on the basis of his name of the links to web pages published lawfully by third parties and containing true information relating to him personally is, at this point in time, incompatible with Article 6(1)(c) to (e) of the directive because that information appears, having regard to all the circumstances of the case, to be inadequate, irrelevant or no longer relevant, or excessive in relation to the purposes of the processing at issue carried out by the operator of the search engine, the information and links concerned in the list of results must be erased.

The judgment constitutes three *performatives* with far reaching consequences: (1) the decision to qualify indexing as 'processing of personal data'; (2) the decision to qualify the provider of a search engine as a data controller; and (3) the decision that the right to have data erased if inaccurate, inadequate, irrelevant or excessive, and the right to object to the processing if the legal ground is the legitimate interest of the controller or a third party, mean that the right of the data subject to be dereferenced must in principle be respected. The Court adds that, in case of this ground, such dereferencing would probably be required if: (a) the legitimate interest of the controller is an economic interest, and if (b) the public interest of access to that information does not overrule the rights of the data subject, noting that this may depend on the celebrity of the data subject. On top of that we should take into account all the decisions that the CJEU did not take, whereas the AG advised them. These implied decisions can *a contrario* also be seen as *performatives*, for instance, (1) the fact that the newspaper lawfully published the data and is allowed to continue processing them (indeed must do so) does *not* imply that indexing by the search engine is therefore lawful, and (2) the fact that the search engine is based on automated processing, without any intent to specifically process personal data, does not imply that they are not a controller.

The decisions made by the Court cannot be reduced to mechanical application (the life of the law is not logic), nor can they be conflated with Schmittian decisionism (the decision space is restricted against an arbitrary choice of action). They are legal written speech acts that decide the reconfiguration of the backend systems of commercial search engines, in the face of the kind of multi-interpretability that is inherent in text-driven normativity. Their effect is performative in the sense described above. I will now compare this performative effect to the effects of the performance of PoJ software.

3. The Performance of Prediction of Judgment Software and its Performative Effect

What would the Court have decided if supposedly 'intelligent' software had estimated that Google is (or is not) to be considered a controller, with an 'accuracy' that is higher than some supposedly relevant 'baseline'. If doctors may at some point be compelled by their insurance company to motivate digressions from computational support systems, will courts be held to supplementary motivation if they digress from predictions on points of law? Should lawyers 'buy into' the discourse that human lawyers are subjective, biased, and limited by their bounded rationality, whereas ML systems will soon outwit them due to their objective output (assuming potential bias can be 'corrected' by those versed in the relevant subfield of CS)? Must we accept that 'distant reading' of legal text will provide a grasp over far more relevant legal textual corpora than any human lawyer could ever hope to achieve?

Ricoeur's work can help to change the frame of reference from that of subjectivity (of human lawyers) versus objectivity (of machines) to that of a dynamic interaction between anticipation and validation, which equates to an iteration of anticipation, contestation, argumentation, and consolidation that culminates in closure. Data-driven prediction engines can trace, mine, and 'read' our anticipatory interactions in the domain of legal decision making, but their anticipations are of another kind than our own. They are mathematical mappings, not a way to navigate their own institutional environment. They simulate our past behaviours, they scale our past, but do not face their future (let alone ours). They have no future, no past, and no present. They have nothing to lose. Whereas some might think that that makes 'them' more objective, in point of fact it makes them dangerously unreliable because they have no clue as to what matters.[108]

4. What We Stand to Lose

In this third part I have argued that modern positive law and the rule of law are historical artefacts, contingent upon the technologies of the printing press, sharing the affordances of their text-driven embodiment. Whereas we often hear that law is slow to catch up with new technologies, always 'regulating' after the fact, and thus incapable of dealing with disruptive innovation, this chapter takes another point of departure. After probing the lure of data-driven technologies for the law and the mathematical and statistical assumptions they build on in the second part, we conducted an in-depth assessment of the affordances of text-driven law. This provides us with a better understanding of law's current mode of existence, while resisting an essentialist take on the way that law exists. The analysis should generate an acuity as to what we wish to *preserve*,[109] in terms of legal protection, legal certainty, and the rule of law, noting that we cannot take for granted that data-driven 'law' will afford similar protection, similar certainty, and similar checks and balances.

Moving from the assumptions of text-driven anticipation to those of data-driven predictions, we may be embracing (1) a reduction of human interaction to mathematical relationships, (2) formalization and disambiguation of both facts and norms, such that they can be made machine-readable, (3) the reconfiguration of legal decision making in terms of correlations and causalities, mapping vocal pitch, political affiliation, or 'word embeddings' as influencers to the binary outcome of a court case, (4) a distinction between content and metadata replacing that between substance and procedure, (5) the idea that computational systems are more objective and less biased (provided the training data have been debiased) than human judges, (6) replacement of interpretation, contestation, and argumentation with regard to both the facts of a case and the applicability and the application of legal norms, by an algorithm

[108] Embodiment matters, as roboticists Pfeifer and Bongard demonstrate in their work on 'understanding by building' artificial intelligence. Full intelligence will depend on an agent being capable of navigating and surviving in their 'real world' environment: R. Pfeifer and J. Bongard, *How the Body Shapes the Way We Think. A New View of Intelligence* (2007). In the same vein, more recently, Cantwell Smith (n. 76).

[109] Maryanne Wolf highlights what she believes we should preserve as key affordances of the 'bookish' mind, based on extensive research into the neuroscience of the human brain: M. Wolf, *Proust and the Squid: The Story and Science of the Reading Brain* (2008).

that was trained on data that is considered relevant and sufficiently complete, with some kind of explanation of why the algorithm came to its conclusion, (7) a type of 'distant reading' that in point of fact collapses the distantiation between author, text, meaning, and reader that was instantiated by the shift from oral to written speech. This way we may give up on (8) the core tenets of the rule of law, notably practical and effective remedies to contest claims of validity regarding both legal norms and legally relevant facts. We may lose the *mode of existence of law* where legal protection is *part of* law's instrumentality rather than an add-on, because this instrumentality is built on legal effect rather than merely brute force, and because legal certainty thrives on the contestability of facts and norms, not on the mechanical application of logical rules. We may even lose the kind of human agency that is constituted by text-driven law, because the radical ambiguity that is inherent in the open texture of legal concepts and legal norms affords a kind of discretion that has to be removed in the process of formalization that is inherent in data-driven predictions.

The final question is whether this is inevitable. Do I confess to technological determinism in summing up all that we stand to lose when shifting from text- to data-driven law?

4. Boundary Work: Legal Protection by Design?

Technological determinism is a trap. It reduces our acuity in relation to the affordances of specific types of technology instead of enhancing it.[110] What we should face, however, is the possibility that due to the assumptions and trade-offs inherent in their design, specific data-driven technologies determine our choice architecture in ways that diminish our agency. This is not merely a technological question as the relevant design, operations and uptake of legal technologies will often depend upon the political economy that informs them. If the market is organized such that companies compete by way of algorithmic optimization of advertising revenue in ways that prioritize extreme content and fake news, it may be very difficult to solve that problem at the level of the technology. The relevant technological solutions will probably require various types of algorithmic censure and moderation, which has radical drawbacks for the freedom of information. Instead, the business model that invites such optimization should be eradicated, noting that a market that invites this kind of

[110] A detailed analysis of the notion of technological determinism in relation to the law can be found in Hildebrandt, *Smart Technologies* (n. 69) ch. 8.

behaviour also invites unhealthy concentration of economic power, inviting a much-needed rethinking of competition law.[111] In short, whether a technology overdetermines individual behaviour and societal interaction is an empirical question that must be addressed by doing more rather than less research. Both the idea that technology is an autonomous force that will necessarily diminish our agency and the idea that technology is in the end a force for good are naïve and lazy shortcuts to unsubstantiated conclusions.

In other work I have advocated the idea of legal protection by design (LPbD) as a way of integrating legal norms at the level of fundamental rights law in the research design and the architecture of data-driven systems (and environments). This requires work at the boundary between law and computer science, rejecting the colonization of law and the rule of law by engineering perspectives though nevertheless respecting the methodological integrity of computing and engineering sciences. In data protection law this approach has been foregrounded for quite some time. For instance, in the *Google Spain v Costeja* case the CJEU required that a search engine provider implements a specified legal right into the design of its system. It is not just that the search engine had to delist a particular search result. Rather, the search engine's backend system had to be reconfigured in such a way that requests similar to that of Mr Costeja could be honoured. Article 7(3) of the GDPR requires that consent for the processing of personal data (for a specific purpose) can be withdrawn as easily as it has been provided. This is not merely a matter of adding a button to a website, but a matter of reengineering the backend system (that is not visible to end-users but crucial for putting an end to processing whenever consent is withdrawn). Under Article 25 GDPR such design choices become part of a general legal obligation for data controllers to ensure that rights of data subjects and legal obligations for controllers are by default and by design integrated into systems that process personal data. This is called data protection by design and could be termed a first instance of LPbD. Interestingly, the obligation is articulated as an obligation to 'implement appropriate technical and organizational measures, such as pseudonymization, which are designed to implement data protection principles, such as data minimization, in an effective manner and to integrate the necessary safeguards into the processing in

[111] See e.g. Khan, 'The Ideological Roots of America's Market Power Problem', 127 *Yale Law Journal* (2018), https://www.yalelawjournal.org/forum/the-ideological-roots-of-americas-market-power-problem; Khan, 'The New Brandeis Movement: America's Antimonopoly Debate', 9(3) *Journal of European Competition Law & Practice* (2018) 131, https://doi.org/10.1093/jeclap/lpy020 (last visited 6 April 2022). Hildebrandt, 'Primitives of Legal Protection in the Era of Data-Driven Platforms', 2(2) *Georgetown Law Technology Review* (2018) 252.

order to meet the requirements of this Regulation and protect the rights of data subject'.[112] The formulation demonstrates that data protection by design is not about 'compliance by design', which is not feasible but also not desirable. It is about a duty for controllers to design their systems in ways that minimize infringements of fundamental rights, while integrating the checks and balances that are inherent in the rule of law. Similarly, LPbD is not about the 'automation of compliance'. It is not about creating an online hyperconnected environment that limits our choice architecture to what is lawful. This would be the inverse of LPbD and closer to 'legal by design' or techno-regulation.[113] It would result in technologies that actually determine us, not because technology necessarily does so but because a particular technology has been designed to do so.

PoJ could be used in a way that aligns with 'legal by design' strategies. For instance, public administration could reject the use of legal remedies if their PoJ software predicts that the complainants will lose their appeal anyway. Courts with a huge backlog might start processing cases via PoJ software and resort to abbreviated procedures to speed up decision making. Insurance companies may use PoJ software to deny claims and force their clients to sign a contract where they waive their right if the software predicts that they will lose their case. Some legal scholars have argued that this would solve many problems and improve legal decision making.[114] I hope that this chapter has convinced the reader this would require a radically different understanding of what counts as law.

LPbD, however, has relevance for PoJ and other data-driven technologies in the legal domain. First of all, the term 'legal' in LPbD does not refer to 'regulation' in the sense of attempts to influence human behaviour, but to law and the rule of law. More specifically, it refers to safeguarding effective and practical exercising of human rights, and instituting checks and balances that provide countervailing powers against big players (including the state). This would mean, first of all, that PoJ software requires not only the highest standards in terms of the underlying research design, but also its testability and contestability, based on a proper understanding of the requirements of confirmatory research design in ML (including its preregistration in e.g. the Open Science Foundation).[115] Second, it would limit and restrict the use of PoJ to decision

[112] Article 25(1) GDPR.

[113] M. Hildebrandt, *Law for Computer Scientists and Other Folk* (2020) ch. 10.

[114] Genesereth (n. 15); Lippe, Katz, and Jackson, 'Legal by Design: A New Paradigm for Handling Complexity in Banking Regulation and Elsewhere in Law', 93(4) *Oregon Law Review* (2015) 831.

[115] Hofman, Sharma, and Watts, 'Prediction and Explanation in Social Systems', 355(6324) *Science* (2017) 486. See Articles 8–15 of the proposed EU AI Act, which integrate this kind of 'by design' requirements as a means to offer legal protection 'by design'.

support, and, for instance, require that those making a decision based on the software (1) understand how it came to its conclusion, (2) combine a keen awareness of 'automation bias' with an effective ability to ignore or overrule the prediction,[116] (3) including the legal power to do so,[117] without an additional burden of argumentation. Third, LPbD would require that the curriculum of law schools is extended to integrate proper training in the data fallacies that hamper both the research design and the outcome of PoJ,[118] while also allowing students to play around with the software until they understand the underlying assumptions and their implications for the claims made in terms of functionality. Clearly, these types of requirements rule out the use of proprietary software that is insufficiently transparent in the above sense of allowing testing and contesting its outcome, while also rejecting non-disclosure agreements (NDAs) that reduce relevant contestability, when contracting with providers of PoJ software. This, in turn, means that lawyers must become aware of the accuracy–reliability trade-off, as discussed above: high accuracy that correlates with diminished or absent interpretability implies problems with reliability. Precisely because we do not know why the system concludes as it does, we cannot be sure its conclusions are valid. That is why we should not buy into the narrative that proprietary software may be more opaque but will nevertheless be more accurate. The latter is an unsubstantiated claim, with high-risk consequences.

Lawyers should get their act together before technology developers—whether or not with the best of intentions—take over and transform law's mode of existence. Technology developers, in the meantime, should help lawyers understand the limits as well as the potential of data-driven AI systems. This is the kind of boundary work that we, lawyers, need to engage in—to guard, protect, and reinvent the boundaries of modern positive law and the rule of law in the face of a potentially disruptive technological managerialism.

[116] Cf. Article 14 of the proposed EU AI Act, on 'Human Oversight', notably paragraph 4.

[117] Cf. the EDPB (formally Article 29 WP), *Guidelines on Automated individual decision-making and Profiling for the purposes of Regulation 2016/679* (2017), at 10 on the question of whether human intervention 'counts' as such: 'The controller cannot avoid the Article 22 provisions by fabricating human involvement. For example, if someone routinely applies automatically generated profiles to individuals without any actual influence on the result, this would still be a decision based solely on automated processing. To qualify as human intervention, the controller must ensure that any oversight of the decision is meaningful, rather than just a token gesture. It should be carried out by someone who has the authority and competence to change the decision. As part of the analysis, they should consider all the available input and output data.'

[118] For succinct explanations of data fallacies for lay persons, see Bransby, 'Data Fallacies to Avoid', *Data Science Central* (2018), https://www.datasciencecentral.com/profiles/blogs/data-fallacies-to-avoid-an-illustrated-collection-of-mistakes (last visited 18 December 2021).

3

Thinking Inside the Box: The Promise and Boundaries of Transparency in Automated Decision-Making

Ida Koivisto

1. Introduction: The End of Human Bias in Law?

Even lawyers cannot escape their humanity. In a famous—and controversial—study of Israeli judges, the admittance of parole crucially depended on whether the judge decided over it before or after having a break.[1] Regardless, whether this study got it right, we can safely say that humans are prone to be affected by their moral and political preferences, different sympathies and antipathies, and even bodily sensations, such as hunger or fatigue. For better or for worse, this is part of what makes us human.

Today, it is hard to maintain a romantic vision of law as a simple, formulaic solution to complex problems in the real world. Informed by legal realism and critical legal studies, we are well aware of the indeterminacy and human bias in law. Law is not a system of flawless logic but a result of political contestation. This fragility also extends to the application of law. In the history of law in action, there are countless examples of bias, favouritism, and different predilections of judges and bureaucrats determining people's rights and duties. This is understandable yet depressing. We have learned to accept this state of affairs, given that a viable alternative has not existed. Instead, we have focused on redress mechanisms. At least, they provide an opportunity for acquiring a second opinion, and ultimately, contestation.

[1] Danziger, Levav, and Avnaim-Pesso, 'Extraneous Factors in Judicial Decisions', 108(17) *Proceedings of the National Academy of Sciences* (2011) 6889. About criticisms of the study, see Glöckner, 'The Irrational Hungry Judge Effect Revisited: Simulations Reveal that the Magnitude of the Effect is Overestimated', 11(6) *Judgment and Decision Making* (2016), 601; Weinshall-Margel and Shapard, 'Overlooked Factors in the Analysis of Parole Decisions', 108(42) *PNAS* (2011) E833; Chatziathanasiou, 'Beware the Lure of Narratives: "Hungry Judges" Should Not Motivate the Use of "Artificial Intelligence" in Law', 23(4), *German Law Journal* (2022) 452.

Ida Koivisto, *Thinking Inside the Box: The Promise and Boundaries of Transparency in Automated Decision-Making* In: *Data at the Boundaries of European Law.* Edited by: Deirdre Curtin and Mariavittoria Catanzariti, Oxford University Press.
 DOI: 10.1093/oso/9780198874195.003.0003

Even though human bias may have been an intrinsic part of our legal system as we know it, the regulative ideal has always been there, guiding us like the flickering shadows in Plato's Cave. We would prefer to eradicate random factors when it comes to making decisions about people's lives. Indeed, in law, *ought* should not be derived from *is*. Even if a judge's rumbling stomach in fact affects their legal deliberation, in law that should not be the case. Law should strive to fulfil its ideals of equality, justice, and predictability; in other words, legal certainty. Hence, efficiency, accuracy, and equality are still *modus operandi* of how to develop law, not the inherent caveats of human decision-making.

If we look at these ideals more closely, we can see that they seem better suited for machines to execute than whimsical humans. Consequently, we might think that replacing humans with machines would make the problems of human inefficiency and bias go away, and additionally, save considerable amounts of money.[2] The steady increase in computing power, the emergence of big data analysis, and artificial intelligence research show much promise in developing less human, more just law application. At break-neck pace, computers seem to be gaining the ability to do things we never thought possible. Should we thus forfeit human decision-making and hand it over to computer programmes and algorithms? Especially in routine cases, automated decision-making (ADM)—computer-based decision-making without human influence—could help us overcome our deficiencies and lead to an increased perception of fairness.[3] So, problem solved?

This seems not to be the case—even if we did not succumb to alarmist thinking and dystopias of machines taking over the world. There is growing evidence that human bias cannot be totally erased, at least for now.[4] It can linger in ADM in many ways, as I will specify later. As a result, it is not clear who is accountable for that. Are the codes involved to blame?[5] Or the creators of those codes?[6] What about machine learning and algorithms created by other algorithms?[7] Most of the time, we do not know answers to these

[2] Sunstein, 'Algorithms, Correcting Biases' (12 December 2018), available at https://ssrn.com/abstract=3300171 (last visited 18 August 2021). For another optimistic view, see Coglianese and Lehr, 'Transparency and Algorithmic Governance', 71(1) *Administrative Law Review* (2019) 1.

[3] See Binns *et al.*, '"It's Reducing a Human Being to a Percentage": Perceptions of Justice in Algorithmic Decisions' (2018), available at https://arxiv.org/pdf/1801.10408.pdf (last visited 18 August 2021).

[4] Castelluccia and Le Métayer, 'Understanding Algorithmic Decision-making: Opportunities and Challenges' (2019), https://www.europarl.europa.eu/RegData/etudes/STUD/2019/624261/EPRS_STU(2019)624261_EN.pdf (last visited 18 August 2021).

[5] Mittelstadt *et al.*, 'The Ethics of Algorithms: Mapping the Debate', 3(2) *Big Data and Society* (2016) 1.

[6] See e.g. Bivens and Hoque, 'Programming Sex, Gender, and Sexuality: Infrastructural Failures in the "Feminist" Dating App Bumble', 43(3) *Canadian Journal of Communication* (2018) 441.

[7] Barreno *et al.*, 'Can Machine Learning Be Secure?' (2006), available at https://dl.acm.org/doi/pdf/10.1145/1128817.1128824?download=true (last visited 18 August 2021).

questions.[8] This difficulty is often referred to as 'the black box problem'. We cannot be sure how the inputs transform into outputs inside the 'black box', and who is to blame if something goes wrong. As the potentially discriminatory nature of algorithmic predictions has been identified as a thorny—and I would claim from the legal perspective, *the* primary—problem in ADM, solutions to tackle that problem are actively sought.[9] In particular, law and regulation are called upon.

However, to date, legally binding regulation is mostly lacking.[10] As the standard lamentation goes, law and regulation are lagging behind technological developments.[11] So far, the EU's General Data Protection Regulation (GDPR) carries the most promise in resolving the problem, as much of ADM is closely linked to processing personal data. However, legitimacy of algorithmic governance is a topical concern also beyond data protection.[12]

Consequently, soft law and self-regulation are resorted to. The number of different codes of conduct (artificial intelligence [AI] ethics) skyrocketed in the years 2018–2019. As an independent non-governmental organization, Algorithm Watch, shows, the number is staggering. These codes of conduct are of various kinds and published by different institutions. Some of them are private (e.g. Partnership of AI—Google, Facebook, Amazon, IBM, Microsoft, Deep Mind), some public (e.g. High-level Expert Group on AI), while some are produced by different kinds of hybrid partnerships.[13] In 2021, the EU published its Proposal for Regulation of the European Parliament and of the Council Laying Down Harmonised Rules on Artificial Intelligence (Artificial Intelligence Act) and Amending Certain Union Legislative Acts ('the AI Act').[14] However, the Act is not yet in force.

[8] Burrell, 'How the Machine "Thinks": Understanding Opacity in Machine Learning Algorithms', 3(1) *Big Data and Society* (2016) 1.

[9] Zarsky, 'The Trouble with Algorithmic Decisions: An Analytic Road Map to Examine Efficiency and Fairness in Automated and Opaque Decision Making', 41(1) *Science, Technology, and Human Values* (2016) 118.

[10] For an overview of pertinent legal questions, see Desai and Kroll, 'Trust but Verify: A Guide to Algorithms and the Law' 31(1) *Harvard Journal of Law and Technology* (2017) 1.

[11] Cohen, however, argues that this assumption is dated and erroneous. It would be better to talk about dynamic interaction between law and technology. J. Cohen, *Between Truth and Power: The Legal Constructions of Informational Capitalism* (2019) at 4–5.

[12] See Danaher, 'The Threat of Algocracy: Reality, Resistance and Accommodation', 29(3) *Philosophy and Technology* (2016) 245.

[13] Algorithm Watch, 'AI Ethics Guidelines Global Inventory' (2019), https://algorithmwatch.org/en/project/ai-ethics-guidelines-global-inventory/ (last visited 18 August 2021).

[14] The EU's AI Act. Commission, 'Proposal for Regulation of the European Parliament and of the Council Laying Down Harmonised Rules on Artificial Intelligence (Artificial Intelligence Act) and Amending Certain Union Legislative Acts' COM/2021/206 final.

What unites both the GDPR, the AI Act, and a great majority of the AI ethics codes of conduct is the call for *transparency*.[15] This is hardly surprising, as the promise of transparency is overwhelmingly positive. Although transparency can be approached in a plethora of ways, as a normative metaphor, its basic idea is simple. It promises legitimacy by making an object or behaviour visible and, as such, controllable. No more black boxes, but X-rayed ones! A metaphoric solution is thus proposed to a metaphoric problem. On a more general level, the call for transparency aims to abolish ignorance and opacity in a society by assuming active and well-informed citizens. At the same time, it presupposes an asymmetrical power structure between the one that exercises power and the one who is subject to it. To be legitimate, this unequal use of power needs to be accountable to the subjects.

As promising as it sounds, the legitimation narrative of transparency cannot really deliver in its quest to resolve the black box problem in ADM. Instead, I will argue that transparency is a more complex ideal than is portrayed in mainstream narratives. My main claim is that, contrary to what mainstream narratives suggest, transparency is inherently performative in nature, and cannot but be so. This performativity goes counter to the promise of unmediated visibility, vested in transparency.[16] Subsequently, in order to ensure the legitimacy of ADM—if we, indeed, are after its legitimacy—we need to be mindful of this hidden functioning logic of the ideal of transparency. As I will show, when transparency is brought to the context of algorithms, its peculiarities will become visible in a new way.[17] In this chapter, I will problematize the promise of transparency as the solution to the black box problem in ADM.

The chapter is organized as follows. First, I will analyse the black box problem theoretically, discussing the logic of discovery and the logic of justification. Which one do we want to 'see' with the help of transparency? I will also illustrate the nature of the black box problem in ADM with the help of examples from the US, Poland, and Finland. Second, I will discuss theoretically the ideal of transparency. As hinted, I argue that it is based on certain hidden functioning mechanisms, stemming from its nature as a visual metaphor, its *icono-ambivalence*, and its performativity. These points of departure lead to an

[15] Hagendorff, 'The Ethics of AI Ethics—An Evaluation of Guidelines' (2019), https://arxiv.org/ftp/arxiv/papers/1903/1903.03425.pdf (last visited 18 August 2021).

[16] See however Albu and Flyverbom, 'Organizational transparency: Conceptualizations, Conditions, and Consequences', 58(2) *Business and Society* (2019) 268, who attribute both verifiability and performativity to transparency.

[17] Ananny and Crawford, 'Seeing Without Knowing: Limitations of the Transparency Ideal and its Application to Algorithmic Accountability', 20(3) *New Media and Society* (2016) 973, at 977–982. Also, Bostrom, 'Strategic Implications of Openness in AI Development', 8(2) *Global Policy* (2017) 135.

overall idea of transparency as an internally contradictory ideal, building on the so called 'truth-legitimacy trade-off'. Third, I will apply this theory. I will discuss it in the context of ADM and more specifically, the GDPR. What functions and expressions do transparency have in that regulation? What are its implications? Fourth, I will draw the discussion together and conclude that, although transparency is widely appreciated, there are weak signals indicating that its major legitimating narrative is not sustainable in the context of ADM.

2. The Black Box Problem

A. Logic of Discovery and Logic of Justification

Before we talk about the black box problem in ADM, a few words about the black box in general are needed. What is it exactly? Why are we using this particular metaphor? Why is it a problem? Or, as Taina Bucher asks, what is at stake in framing algorithms in this way, and what might such a framing possibly distract us from asking? Although the black box would well deserve critical deconstruction in the same way as the notion of transparency, that cannot be done fully here.[18] That said, we will start by busting two common myths about the black box.

First, the metaphor of a black box need not have anything to do with technology, although technology is the context in which it is most often mentioned. Instead, a black box simply refers to a condition whereby the way in which an input translates into an output is unknown or un-knowable. That is to say, a human judge makes a black box too. Indeed, the way in which human data processing works, is hardly any clearer to us than black box algorithms.[19] Second, despite its common negative connotation—rendering the unknown an epistemological problem[20]—the black box can also be seen as value-neutral. For example, it is often approached neutrally in computer science, as a feature of a system. A black box does not need to arouse protest. The lack of transparency only becomes a problem if the outputs prove to be undesirable.

A black box may be a black box to itself, too. A judge does not really know, let alone be able to express, how her neurons are shooting when she is

[18] Bucher presents a critical genealogy of the metaphor. T. Bucher, *If… Then. Algorithmic Power and Politics* (2018) 44.

[19] As a societal phenomenon, see F. Pasquale, *The Black Box Society: The Secret Algorithms That Control Money and Information* (2015).

[20] Bucher (n. 18) 44.

pondering the intricacies of a case. Something happens in the brain and different connections are brought into consciousness. This process is unfathomable even when it is happening within our own brain. Similar processes may take place in computer systems, in particular in machine learning and deep learning neural networks—i.e. software that learns by itself through inferring regularities in provided training data.[21]

There is a catch, though. Some of us would be ready to argue against that: judges do need to know how they are solving the case. The same applies for ADM—reasons must be given for the decision to be acceptable. This is exactly why we call for transparency and giving reasons as a condition for judicial legitimacy. If that were not the case, anything would go. True, judges do need to be able to explain themselves. Nevertheless, we need to make an important distinction, which is known in philosophy of science as *the logic of discovery* and *the logic of justification.*

What do these logics mean and how do they differ from each other? The logic of discovery is a description of the empirical process by which one's brain automatically finds patterns, similarities, and connections between perhaps seemingly unrelated things. This logic can be hard to account for. How, indeed, can we know or explain why certain ideas and associations rush into our consciousness following certain stimulus in a given moment? We cannot. Even if we could do that, the explanation might sound random and weird. Indeed, how do we convince someone that the taste of a madeleine dipped in tea brings an entire array of memories to our own mind?

Hence, the logic of discovery does not seek to convince others. It just describes how a heuristic process goes. Not so for logic of justification, which does attempt to convince. It is no less than the basic principle that underpins legal argumentation or giving reasons for a decision. According to the logic of justification, we need to justify, step by step, why the associations we make should be accepted, why the suggested correct answer to a given question is indeed correct. This is premised on the idea of shared understanding of how logical reasoning should take place.

As a result, the logic of justification is not limited to the way in which our private associations are built. Therefore, if we want to convince others with our argument, we need to make our thinking look like it was following a

[21] On the different transparency standards on humans and machines, see Zerilli *et al.*, 'Transparency in Algorithmic and Human Decision-Making: Is There a Double Standard?', 32(4) *Philosophy and Technology* (2018) 661. Analysis of AI opacity, see Carabantes, 'Black-box Artificial Intelligence: An Epistemological and Critical Analysis', 35 *AI and Society* (2019) 309. See also Lipton, 'The Mythos of Model Interpretability', *arXiv:1606.03490* (2017).

predetermined, rational logic, and only that logic, even if the logic of discovery would suggest otherwise. The logic of discovery may be of interest to a psychoanalyst, but hardly a subject of a legal decision. As philosopher Karl Popper argues, 'My view of the matter ... is that there is no such thing as a logical method of having new ideas, or a logical reconstruction of this process. My view may be expressed by saying that every discovery contains "an irrational element", or "a creative intuition" in Bergson's sense.'[22]

How do the logic of discovery and the logic of justification relate to the question of the black box? What is their explanatory power in this context? As mentioned, a black box need not be approached as a problem. However, if we do so, implying that we should attempt to get rid of it, we covertly encounter the question of the two different logics. By opening the box, or making it transparent, we want to see the way in which the inputs translate into outputs. To that end, we need to specify which logic we want to see: the logic of discovery or the logic of justification?

As explained, the logic of discovery and logic of justification are subject to different kinds of rationalities. The first is purely descriptive or empirical while the second is normative and somewhat formulaic. Logic of discovery is the process of emerging ideas—however irrational or haphazard this process would be—whereas the logic of justification aims for general acceptance, following certain rules.

Would we want to know how the black box actually operates, regardless of whether we can understand the process? Alternatively, do we want the box to explain and justify itself, to convince us of why it follows the exact steps it does, and why we should accept its outputs? This distinction is helpful although, to my knowledge, it has not been applied in this context before. I will come back to this theme when discussing the transparency requirements laid down in the GDPR.

B. Examples of the Black Box Problem in ADM

To summarize, the black box need not to be a problem per se. However, we speak of 'a problem' in the context of algorithms and ADM for very good reasons—biases and other harms do happen.[23] As Frank Pasquale states, black

[22] K. Popper, *Logic of Scientific Discovery* (2nd ed., 2002) at 7–8.

[23] An illustrative inventory of the potential algorithmic harms, see Future of Privacy Forum, 'Unfairness by Algorithm: Distilling the Harms of Automated Decision-Making' (2017), https://fpf.org/wp-content/uploads/2017/12/FPF-Automated-Decision-Making-Harms-and-Mitigation-Charts.pdf (last visited 18 August 2021).

boxes must be exposed to counteract any wrongdoings, discrimination, or bias these systems may contain: 'algorithms should be open for inspection—if not by the public at large, at least by some trusted auditor'.[24]

Where do these potential wrongdoings come from? At least from two directions.[25] First, the code on which the ADM system is based can be poorly designed. That is to say, the coders may, deliberately or unbeknownst to themselves, favour choices that advantage some people over others.[26] This kind of bias is similar to those of the described judges: they are also affected by attitudes, preferences, and bodily sensations—not to mention certain background variables such as gender, religion, ethnicity, or culture.[27] These things may further affect the code, resulting in outputs that may be biased or otherwise unanticipated.

Second, particularly when it comes to machine learning and deep learning neural networks and big data, the bias shifts its shape. The human bias may be represented by data itself.. As learning algorithms need large amounts of data to recognize patterns in it, these patterns may prove discriminatory, crucially, because we humans are the source of those data. It reflects who we are and how we tend to behave—not how we should behave. It thus derives *ought* from *is*. When these outputs based on the skewed inputs are used as a basis for future predictions, they may actually reproduce the bias in it, and thus create self-fulfilling prophesies ('garbage in, garbage out').[28] Even if we have a neutral process, we do not necessarily end up with a neutral outcome.

Let us approach these questions through examples. It is worth noting, though, that these examples do not relate directly to the GDPR and its transparency requirements, but rather illustrate the wider societal context, which makes the meaning of those requirements more understandable. The best-known example comes from the US: an article by *Pro Publica* created a scandal in 2016.[29] The article discusses the software used for assessing the recidivism

[24] Pasquale (n. 19) at 141.

[25] See Yeung, 'Why Worry about Decision-Making by Machine?' in K. Yeung and M. Lodge (eds), *Algorithmic Regulation* (2019) 21–48.

[26] C. O'Neil, *Weapons of Math Destruction: How Big Data Increases Inequality and Threatens Democracy* (2017); V. Eubanks, *Automating Inequality: How High-Tech Tools Profile, Police, and Punish the Poor* (2018).

[27] There has even been discussion over racist soap dispensers, which allegedly do not recognize dark skin to work.

[28] See Kerr, 'Prediction, Pre-emption, Presumption: The Path of Law after Computational Turn', in M. Hildebrandt and K. de Vries (eds), *Privacy, Due Process and the Computational Turn: The Philosophy of Law Meets the Philosophy of Technology* (2013) 91.

[29] Angwin *et al.*, 'Machine Bias' (2016), https://www.propublica.org/article/machine-bias-risk-assessments-in-criminal-sentencing (last visited 18 August 2021). See also Chouldechova, 'Fair Prediction with Disparate Impact: a Study of Bias in Recidivism Prediction Instruments', 5(2) *Big Data* (2016) 153.

potential of captive perpetrators in several states of the US. The idea was to give a person a numeric score, ranging from 1 (low risk) to 10 (high risk), reflecting the likelihood of re-offending. This score was further used, for example, to assess whether or not the person could be granted parole or be released prior to trial. The idea behind this is understandable: by achieving accuracy by ADM, it would lower crime and state costs, by separating low-risk prisoners from the high-risk ones, and releasing those considered low risk.

Nevertheless, the reality was less rosy, as was noticed by *Pro Publica* in its investigation. The algorithm systematically discriminated against blacks, giving them significantly higher risk scores than whites on average. NorthPointe, the enterprise which had created it, claimed the algorithm was a trade secret. Thus, it was impossible to know in what way it concluded that blacks were more like to reoffend than whites, and how the scores were actually calculated.

Certainly, it was not explainable by the previous criminal history of the people processed; rather, the history and the score clearly did not match. The set of questions, on which the score was at least partially based, did not include race. However, it did include questions mapping the potential rehabilitation needs of the person, such as questions of drug abuse and incarcerated friends, which nevertheless seemed to correlate with race.[30] Some backlash against the scoring system has emerged. There was even a court case against the use of the algorithm (*State v. Loomis*) as an alleged violation of Mr. Loomis' due process rights.[31] However, the court concluded that the use of the software was possible so long as the decisions were not solely based on it.[32]

Let us take another example from Poland. The Polish Ministry of Labour and Social Policy introduced a new system of granting unemployment benefits in 2014. It was based on a survey and an interview, which functioned as input of a score. People who were unemployed needed to fill in a form with a set of questions, indicating, for example, the reason for unemployment. Although

[30] A similar case was found in the US healthcare system, in which a commercial algorithm concluded on the basis of medical costs data that black patients need less medical care than whites. The reason for this turned out to be that blacks were previously granted less treatment than whites, not that they would be healthier. By inductive reasoning, the algorithm started to reproduce that pattern. Obermeyer et al., 'Dissecting Racial Bias in an Algorithm Used to Manage the Health of Populations', 366(6464) *Science* (2019) 447.

[31] See further, Liu, Lin, and Chen, 'Beyond *State v. Loomis*: Artificial Intelligence, Government Algorithmization and Accountability', 27(2) *International Journal of Law and Information Technology* (2019) 122.

[32] From a Freedom of Information Act point of view in the US, see Fink, 'Opening the Government's Black Boxes: Freedom of Information and Algorithmic Accountability', 21(10) *Information, Communication and Society* (2018) 1453. Later, the discourse has been diversified, and the 'anti-discrimination' discourse is considered sometimes too simplistic, overlooking, for example, questions of intersectionality. See Hoffmann, 'Where Fairness Fails: Data, Algorithms, and the Limits of Antidiscrimination Discourse', 22(7) *Information, Communication and Society* (2019) 900.

there was blank space left for answering seemingly open-ended questions, in reality there were 22 predefined answers to those questions. The questionnaire also did not recognize certain reasons, such as homelessness or ethnic origin or being a convicted felon, as a valid reason, although in practice these were major employability impediments in the Polish labour market.

According to the acquired score, the applicants were sorted into three different categories. The first category of people was considered the most employable, having a high educational level and unemployment stemming from some haphazard personal or market reason. They were only 2 per cent of the applicants. The second category of applicants was somewhat worse off, although still having some important skills (65 per cent). They were considered potentially in need of some additional education, skills, and support. The last category was the most problematic. It consisted of people on whom more of life's adversities seemed to accumulate: illness, drug abuse, lack of education, marginalization (33 per cent).[33]

Each of these categories were entitled to a different menu of benefits according to their needs. However, also in this case, there were hidden problems. Namely, there was virtually no possibility of contesting one's categorization; no information was available on the scoring rules. In addition, the array of different benefits and other supporting services were unevenly distributed so that they were the least available to the third category of people, who obviously needed them the most. In other words, the system was largely considered discriminatory, lacking transparency, and infringing data protection rights; all major concerns in the GDPR. This system of organizing unemployment governance caused resistance, most prominently by a civil society organization. In the end, Poland's constitutional court found that the system breached the constitution, although mostly due to formal reasons. As a result, the scoring system was abolished in 2019.[34]

The third example comes from Finland. Unlike the two previous examples, this case took place in a commercial context. It concerned internet commerce and different financing options while purchasing building materials online. The applicant was a man, living in rural Finland. His mother tongue was Finnish, as is the case with the vast majority of Finns. He had no prior record

[33] See Jędrzej, Sztandar-Sztanderska, and Szymielewicz, 'Profiling the Unemployed in Poland: Social and Political Implications of Algorithmic Decision Making' (2015), https://panoptykon.org/sites/default/files/leadimage-biblioteka/panoptykon_profiling_report_final.pdf (last visited 18 August 2021).

[34] Jedrzej, 'Poland: Government to Scrap Controversial Unemployment Scoring System' (2019), https://algorithmwatch.org/en/story/poland-government-to-scrap-controversial-unemployment-scoring-system/ (last visited 18 August 2021).

of disruptions of payment, or any problems in his credit history. These facts proved relevant, as he was denied the option of a partial payment arrangement. The decision was reached by using statistical methods in the ADM of the bank that was cooperating with the construction materials company.

According to the statistics used as the basis to create the algorithm, Swedish speakers and women were more likely to pay back their loans than Finnish speakers and men. The algorithm was found to favour Swedish-speaking women over Finnish-speaking men. In other words, the applicant was denied a financing option because of his gender, age, place of residence and mother tongue, and their cumulative effect. The rejection of the loan application was thus caused by profiling, not an individual assessment of creditworthiness. The case was considered both by the antidiscrimination ombudsman and, due to her initiative, the National Non-Discrimination and Equality Tribunal of Finland. The tribunal found the firm guilty of multi-reason discrimination. It was given a fine and ordered to discontinue the discriminatory practice.[35]

These examples are by no means exhaustive. On the contrary, with the increasing use of ADM, more similar cases are emerging. Although the three examples presented above are quite different in context and consequence, they also share some important similarities. First, the examples represent the larger development of the emergence of a 'scored society', a new way of quantifying and ranking people.[36] These resulting profiles are made of stereotypes and profiles of individuals based on certain characteristics, such as wealth, gender, habits, education, etc. Profiling requires individual information. This information, however, leads to simplification and generalization—to the treatment of people as representatives of a certain category rather than unique individuals.[37] Some of these profiles have proven discriminatory, as illustrated.

This brings us to the second similarity: there is a lack of information about the scoring rules. Accordingly, there were only limited possibilities to react to the breach of individual rights. It can even be unclear whether any rights have indeed been violated. This conversely underlines the attractiveness of transparency as a legitimating ideal in ADM. Third, they all have caused backlash and protest. With varying success, we can see that there are remedies available. It is debatable, though, whether they are well suited to the legal problems of a

[35] Register number: 216/2017, Date of issue: 21 March 2018, https://www.yvtltk.fi/en/index/opinionsanddecisions/decisions.html (last visited 18 August 2021).

[36] Citron and Pasquale, 'The Scored Society: Due Process for Automated Predictions', 89(1) *Washington Law Review* (2014) 1.

[37] For an overview on profiling see M. Hildebrandt and S. Gutwirth (eds), *Profiling the European Citizen*: Cross-*Disciplinary Perspectives* (2008).

scored society. How many problems like the described examples go completely unnoticed?

In the context of people's rights, possibilities, and equal treatment, the black box indeed looks like a problem rather than just a neutral feature. The algorithms in use are not available, visible, or understandable to the people who, however, are subjects to their silent and seemingly unerring power. This may lead to potential approval of unjustified categorizations and treatment, if the black box just produces a score or the loss of an opportunity without giving reasons why that is so. Neither logic of discovery nor logic of justification can be seen: there is no transparency. In the following, I analyse the ideal of transparency more closely.

3. Transparency and its Covert Human-Faced Logic

As mentioned, transparency carries much promise in solving the black box problem. In Ananny and Crawford's words, 'The more that is known about a system's inner workings, the more defensibly it can be governed and held accountable.'[38] Depending on the context, transparency can mean different things in ADM. It can be associated to source code publicity, auditing, and impact assessment, to mention but a few.[39]

On a more fundamental level, however, transparency is a major socio-legal ideal, which seldom encounters resistance or questioning. It assumes that when we see by ourselves, we can understand what is happening. By virtue of this eye witnessing, we can further fix what needs to be fixed. In public policy context, this general promise has been inherent in this justificatory narrative of transparency from its very inception—from the era of the Enlightenment, that is.[40] It contrasts with the ideal of secrecy and relies on democratic monitoring of power. It presupposes that citizens have a legitimate right to know how power is exercised upon them, and that they are willing and able to use that right. Similarly, algorithmic transparency follows a simple logic: if we

[38] Ananny and Crawford (n. 17) 2. See also Laat, 'Algorithmic Decision-Making Based on Machine Learning from Big Data: Can Transparency Restore Accountability?', 31(4) *Philosophy and Technology* (2018) 525.

[39] Felzmann *et al.*, 'Robots and Transparency: The Multiple Dimensions of Transparency in the Context of Robot Technologies', 26(2) *Institute of Electrical and Electronics Engineers Robotics and Automation Magazine* (2019) 71.

[40] Hood, 'Transparency in Historical Perspective', in C. Hood and D. Heald (eds), *Transparency—Key to Better Governance?* (2006) 3, at 6–7; Baume and Papadopoulos, 'Transparency: from Bentham's Inventory of Virtuous Effects to Contemporary Evidence-based Skepticism' 21(2) *Critical Review of International Social and Political Philosophy* (2018) 169.

could only open up the algorithmic black boxes and see their inner workings we could make sure they are fair.[41] The unknown—including the black box—is thus considered problematic because it obscures vision; it is particular kind of secrecy. Like that, it undermines the Enlightenment imperative of *sapere aude*, 'dare to know', 'have the courage, the audacity, to know'.[42] Thus, transparency is regarded as an apt cure for this, as it specifically promises clear vision.

Nevertheless, transparency has proven more complex than its promise suggests. In order to delve into the potential of transparency to solve the black box problem, we need to discuss the hidden functioning logic of transparency on a more fundamental, theoretical level. In the following, I will approach this logic from three angles, which address the basic assumptions of the transparency ideal: transparency as a visual metaphor; transparency as an icono-ambivalent ideal; and the latent conjunction between transparency and intentionality. This all will lead to an overall idea, which I call the *human-faced logic of transparency*.[43] Although not restricted to the context of digitalization, this logic has quite dramatic consequences concerning the general promise vested in transparency, and consequently, the specific promise in ADM.

First, let us start with the metaphor. We can notice that as a concept, transparency appeals specifically to our vision, our ability to see things with our own eyes. We cannot hear transparency, nor smell or taste it. Therefore, it could be called a visual or an ocular-centric arrangement. Perhaps, we can better grasp this idea when we think of transparency as looking through a window. Something is made directly and intentionally visible to the viewer, which otherwise would stay hidden, either spontaneously (something cannot be seen easily) or deliberately (something is kept out of sight). Without transparency, we cannot see, but with transparency, we can.[44]

This promise underpins transparency as a metaphor. It requires that transparency is approached as a figurative placeholder for different practices, which provide information about its object. The visual undertow of transparency makes it understandable and attractive to us even in cases when we are talking about abstractions such as governance. So long as we can witness the reality with our own eyes, we do not need verbal explanations, which are, by virtue

[41] Lepri *et al.*, 'Fair Transparent, and Accountable Algorithmic Decision-making processes', 31(4) *Philosophy and Technology* (2018) 611.

[42] Bucher (n. 18) 44. *Sapere aude* is particularly known from Immanuel Kant's thinking.

[43] For the outline of the theory, see Koivisto, 'The Anatomy of Transparency: The Concept and its Multifarious Implications', EUI Working Paper MWP 2016/09, https://cadmus.eui.eu/bitstream/handle/1814/41166/MWP_2016_09.pdf?sequence=1&isAllowed=y (last visited 18 August 2021).

[44] Christensen and Cornelissen, 'Organizational Transparency as Myth and Metaphor', 18(2) *European Journal of Social Theory* (2015) 132, at 133.

of transparency, indirectly considered less reliable than direct visual observation. This is the very core, I argue, why it is so appealing to us. Seeing by oneself seems to be self-authenticating: seeing is understanding, understanding is seeing.

However, transparency is not only a metaphor. Additionally, the literal meaning of transparency belongs to its functioning mechanisms. Sometimes transparency is organized as direct see-ability. This can be exemplified by glass walls or roofs of public buildings.[45] They allow people to see what is happening in the chambers of powers. Transparency can thus work as inspective architecture. As a result, transparency oscillates between two functionalities: transparency as actual, visual see-ability allowed by an optical arrangement and transparency as a metaphor for verbal practices of self-reporting.

When referring to a governance ideal, transparency can thus mean both *actual, material transparency* and *metaphorical, as if transparency*. The *as if* aspect of transparency becomes understandable when we refer to see-ability or knowability of abstract things, which typically lack physical appearance. What is there to see when we talk about abstractions, such as governance or decision-making? Indeed, nothing. Social constructs such as governance only exist in our collective imagination and can only be understood through symbols and hints. For example, how could we use transparency to see something as abstract as a person's recidivism risk?

This oscillation between literal and metaphorical meaning[46] brings us to the second, not obvious aspect of transparency: its icono-ambivalence. This conceptualization is my own, although it is loosely inspired by Bruno Latour's concept of *iconoclash*, our simultaneous reliance on and suspicion of images.[47] What does the neologism icono-ambivalence mean? It refers to another, internal duality of transparency: on the one hand, transparency is ideologically *iconoclastic*. It is suspicious of images, explanations, and mediation—ultimately, humans. It attempts to strip governance from all kinds of obfuscating veils: secrecy, appearances, and concealment. It promises to allow governance itself to emerge in its pure essence before the eyes of the viewer. Following that reasoning, the transcendence of governance, if you will, would take care of

[45] See Rowe and Slutzky, 'Transparency: Literal and Phenomenal', 8 *Perspecta* (1963) 45; Fisher, 'Exploring the Legal Architecture of Transparency', in P. Ala'i and R. Vaughn (eds), *Research Handbook of Transparency* (2014) 59.

[46] Alloa, 'Transparency: A Magic Concept of Modernity', in E. Alloa and D. Thomä (eds), *Transparency, Society and Subjectivity: Critical Perspectives* (2018) 21, at 31–32. Also Flyverbom, 'Transparency: Mediation and the Management of Visibilities', 10 *International Journal of Communication* (2016) 110, at 113.

[47] Latour, 'What Is Iconoclash?', in B. Latour and P. Weibel (eds), *Iconoclash: Beyond Image Wars in Science, Religion, and Art* (2002) 14

its own representation so long as the impediments blocking its visibility for the viewer were removed. In the context of ADM, opening a black box would represent such iconoclastic thinking: the black box hinders us to see the inner workings of the algorithmic system.

On the other hand, I argue, transparency is also *iconophilic* and necessarily so. Iconophily means love for or acceptance of images and representation. If iconoclasm is the ideological aspect of transparency, iconophily is its unescapable practicality. In many cases, there is nothing to show, to emerge, without conscious efforts and constructs. Therefore, transparency needs to rely on images, metonymically understood: illustrations, statistics, reports, memoranda, etc.—conscious, constructed appearances, mostly falling into the category of documents. In the context of ADM, providing a description, an illustration, or an explanation on the algorithm would represent an iconophilic approach to transparency.

In this sense, transparency needs to rely on people and their mimetic abilities, their capabilities to 'capture' the essence of governance and to communicate it to the public. The iconophilic aspect of transparency thus refers to the accessibility of those created illustrations of intangible abstractions. For example, a score of one's employability is an iconophilic expression of a social construct, which does not exist naturally in the world. The icono-ambivalence of transparency leads to a paradox: transparency means, in Emmanuel Alloa's words, mediated immediacy.[48] It both is, and it needs to be, constructed.

The complexity of transparency does not end there, however. As mentioned, transparency is associated with legitimacy: it is generally considered desirable. Transparency is good, whereas the lack of transparency is bad. How does this legitimating effect work?[49] To answer that, we need to address the third aspect of the hidden functioning logic of transparency, namely that of intentionality. We can detect the significance of intentionality with careful analysis of language. Although in public discourse transparency is almost entirely treated as a positive thing—regardless of whether it is seen as iconophilic or iconoclastic—it also entails a negative connotation.

It is important to notice that transparency is not only a virtue, but under certain circumstances, a sign of failure. This contention has its roots in a linguistic observation, available for anyone to test: 'You are so transparent! I can see through you!', we might say, when we notice someone's failure to come

[48] Alloa (n. 46) at 21–55.

[49] Curtin and Meijer, 'Does Transparency Strengthen Legitimacy?', 11(2) *Information Polity* (2006) 109. See also de Fine Licht, *Magic Wand or Pandora's Box? How Transparency in Decision Making affects Public Perceptions of Legitimacy* (2014).

across in a certain, predetermined way. In that case, the attempt is implausible to the extent that we cannot but see the 'truer truth' behind that leaking appearance, or at least we think we do. Perhaps counter-intuitively, we resent this revelation. We prefer hidden motives to be hidden, and value transparency only when it is intentional. This negative if not pejorative connotation of transparency is completely unnoticed and consequently untheorized in current academic literature on transparency.

Hence, transparency is regarded as a value when it is consciously created or allowed but frowned upon when it is a sign of involuntary revelation, signifying the incapability to keep hidden things hidden. Unintentional transparency refers to the lack of control, which we tend to abhor. This intentionality is the key to the paradoxical, and as was mentioned, the human-faced nature of the ideal of transparency. This dynamic of transparency has largely remained unexplored in the academic literature on transparency. However, it has huge implications when we think about the promise and beliefs vested in transparency.

This is to say, transparency, both referring to social life and as a governance ideal, is closely linked to prestige, appearance, favourable impressions, and in case of failure, loss of strategy, or the emergence of shame. Involuntary transparency makes one appear in an unplanned way. It is about mediating of what can be seen. In other words, it is about managing visibilities.[50] The key word that captures this dynamic is *impression management*. It is a term coined by social psychologist Erving Goffman in his seminal work *Presentation of Self in Everyday Life* (1956). In it, he explains how social life is, and cannot but be, performative in nature: we carefully plan how we want to appear to others, and what part of our lives we want to keep to ourselves, in turn. This enables us to have a face, a social persona. In that way, transparency is a narcissistic ideal.

I argue that a similar mechanism is characteristic of institutions. They, too, have an interest to uphold a certain image, a certain face, to control what information they release. If that were not the case, information leaks, for example, could not lead to such scandals as they often do. As a result, it is possible to hypothesize that the use of different transparency practices—whether physical or metaphorical, iconoclastic or iconophilic—are motivated by this very goal: to appear in a favourable light.

If we take this idea to the extreme, we reach a rather radical conclusion. The ultimate logic of transparency can be called *the truth-legitimacy trade-off*. It means that by intentional transparency more legitimacy is achieved, but most

[50] See Flyverbom (n. 46) at 110, also Flyverbom, *The Digital Prism: Transparency and Managed Visibilities in a Datafied World* (2019).

probably, it is based on a carefully curated picture of reality. If, in contrast, there is no such curation, there will be more extensive access to information, but most probably, less legitimacy, because the less flattering elements of reality would also be subject to external gaze. This is premised on the idea that only intentional transparency is capable of creating legitimacy. The image created by transparency is designed to be seen, it delivers managed visibilities.

In the context of this chapter, it is not possible to delve into this human-faced logic of transparency more deeply. That said, the most important implication of the logic needs to be highlighted: transparency as an ideal is not neutral visibility or an undistorted flow of information. When something is framed as 'transparency', it is also planned to deliver a particular kind of message, to enable its deliverer to uphold a persona, a face. This message may be constructed or allowed to emerge, depending on the context. In any case, the release is controlled. In other words, we do not only see through transparency, we also see the created transparency, which makes the medium the message.

In the context of ADM, the human agent caring about her appearance to others may be distant if not, in some cases, completely absent. Regardless, the main feature of planned visibilities remains, as I will argue in the following. For example, if a scoring algorithm for creditworthiness, software was deliberately revealed in the name of transparency, that could increase the legitimacy of the releasing institution. If it were leaked, instead, we would be equally informed but most likely less impressed; we would assume they have something to hide.[51] However, in ADM, the particular object of transparency—an algorithm—complicates the issue further. It proves the insufficiency of transparency as a cure-all concept. This will be discussed in the following.

4. The EU's General Data Protection Regulation: Law Coupling Transparency and ADM

A. Transparency Portrayed in the GDPR

I have now presented some of the key factors of my general theory of transparency as a socio-legal ideal. These factors function as tools for analysis in assessing the potential of transparency to solve the black box problem in ADM.

[51] See Gibbs, 'Sigmund Freud as a Theorist of Government Secrecy', 19 *Research in Social Problems and Public Policy* (2011) 5, at 15: 'The underlying principle in law, psychology and historical research is the same: When people make declarations that go against their interest, such declarations have high credibility.'

What happens to the human-faced logic of transparency, if, at least seemingly, humans are no longer always the gatekeepers of information and the managers of impression? Is there anyone to reveal or conceal? Alternatively, does human mediation govern transparency also in ADM; if so, what follows from that? What is the role of law in this? To analyse this field of questions, we need to move to a somewhat more concrete level of discussion. As mentioned, the EU's GDPR attempts to solve the black box problem with the help of transparency. Therefore, it is worth a closer look. How is transparency portrayed in it and the ADM regulations it includes?[52]

GDPR has been applied since May 2018. As is widely known, it has changed the data protection regime in the EU, not least due to the increasing use of ADM.[53] The aim of the GDPR is to 'harmonize data privacy laws across Europe, to protect and empower all EU citizens' data privacy, and to reshape the way organizations across the region approach data privacy'.[54] Most crucially, it has created new rights for data subjects and new duties for data controllers. It is also built on a risk-based approach, which obliges the data controllers to assess the effects of processing personal data. The regulation is extensive, complex, and, I would maintain, somewhat difficult to decipher. Consequently, it includes many interesting research themes and, indeed, the amount of academic writing on the topic is on rise.

In ADM, the questions of privacy and data protection go hand in hand with the call for transparency. Transparency is expected from the data controllers and from ADM, and data protection and privacy are demanded for the data subjects. This is because algorithmic models—such as different scoring and profiling tools employed in ADM—typically feed on huge amounts of personal data. That is necessary for them to form accurate outputs, as was illustrated through the examples above. Those personal data further originate from data subjects, and they are valuable raw material for a data-driven economy. Therefore, we should be keenly interested in how these data are gathered and handled. How can we know whether there is an illegal or unethical bias involved?[55] As presented, we often cannot. This ignorance is a growing legal

[52] For a detailed analysis on transparency in GDPR, see Felzmann *et al.*, 'Transparency You Can Trust: Transparency Requirements for Artificial Intelligence between Legal Norms and Contextual Concerns', 6(1) *Big Data and Society* (2019).

[53] The EU's AI Act (n. 14), see also White Paper On Artificial Intelligence—A European approach to excellence and trust, Brussels, 19.2.2020 COM(2020) 65 final, https://ec.europa.eu/info/sites/info/files/commission-white-paper-artificial-intelligence-feb2020_en.pdf (last visited 18 August 2021).

[54] European Parliament, 'The Implementation of the Data Protection Package-At the Eve of its Application' (15 May 2018), https://www.europarl.europa.eu/committees/en/libe/events-nationalparl.html?id=20180419MNP00301 (last visited 18 August 2021).

[55] See further e.g. Hacker, 'Teaching Fairness to Artificial Intelligence: Existing and Novel Strategies Against Algorithmic Discrimination Under EU Law', 55(4) *Common Market Law Review* (2018) 1143.

concern, to which the call for transparency is closely connected. Would it help, then, if the data processing were made transparent to the data subjects? It is believed so.

This belief in transparency has strong institutional support in the GDPR. Transparency is one of the key principles of the entire Regulation along with fairness and lawfulness.[56] ADM, in turn, is regulated specifically in Article 22 (Automated individual decision-making, including profiling).[57] Although as a main rule, the Article defines a right not to be subject to ADM alone when there are legal or similar kinds of effects on the individual, it also defines a number of exceptions when it is, in fact, allowed. Some writers even argue that this hollows out the entire right not to be subject to ADM, making the exceptions the main rule.[58] However, when ADM is applied by virtue of the exceptions laid down in Article 22, it does not mean that data controllers can forget about the related data protection issues, including the call for transparency. Indeed, it can be argued that these very exceptions make transparency relevant in ADM.

As mentioned before, the background assumption in the call for transparency is an asymmetrical power structure. Here, that structure emerges between the data controller and the data subject. Therefore, accountability mechanisms are needed. To that end, Article 22 needs to be read together with Articles 13–15, which regulate the rights of the data subject to information and access to personal data.[59] The idea is that a data subject should be sufficiently informed about how her data are being handled, also when ADM is in question.

When it comes to the black box problem and transparency as its potential solution, there is a specific formulation in Articles 13–15 which is worthy of closer analysis. That is to say, those articles require 'meaningful information about the logic involved' as a right of the data subject to ensure fair and transparent processing. The formulation is virtually identical in all of the Articles 13–15. In Article 13(2)(f), for example, it says that:

[56] 'Personal data shall be processed lawfully, fairly and in a transparent manner in relation to the data subject ('lawfulness, fairness and transparency').' Council and Parliament Regulation 2016/679, OJ 2016 L119/1 ('GDPR') 5(1) (a).

[57] See Temme, 'Algorithms and Transparency in View of the New General Data Protection Regulation', 3(4) *European Data Protection Law Review* (2017) 473.

[58] Brkan, 'Do Algorithms Rule the World? Algorithmic Decision-making and Data Protection in the Framework of the GDPR and Beyond', 27(2) *International Journal of Law and Information Technology* (2019) 91, at 119–120.

[59] Information to be provided where personal data are collected from the data subject, Art. 13(2)(f) GDPR; Information to be provided where personal data have not been obtained from the data subject, Art. 14(2)(g) GDPR; Right of access by the data subject, Art. 15(1)(h) GDPR.

> In addition to the information referred to in paragraph 1, the controller shall, at the time when personal data are obtained, provide the data subject with the following further information necessary to ensure fair and transparent processing:
>
> (f) the existence of automated decision-making, including profiling, referred to in Article 22(1) and (4) and, at least in those cases, meaningful information about the logic involved, as well as the significance and the envisaged consequences of such processing for the data subject.

We can notice that information is required both of the existence of ADM, and in that case, at least, meaningful information of the logic involved and the envisaged consequences of such processing for the data subject. In other words, the data controller needs to consider the entire lifespan of the ADM and provide information extensively, although some of it might be speculative. Additionally, Article 12 specifically defines transparent information: 'The controller shall [provide information] in a concise, transparent, intelligible and easily accessible form, using clear and plain language, in particular for any information addressed specifically to a child ....'

Regardless of these many paragraphs, the extent and the quality of information furnishing obligations has proven somewhat unclear. In academic literature, the enigmatic formulation of 'meaningful information' has caused much debate: do these mentioned paragraphs together create a right to explanation when ADM is being used? Some authors argue that no such right exists based on the wording of the regulation.[60] Some writers, in turn, state that a systemic reading is necessary instead, in particular, when the Articles 22 and 13–15 are read together with the recitals 71–72.[61] As Maja Brkan summarizes, 'the basic dilemma that the overview of the literature reveals is the quest whether the so called "right to explanation" would be a right that is read into another existing GDPR right, such as the right to information or access, or whether such a "right to explanation" could potentially be created in addition to other existing rights from the binding provisions of the GDPR.'[62]

[60] Wachter, Mittelstadt, and Floridi, 'Why a Right to Explanation of Automated Decision-Making Does Not Exist in the General Data Protection Regulation', 7(2) *International Data Protection Law* (2017) 76.

[61] Malgieri and Comandé, 'Why a Right to Legibility of Automated Decision-Making Exists in the General Data Protection Regulation', 7(4) *International Data Protection Law* (2017) 243; Goodman and Flaxman, 'European Union Regulation on Algorithmic Decision-Making and a "Right to Explanation"', 38(3) *AI Magazine* (2017) 50; Selbst and Powles, 'Meaningful Information and the Right to Explanation', 7(4) *International Data Protection Law* (2017) 233; Edwards and Veale, 'Enslaving the Algorithm: From a "Right to an Explanation" to a "Right to Better Decisions"', 16(3) *Institute of Electrical and Electronics Engineers Security and Privacy* (2018) 46.

[62] Brkan (n. 58) at 111.

I am not delving into the debate on 'right to explanation' more deeply. However, the mere emergence of it is symptomatic. Transparency and 'meaningful information' should constitute the general ethos of the regulation, and yet their formulations are so vague that there is uncertainty about the very existence of the right to explanation.[63] The deeper question is, therefore, whether the transparency formulations laid down in the GDPR are serving their purpose or not. Some of the confusion may stem from the fact that the regulation does not only define the quantity of information but also the quality of it. This is particularly visible in the context of the right to explanation. Not only does information about the logic involved need to be at hand, it needs to be meaningful[64] and, in the light of Article 12, 'concise, transparent, intelligible and easily accessible form, using clear and plain language'.

It seems that in the GDPR, transparency is regarded both as an umbrella concept, under which the access to information rights may be gathered, and an interpretative principle, which should inform all personal data processing, and the quality of provided information, which the access to information rights concretize. Is 'meaningful information', thus, an expression of the general principle of transparency (see Articles 13–15: '... to ensure transparent ... processing'), or is it ultimately something else? The entire question leads us back to the question of what kind of information we are after.[65]

B. Transparency as Showing or Explaining its Object?

To understand better the functioning mechanism of transparency in the GDPR and the black box problem, we need to return to the questions of *the logic of discovery* and *the logic of justification*, which were already briefly discussed. The distinction becomes important in assessing the way in which information can be transparent or meaningful. Namely, what is pursued through the call for transparency is often, in fact, a conceivable message. How do the operations in

[63] Wachter, Mittelstadt, and Russell, 'Counterfactual Explanations Without Opening the Black Box: Automated Decisions and the GDPR', 31(2) *Harvard Journal of Law and Technology* (2018) 841: 'Meaningful information about the logic involved' is said to require only clarifying the categories of data used to create a profile; the source of the data; and why this data is considered relevant as opposed to a detailed technical description about how an algorithm or machine learning works. See also de Vries, 'Transparent Dreams (Are Made of This): Counterfactuals as Transparency Tools in ADM', 8(1) *Critical Analysis of Law* (2021) 121.

[64] Malgieri and Comandé discuss the question of 'meaningfulness' of information from different angles. Malgieri and Comandé (n. 61) at 256–258.

[65] How these ideas have been conceived in different EU member states, see Malgieri, 'Automated Decision-making in the EU Member States: The Right to Explanation and Other "Suitable Safeguards" in the National Legislations', 35(5) *Computer Law and Security Review* (2019) 1.

a black box affect my legal standing? Interestingly, the wording in Articles 13–15 specifically mandates expressing the 'meaningful information about logic involved' in ADM. Is it the logic of discovery or logic of justification, or a logic of some other kind? Do we need the black box to reveal or to justify itself?

Against the described backdrop, it is not clear what the right to explanation—or whatever it is called—signifies. For example, in Finland, where legislation to enable automated decisions in public administration is currently being drafted, the GDPR formulations have caused confusion. According to a recent preparatory memorandum: 'Thus far, it is not known how the requirement of "meaningful information of the logic involved" should be understood. The Chancellor of Justice has regarded decision rules and algorithms used in ADM as meaningful information. However, EU legislation cannot be explained or interpreted in domestic legislation, which is why the interpretation of those requirements is the responsibility of the authorities employing ADM.'[66]

This uncertainty of the meaning of those GDPR formulations leads us to ask, what would a data subject want or need to know.[67] To answer that, we need to approach the question from the data subject's point of view. Assumedly, she would not be primarily interested in the ADM per se, out of sheer human interest. Instead, she would probably be more interested in why it was applied to her, how the result of it was achieved, and how it affects her: for example, why she reached a certain recidivism score or why she was put in a particular category as a job applicant.

The WP29 guidelines on the use on ADM state that: 'The GDPR requires the controller to provide meaningful information about the logic involved, not necessarily a complex explanation of the algorithms used or disclosure of the full algorithm. The information provided should, however, be sufficiently comprehensive for the data subject to understand the reasons for the decision.'[68] With the help of the provided information, the data subject could then assess whether she approves the automated decision or not, whether she wishes to contest it, and whether she wants to have a human intervention. In this form, we encounter the standard legitimating narrative of transparency: when we see, we can control, and possibly, change whatever is found unsatisfying.

[66] Hallinnon automaattista päätöksentekoa koskevaa yleislainsäädäntöä valmisteleva työryhmä: Hallinnon automaattinen päätöksenteko. Käyttöalaa ja läpinäkyvyyttä koskevat säännösluonnokset. Oikeusministeriö. Muistio 31.5.2021 (Memorandum by the Working Group Preparing General Legislation for ADM in Public Administration, Finnish Ministry of Justice, May 31, 2021) (translation by the author).

[67] See Brkan (n. 58).

[68] WP29, 'Guidelines on Automated individual decision-making' (3 October 2017, last revised and adopted 6 February 2018), at 25, https://iapp.org/media/pdf/resource_center/W29-auto-decision_profiling_02-2018.pdf (last visited 18 August 2021).

The meaningfulness of information is thus assumed to avoid the effects of the black box problem. As Bucher argues, when algorithms are conceptualized as black boxes, they are simultaneously understood as a problem of the unknown. This does not simply mean the lack of knowledge or information; rather, the black box points to a more specific type of unknown. The dominant discourses of transparency and accountability suggest that in fact, algorithms are *knowable known unknowns.* They are knowable if the right resources are provided. This is further done, as the mainstream narrative goes, by opening the black boxes.[69]

However, it is possible to argue that in the context of ADM, the standard promise of transparency is not necessarily entirely valid. For example, if the algorithm considering Swedish-speaking women to be more reliable than Finnish-speaking men was revealed, would understanding and legitimacy follow? Ananny and Crawford argue that to 'look inside the black box' may be too limited a demand. The metaphor is unsuitable when we are talking about something as complex as algorithmic systems. It suggests falsely easy certainty, which would follow from looking, and ignores the ideological and material complexities involved in ADM. Furthermore, the promise of 'seeing is understanding' may fail in the call for accountability; its object is hard to decipher and be held accountable.[70]

Similarly, Wachter, Mittelstadt, and Russel remain sceptical about the 'look inside the black box' approach. However, instead of the danger of 'easy certainty' and simplification, they think that opening the black box would lead to unnecessary complexity and leave the data subject confused about what is going on. They state that although interpretability is desirable, explanations can, in principle, be offered without opening the black box. In their view, less weight should be put on the data subject's ability to understand—whether through looking inside the box or being provided with an explanation—and more on how explanations are to empower data subjects to act towards their specific goals.[71]

These criticisms point in the same direction: seeing inside the black box does not necessarily lead to understanding, and understanding does not necessarily lead to control or other type of action.[72] Consequently, understanding

[69] Bucher (n. 18) 43.

[70] Ananny and Crawford (n. 17) at 10.

[71] Wachter, Mittelstadt, and Russel (n. 63) at 843: 'We propose three aims for explanations to assist data subjects: (1) to inform and help the subject understand why a particular decision was reached, (2) to provide grounds to contest adverse decisions, and (3) to understand what could be changed to receive a desired result in the future, based on the current decision-making model.'

[72] See also Macgregor, Daragh, and Ng, 'International Human Rights Law as a Framework for Algorithmic Accountability', 68(2) *The International and Comparative Law Quarterly* (2019) 309.

has become a concern. The debate on the right to explanation can be considered one aspect of this. Also, conceptually, understanding has partially started to diverge from the vocabulary of transparency. Provided information needs to be *meaningful* and *transparent*, as it is conceptualized in the GDPR. Additionally, other similar conceptualizations have lately emerged into the discourse: *explainability*, *interpretability*, *intelligibility*, *explicability*, *understandability*, and *comprehensibility*. These concepts imply that transparency is not enough to guarantee understanding.[73]

Hence, more than transparency is needed, but that 'more' can be malleable to many purposes.[74] This is readily explainable with the help of my theory, presented above. If transparency is conceived as a purely iconoclastic ideal, which, by virtue of this, lets its object (such as an algorithm) merely 'shine through' transparency, it would not do much work. It would not be able to deliver and fulfil its promise. The revelation through the iconoclastic mechanism—removing the obstacles of visibility (the 'opening the box' approach)—would not necessarily communicate anything to an average data subject. The revealed information would be highly esoteric, comprehensible only to experts. The underlying promise of transparency, 'understanding is seeing', would be thus jeopardized. Indeed, in the context of ADM, seeing seldom constitutes immediate understanding to a layperson but instead leaves one puzzled by confusing information, perhaps comparable to a text in a foreign language. As Ananny and Crawford argue, transparency may privilege seeing over understanding.[75]

Thus, whether we talk about transparency or the right to explanation, or meaningful information about the logic involved, we need to consider the question of iconophily and the necessary human involvement it entails. We can also assume that ADM is not naturally attuned to consider meaningfulness of information from the point of view of human comprehension.[76] This human intervention may shift transparency again towards understandability. This may be problematic, because ideologically, transparency specifically privileges immediate seeing over more mediated verbal explanations, descriptions, or illustrations. If transparency becomes a synonym of explanation, it inevitably loses something from its legitimating power. The core promise of transparency 'do

[73] See e.g. Olsen *et al.*, 'What's in the Box? The Legal Requirement of Explainability in Computationally Aided Decision-Making in Public Administration', 162 *iCourts Working Paper Series* (2019).

[74] See Buhmann, Paßmann, and Fieseler, 'Managing Algorithmic Accountability: Balancing Reputational Concerns, Engagement Strategies, and the Potential of Rational Discourse', 163 *Journal of Business Ethics* (2020) 265.

[75] Ananny and Crawford (n. 17) at 8–9.

[76] de Fine Licht and de Fine Licht, 'Artificial Intelligence, Transparency, and Public Decision-making', 35 *AI and Society* (2020) 917.

not believe what I say, see for yourself' would thus be transformed to 'do not believe what you see, let me explain instead'.

However, as presented, the iconophily—transparency requiring constructs in order to create a visible appearance—together with the intentionality of transparency, enables the consideration of human understanding and its limitations. On the one hand, it may produce information that is meaningful from an average data subject's point of view and creates legitimacy like that. For example, a simple enough explanation of the logic involved in ADM may make it easier for a data subject to understand and accept. On the other hand, it is potentially also a forum of impression management logic. The more human mediation and human involvement there is, resulting in carefully managed visibilities, the more legitimacy may be produced. At the same time, this may also mean less 'truth', when the intricacies of the black box cannot, by being exposed, necessarily communicate anything (the truth-legitimacy trade-off).

5. Conclusions: Has ADM Broken the Promise of Transparency?

In this chapter, I have discussed the ideal of transparency as a suggested solution to the black box problem in ADM. According to its promise, transparency would open or X-ray black boxes. This would enable data subjects to look at what is inside the boxes and perhaps question and change their inner workings. As I have explained, the main narrative of transparency has been adopted from the discourses of public law and governance into the discourses of ADM, algorithmic governance, and regulation. Despite its well-institutionalized and seldom questioned promise, transparency is, I argued, more complex an ideal than the popular opinion acknowledges. I claimed that transparency is covertly a human-faced ideal, due to its basis in a visual metaphor, icono-ambivalence, and the connection between intentionality and legitimacy.

As I have argued, even as an institutional value, transparency is underpinned by attempts of impression management and the avoidance of losing face, even if that face belongs to an institution.[77] I argue that the deep structure of transparency is ultimately control. Only controlled information release can create the promised and desired legitimacy. If that is not the case, the agent releasing

[77] For example, as Monika Zalnieriute demonstrates, technology companies may boost their legitimacy by 'transparency washing', ostentatious adoption of transparency policies. Zalnieriute, '"Transparency-Washing" in the Digital Age: A Corporate Agenda of Procedural Fetishism', 8(1) *Critical Analysis of Law* (2021) 139.

the information could not influence the impression it gives and would thus be unable to govern its image (the truth-legitimacy trade-off of transparency).

This complexity of transparency as an ideal is surreptitiously surfacing in the current discourses and even regulation on ADM, the EU's AI Act as the most recent example. Although transparency is called for in regulation concerning ADM and AI, it seems to be considered increasingly insufficient in addressing the core issues of the black box problem. As a sign of this, there are attempts to complement and/or to replace the concept of transparency with some other more fitting terminology such as a right to explanation, explicability, or understandability, which would better consider the recipient of the information. On a theoretical level, the conceptual plurality does work better in differentiating the logic of discovery from the logic of justification.

Nonetheless, the term transparency still seems to carry a justificatory promise that other terms do not. This is visible, for example, in the vocabulary of the GDPR as well as in the EU's AI Act, in which transparency specifically is one of the key principles, trickling down to more concrete information release practices. The history of transparency is longer than the other similar concepts, and it is closely linked to democracy and citizen participation. Transparency has the potential to empower to action—after all, it is a mechanism of control—because it assumes that everyone can understand by seeing and then taking necessary action. Understandability, in turn, has the potential to make people passive recipients of simplified information, being increasingly dependent on translating intermediaries. Additionally, the idea of immediate visibility inherent in transparency has emancipatory potential different from the mentioned neighbouring concepts. Explanation includes more human influence than sheer transparency, however illusory.

The extent to which the performative logic of transparency fuels the attempts to replace the term needs to be further analysed. How well is it recognized in those newer terms? It is important to notice that (human?) mediation is needed in the process of 'translating' the inner workings of the black boxes into a form understandable to a layperson.[78] Bucher explains how critics of the Enlightenment vision have been suspicious of the notion of revealing or decoding inner workings. The assumption is that a kernel of truth would just be waiting to be revealed by a mature and rational mind. In the Kantian tradition, she continues, the audacity to know is not only directly linked to rationalism but also to the quest for the condition under which true knowledge is

[78] See Koulu, 'Proceduralising Control and Discretion: Human Oversight in Artificial Intelligence Policy', 27 *Maastricht Journal of European and Comparative Law* (2020) 720.

possible. In this way, black boxes threaten the very possibility of knowing the truth.[79]

To what extent is this translation a matrix of impression management logic? How much is lost in translation, and how much should one anticipate those potential explanations serve the interest of the data controller? These questions require more work to be answered. Maybe black boxes even represent, in Elena Esposito's words, *divinatory rationality*. In pre-modern times, the mystery of the oracle was the guarantee of the rationality of the procedure. It was convincing and reliable precisely *because* humans lack the ability to understand the logic of the world, not despite that.[80] In a similar vein, in Socratic tradition the unknown was considered the prerequisite for wisdom, not a hindrance to it.[81]

An important feature of transparency's problems in the context of ADM stem from the fact that impression management logic cannot take place effortlessly. It requires assessing the effects of the release. How would they influence the desired impression? ADM lacks the sense of common decency and the understanding of when to interpret things to the letter and when more liberally. It lacks the human capability to steer through varying contexts with a compass such as the law or, indeed, transparency; in other words, it lacks practical wisdom. That feature would make it hard to create transparency by design, transparency which would not include this kind of ex post evaluation (i.e. meaningful information about the envisaged consequences). As Riikka Koulu shows, the effects of transparency by design depends on how transparency is interpreted: in the context of algorithmic systems, it is further interlinked with the ways in which those systems are designed. However, the GDPR, for example, remains silent on such design processes.[82]

In the end, the entire binary distinction between humans and machines may prove problematic. To the extent that transparency is seen as human-faced, it presupposes people who are concerned about their impression.[83] If transparency is seen as a tool for representation, whether in terms of sincere mimicking, impression management, or full-fledged distortion, it still relies on the idea of the reality principle: that there is a ground truth to be represented—be it something highly abstract, such as a computer algorithm—and that truth

[79] Bucher (n. 18) at 44.
[80] Esposito, 'Digital Prophesies and Web Intelligence', in M. Hildebrandt and K. de Vries (eds), *Privacy, Due Process and the Computational Turn: The Philosophy of Law Meets the Philosophy of Technology* (2013) 121, at 129–132.
[81] Bucher (n. 18) at 44.
[82] Koulu, 'Crafting Digital Transparency: Implementing Legal Values into Algorithmic Design', 8(1) *Critical Analysis of Law* (2021) 81.
[83] Albu and Flyverbom (n. 16).

can be delivered and understood.[84] What would it imply from the perspective of transparency's legitimating promise if human were removed from the equation? Are we left with governance which no longer needs humans as its agents? Would such governance promise acceptability precisely because of the lack of ever so dubious and self-interested humans?

These questions are tricky for several reasons. First, regardless of the impressive technological development of our time, machines are only capable of restricted functions. However, according to the most radical visions of singularity, once created by human beings with human desires, algorithms may become increasingly independent from their makers.[85] This would cause problems of predictability, fairness, and legitimacy, thus forming, in Danaher's words, 'the threat of algocracy'.[86] In this process, humans could lose their monopoly to control and understand algorithms. Algorithms could become independent to the extent that they themselves create new algorithms, even audit other algorithms.

Second, there is no reason to assume that algorithms in ADM would necessarily 'think' like humans.[87] It would be hard to imagine that algorithms would desire other algorithms' approval, would want to be in contact with them and belong to the community of other algorithms. There is neither a reason to assume that they would want to be seen in a favourable light by other algorithms, to have high status in the algorithmic community, and avoid being shamed in front of other algorithms. Just by this little thought experiment, our own humanity, having a core of a social animal, becomes sufficiently clear. It is easy to see how transparency practices work through our human way of thinking and acting.

Maybe we should adopt a science and technology studies inspired approach and question the entire human-machine distinction and test what would happen to transparency.[88] As Ananny and Crawford state, 'We suggest here that rather than privileging a type of accountability that needs to look inside systems, that we instead hold systems accountable by looking across them—seeing them as sociotechnical systems that do not contain complexity but enact complexity by connecting to and intertwining with assemblages of humans and non-humans.'[89] To some extent, this is already happening. For example,

[84] Koivisto, 'The Digital Rear Window: Epistemologies of Digital Transparency', 8(1) *Critical Analysis of Law* (2021) 64.
[85] See N. Boström, *Superintelligence: Paths, Dangers, Strategies* (2014).
[86] Danaher (n. 12) at 245.
[87] Burrell (n. 8).
[88] Hansen, 'Numerical Operations, Transparency Illusions and the Datafication of Governance', 18(2) *European Journal of Social Theory* (2015) 203.
[89] Ananny and Crawford (n. 17) at 2.

a discussion of explainable AI (XAI) has emerged. Perhaps in the future, the limits of human understanding can be considered in designing new AI systems from the very inception.[90]

That said, it seems impossible to permanently eradicate black boxes in decision-making. Whether we are talking about hungry judges or algorithms, which covertly privilege certain people over others, or even some kind of hybrid transcending the human–machine distinction, the complexity of decision-making cannot be reduced to simple steps of reasoning without something being lost. Following Bucher, mythologizing the inner workings of machines is not helpful. Neither should we think that algorithmic logics were somehow more hidden and black-boxed than the human mind, which is, as explained, a black box too.[91]

The best we can achieve, in the end, are descriptions of logics to justification. Logic of discovery may remain unfathomable to us, and may even be increasingly so, as machine learning models proliferate. This, in turn, may bifurcate the two realms of what happens in reality and what is conceivable to us. It seems that we want to both go beyond human understanding and to keep it as the guiding principle of ADM. In consequence, there may be less and less use for the ideal of transparency, or it will be reduced to its iconophilic aspect. Therefore, it needs to be carefully assessed, whether transparency as a value is worth promoting in the context of ADM, or should we admit its failure in coupling understanding with seeing. As technological development continues, perhaps explainability is as good as it can get.

[90] See e.g. Hagras, 'Toward Human-Understandable, Explainable AI', 51(9) *Computer* (2018) 28; Adadi and Berrada, 'Peeking Inside the Black-Box: A Survey on Explainable Artificial Intelligence (XAI)', 6 *Institute of Electrical and Electronics Engineers Access* (2018) 52138; Waltl and Vogl, 'Increasing Transparency in Algorithmic- Decision-Making with Explainable AI', 42 *Datenschutz Datensich* (2018) 613.

[91] Bucher (n. 18) at 60.

4

Post-GDPR Lawmaking in the Digital Data Society: Mimesis without Integration. Topological Understandings of Twisted Boundary Setting in EU Data Protection Law

Paul De Hert[*]

> In mathematics, topology (from the Greek words τόπος, 'place, location', and λόγος, 'study') is concerned with the properties of a geometric object that are preserved under continuous deformations, such as stretching, twisting, crumpling, and bending.
>
> (Wikipedia)

1. Prelude: My Past Paper on Regulatory Data Protection Approaches

In the past, I looked at the conspicuous absence of terms like 'big data' and 'data analytics' in the major data protection instruments that saw the light between 2016 and 2018 at the level of the European Union (EU) and the Council of Europe (CoE).[1] Crucially, a Bourdieusian grid provided me with a theoretical

[*] The author wants to thank Cristina Cocito (FRC, VUBrussels), Andrés Chomczyk Penedo (LSTS, VUBrussels), Dimitra Markopoulou (LSTS, VUBrussels), Juraj Sajfert (LSTS, VUBrussels), George Bouchayar (LSTS; VUBrussels and University of Luxemburg), Taner Kuru (Tilburg University), Onntje Hinrichs (LSTS, VUBrussels), and Dr. Richa Kumar (Trilateral). I would like to honour my collaboration with Vagelis Papakonstantinou (LSTS, VUBrussels) over the past years. Some of the ideas presented here are the result of our discussions and blogs. The author uses both singular ('I') and plural ('we') tenses. It came naturally and he hopes the readers will understand.

[1] De Hert and Sajfert, 'Regulating Big Data in and out of the Data Protection Policy Field: Two Scenarios of Post-GDPR Law-Making and the Actor Perspective', 5(3) *European Data Protection Law Review* (2019) 338.

Paul De Hert, *Post-GDPR Lawmaking in the Digital Data Society: Mimesis without Integration. Topological Understandings of Twisted Boundary Setting in EU Data Protection Law* In: *Data at the Boundaries of European Law*. Edited by: Deirdre Curtin and Mariavittoria Catanzariti, Oxford University Press. © Paul De Hert 2023. DOI: 10.1093/oso/9780198874195.003.0004

lens through which to view conflicts and collaborations between various agents that inhabit the various departments and agencies at the European level. In mapping the conflictual and collaborative elements of the (non)-regulation of these novel data-driven economy phenomena, the study identified two regulatory approaches that were competing with each other in the drafting era: firstly, taming the big data and other data-driven phenomena with existing data protection legislations or ignoring their presence when regulating data protection, and secondly, addressing data-driven practices and challenges in a more granular way in more regulatory frameworks other than the traditional data protection platforms.

Europe's basic texts of data protection, namely, the EU General Data Protection Regulation (GDPR)[2] and the CoE Convention 108+,[3] illustrate the first 'hands-off' approach: new data-driven practices are not addressed specifically. The underlying feeling of these instruments is that classical data protection principles 'will do the job', a feeling supported by those agents and actors who are of the view that existing data protection law is sufficient.[4]

The second approach is reformation outside the data protection legal canon where aspects of the data-driven society are addressed in the most unlikely regulatory frameworks.[5]

[2] Regulation (EU) 2016/679, OJ 2016 L 119/1.

[3] Convention for the Protection of Individuals with Regard to the Automatic Processing of Individual Data, 1981 ETS 108.

[4] By probing further into the view of 'sufficiency of existing data protection laws', the study highlights that in fact, these actors and agents are grappling with the enormity of the social and economic implications of big data resulting in the conspicuous absence of regulations on big data. This hesitation has resulted in addressing big data concerns on the side-lines and references to these can be found in Working Party 29, Directive 95/46/EC, Recital 26 GDPR, Article 6(4) GDPR, and Article 10 Convention 108+.

[5] Using the lens of the data protection field, the study looks at the measures steered by EU departments such as DG CONNECT and DG GROW where big data has been present. These include: Communication from the Commission to the European Parliament, the Council, the European Economic and Social Committee and the Committee of the Regions: Towards a thriving data-driven economy, 2 July 2014, COM(2014) 442 final; Directive (EU) 2019/770 of 20 May 2019 concerning contracts for the supply of digital content and digital services, OJ 2019 L 136/1; Directive (EU) 2019/790 of the European Parliament and of the Council of 17 April 2019 on copyright and related rights in the Digital Single Market and amending Directives 96/9/EC and 2001/29/EC, OJ 2019 L 130/92; Directive (EU) 2019/1024 of the European Parliament and of the Council of 20 June 2019 on open data and the re-use of public sector information, OJ 2019 L 172/56; Regulation (EU) 2018/1807 of the European Parliament and of the Council of 14 November 2018 on a framework for the free flow of non-personal data in the European Union, OJ 2018 L 303/59; Directive (EU) 2015/2366 of the European Parliament and of the Council of 25 November 2015 on payment services in the internal market, amending Directives 2002/65/EC, 2009/110/EC and 2013/36/EU and Regulation (EU) No 1093/2010, and repealing Directive 2007/64/EC, OJ 2015 L 337/35, and High-Level Expert Group on Artificial Intelligence (AI HLEG), Ethics Guidelines for Trustworthy AI (2019), https://ec.europa.eu/futurium/en/ai-alliance-consultation/guidelines#Top (last visited 18 June 2019). The AI HLEG was established by the European Commission in June 2018 to support the implementation of its Strategy on Artificial Intelligence and to prepare two deliverables: (1) AI Ethics Guidelines and (2) Policy and Investment Recommendations. See on the composition of the expert group with no representatives of the European Data Protection Supervisor (EDPS) or the Data Protection Authorities (DPAs), European Commission,

While mapping these two approaches and looking at a first set of EU post-GDPR laws, I brought to the fore the politics and power that shape the creation of laws and I was able to highlight both the heterogeneity of the EU and the Council of Europe (CoE), and the differences between the two regional organizations.[6]

The complexity of the EU regulatory machinery is furthermore intensified by the particularities of the European Commission, at least from a traditional constitutionalist viewpoint. This strange heterogeneous body, 'shooter of ideas' and 'agenda setter', has key elements of legislature and executive blended in its role. Crucial here is to understand that the Commission consists of several departments (DGs or directorates general) and is complemented by a range of agencies.[7] In order to grasp a complete picture of the emergence of the data protection regulatory framework, one needs to look at the whole of actors and agents, and their interests and motivations.[8] The state or in this case,

High-level expert group on artificial intelligence, https://ec.europa.eu/digital-single-market/en/high-level-expert-group-artificial-intelligence (last visited 18 June 2019).

[6] I concluded that the EU should not be understood as an international organization like the CoE but as a state in itself (in the sense given to it by Bourdieu in *On the State*, n. 9). For instance, the creation of soft laws plays out differently at different levels. At CoE level, one witnesses a definite hardening of soft laws. The European Court of Human Rights (ECtHR) is an eminent CoE body and it is organized such that a binding interpretation of one of the CoE recitals or CoE soft law instruments renders it as a hardened, binding law. On the other hand, at EU level, the process of hardening of the soft law is not that visible. Further differences can be explained by elaborating the different organizational and agential elements of these organizations. The CoE is organized as a classical international organization with a high impact role for agents whose meetings and collaborations are often defined by secrecy and confidentiality. In contrast to the CoE, the EU under the rubric of the Lisbon Treaty has a more classical model of lawmaking with the European Parliament representing the European demos, the Council representing the Member States, and the Commission which works as an initiator. Notwithstanding the constitutionalist structure defined by Lisbon, some secrecy at EU level is created by the involvement of specific actors like the rotating Presidency of the Council, the Rapporteur and the Shadow Rapporteurs in the European Parliament, and the different Council formations (national experts, counsellors, and the ambassadors in COREPER, the Committee of the Permanent Representatives of the Governments of the Member States to the EU).

[7] See the list of 56 Departments and Executive agencies of the Commission, European Commission, *Departments and executive agencies*, https://ec.europa.eu/info/departments_en (last visited 26 May 2021).

[8] Trying to understand policy making in the EU data protection sphere by looking only at Directorate-General JUST (Justice and Consumers), author of the GDPR, and by neglecting the respective agendas of Directorate-Generals such as CONNECT (Communications Networks, Content and Technology), COMP (Competition), ENER (Energy), FISMA (Financial Stability, Financial Services and Capital Markets Union), GROW (Internal Market, Industry, Entrepreneurship and SMEs), HOME (Migration and Home Affairs), Directorate-General, MOVE (Mobility and Transport), RTD (Research and Innovation) and other directorates and agencies is too narrow. When European banks find difficulties with Facebook's project to start producing its own payment system (implying a lot of personal data processing), they go to DG FISMA and not to DG JUST. If there are data protection problems with the Directive (EU) 2015/2366 of Payment Services (n. 5), it is because DG FISMA was the fiduciary and not DG JUST who proposed the GDPR. Similar story for stakeholders regarding automated cars, health, and drones—all go to their respective platforms.

the Commission, with its institutions acts as an 'organized fiduciary' and as a 'viewpoint on viewpoints', as Bourdieu coins it.[9]

2. About This Chapter: Preserving the Boundaries of Data Protection Law in Post-GDPR Laws

In this contribution I intend to push the research further while fully concentrating on EU developments. I look at a second set of post-GDPR laws, while preserving my initial questions about how the different regulatory actors involved in EU law consider the data protection principles as spelled out in the GDPR:

1. Do they take these principles into account?
2. Only by lipreading or mimetics or is there a genuine effort to apply data protection (substantive integration)?
3. If there is anything like an integrative effort, what form does it take: vague or precise (formal integration)?
4. If so, what explains the EU approach and, eventually, how ought it change? How should they do it in my view?

My approach is topological in the sense that I am interested in understanding how the boundaries and other properties (read 'rules and principles') of data protection law are preserved under the continuous regulatory deformations (applying, stretching, twisting, crumpling, and bending) through the multiple post-GDPR laws. My main finding is that boundaries and properties are not always well preserved in the process of continuous lawmaking of the digital data society. Integration, denial, or mimetics? (See on these terms below.) That is the theme of this contribution. All post-GDPR laws—four in total—are discussed in terms of background and their data protection deformations. For lack of space, more concrete analysis of specific legal provisions in the EU laws discussed is not provided for, although it would make the argument stronger. Our first case study (on the cybersecurity directive) will be a bit more extensive to suggest the analytical approach and structure to follow in a longer study.

We open with an example of *ex during* or *eodem tempore*[10]-GDPR law-making in the EU, in this case Network and Information Security (NIS)

[9] P. Bourdieu, *On the State. Lectures at the Collège de France 1989–1992* (2012), at 23–44.
[10] Note that there is no Latin 'ex' word for this category.

or Cybersecurity Directive (section 3).[11] Then follow three shorter ex post studies: the EU regulations on drones (section 4), the proposed Data Governance Act (DGA) (section 5),[12] and the AI Ethical Aspects Resolution and (proposed) Regulation (section 6).[13] In each section, I will look at the explicit connections with the GDPR. At the same time, these short descriptions also allow us to capture how regulators are addressing contemporary data-driven practices more explicitly in this era of the post-GDPR drafting.

The case study descriptions are rather flat. The more critical analysis of these case studies, bringing to the fore their salience for the general theme of this contribution, is reserved for section 7. We do not discuss all post-GDPR digital society related laws for lack of space, but the scheme of analysis proposed can be used for analysing them. We will refer to laws that are not the object of a case study here where necessary (such as the Digital Services Act [DSA][14] and the Digital Markets Act [DMA][15]).

Are all these initiatives the result of harmony and coordination with the GDPR rules and principles or rather of conflicts and deviations? In section 7, I introduce the theme of *GDPR mimesis* that, in my view, enriches the denial/integration discussion. On the internet *mimesis* is characterized as a term that carries a wide range of meanings in literary criticism and philosophy, including imitation, non-sensuous similarity, receptivity, representation, mimicry, the act of expression, the act of resembling, and the presentation of the self.[16] *Mimicry* is the act, practice, or art of mimicking and in biology stands for the resemblance of one organism to another or to an object in its surroundings for concealment and protection from predators.[17] I like the biological definition of *mimicry* and, in general, the element of ridiculing suggested by the term, but I will use for communicative purposes the more neutral term *mimesis*. Together with Papakonstantinou, I distinguish between three forms: definitional,

[11] The analysis is somewhat detailed to introduce the core theme of this study (integration).

[12] Commission, 'Proposal for a Regulation of the European Parliament and of the Council on European data governance (Data Governance Act)', COM/2020/767 final, recently adopted as Regulation (EU) 868/2022 of the European Parliament and of the Council of 30 May 2022 on European data governance and amending Regulation (EU) 2018/1724 (hereinafter, Data Governance Act).

[13] EP Resolution of 20 October 2020, Framework of ethical aspects of artificial intelligence, robotics and related technologies, 2020/2012(INL).

[14] Proposal for a Regulation of the European Parliament and of the Council on a Single Market for Digital Services (Digital Services Act) and amending Directive 2000/31/EC, COM(2020) 852 final.

[15] Proposal for a Regulation of the European Parliament and of the Council on contestable and fair markets in the digital sector (Digital Markets Act) COM(2020) 842 final.

[16] Wikipedia, 'mimesis', https://en.wikipedia.org/wiki/Mimesis (last visited 26 May 2021).

[17] The Free Dictionary, 'mimicries', https://www.thefreedictionary.com/mimicries (last visited 26 May 2021).

substantive, and symbolic mimesis.[18] These terms will be further clarified with illustrations taken from our findings on the DGA (section 5). Problems with mimesis are identified in section 7 with a strong insistence on the value of integration that has been often neglected in the laws that I discussed.

Subsequent sections will, relying on 'law in context' literature, formulate several alternative explanations for the current twisted landscape of data protection lawmaking in Europe (section 8 and following). I will discuss the specific nature of EU regulation as a first factor (section 8), then focus on the regulatory reality of mixing laws and regulations with other regulatory instruments (section 9) but also on the all too human phenomenon of lack of creative thinking of regulators when confronted with new developments (section 10).

The explanations offered in these sections will furnish us with a more realistic understanding of regulatory change, which is not the same as bland acceptance of the outcomes. This study is opposed to *mimicry*, prudent with *mimesis*, and in favour of careful *integration* of legal rules in a pre-existing framework of GDPR principles and rules. Only then, boundaries of data protection law will be able to function properly. The study concludes by advancing a perspective on regulatory change in EU lawmaking (section 11).

3. NIS Directive: Common Objective, No Integration (Case Study 1/*Eodem Tempore*)

A. Background

As early as 2009, the EU Commission, under the direction of two different DGs, the DG CONNECT and the DG JUST, began its consultation on the legislative process that eventually led to the adoption of the Network and Information Systems Directive (NIS Directive)[19] and the GDPR. As regards the Directive, in 2009 the Commission published its Communication on the protection of critical information infrastructure against large scale cyber-attacks and disruptions.[20] A more concrete approach was adopted with the Commission's

[18] Papakonstantinou and De Hert, 'Post GDPR EU laws and their GDPR mimesis. DGA, DSA, DMA and the EU regulation of AI' (1 April 2021) *European Law Blog*, https://europeanlawblog.eu/2021/04/01/post-gdpr-eu-laws-and-their-gdpr-mimesis-dga-dsa-dma-and-the-eu-regulation-of-ai/ (last visited 26 May 2021).

[19] Directive (EU) 2016/1148, OJ 2016 L 194/1. See Markopoulou, Papakonstantinou, and De Hert, 'The New EU Cybersecurity Framework: The NIS Directive, ENISA's Role and the General Data Protection Regulation', 35(6) *Computer Law & Security Review* (2019) 105336.

[20] Communication from the Commission to the European Parliament, the Council, the European Economic and Social Committee and the Committee of the Regions on Critical Information

Proposal for a Directive, which was released in 2013.[21] From 2013 to 2015 the Commission, the Council and the Parliament discussed intensely the draft put forward by the Commission and these discussions resulted in the NIS Directive that entered into force in July 2016. The deadline for national transposition by the EU Member States was 9 May 2018.

We briefly recall the chronological facts about the birth of the GDPR in a footnote,[22] to highlight the progression in parallel of the two lawmaking processes. Yet, the two processes happened completely independently. This is depicted in their texts as they hardly acknowledge one another.[23]

The reasons behind this detached approach while negotiating the two documents, that are, at least by appearances, related,[24] may only be assumed.[25] There is no doubt that the two documents should have been better aligned and integrated. Not so much because of their scope, aim, or purpose,[26] but because of practical reasons: it is possible and frequent that network and information systems are used for the processing of personal data: Does this lead to

Infrastructure Protection—"Protecting Europe from large scale cyber-attacks and disruptions: enhancing preparedness, security and resilience"{SEC(2009) 399}{SEC(2009) 400}.

[21] Proposal for a Directive of the European Parliament and of the Council concerning measures to ensure a high common level of network and information security across the Union/* COM/2013/048 final—2013/0027 (COD) */.

[22] The GDPR, replacing the first EU data protection law (Directive 95/46/EC, OJ 1995 L 281) was the result of a long process as well, started in 2009, through a relevant public consultation launched by the Commission. This was followed by a Communication released by the Commission in 2010. After receiving comments from all major participants in the process, this stage was concluded in 2012 with the publication by the Commission of the first draft on a Regulation. Owing to significant delay by the Council, the process was finalized three years later, in December 2015. The Regulation was published in April 2016 with effect from 25 May 2018.

[23] In particular, the NIS Directive refers to processing of personal data in its Article 2, where it is stated that 'processing of personal data pursuant to this Directive shall be carried out in accordance with Directive 95/46/EC'. A very generic reference let alone outdated, given that the GDPR was already published. Reference to personal data in the context of NIS is also made where cooperation with data protection authorities when addressing incidents resulting in personal data breaches is regulated (Art. 15 para. 4). From its part, the GDPR takes account of cybersecurity-related processing, only for its own aims and purposes, for example when clarifying that 'processing of personal data to the extent strictly necessary and proportionate for the purposes of ensuring network and information security constitutes a legitimate interest of the data controller concerned', also listing CERTs and CSIRTs among recipients of these clarifications (Preamble 49).

[24] Both have very similar provisions that impose adopting security measures and policies, adopting security breach notification, setting up supervisory authorities, and foresee a sanction mechanism.

[25] Whether this approach was the right one is a question that cannot be answered easily. As far as the 'why' is concerned, what instantly comes in mind, is the practical dimension of the question. Two processes run in parallel, by separate DGs, under different responsible teams, each of which had its own agenda. Also, at the Council, different Groups worked on each text in parallel but never interacted.

[26] In the GDPR it is personal data protection as a fundamental right in Article 16 Treaty on the Functioning of the European Union (TFEU). In the NIS Directive it is the security of networks. Consequently, the two documents do not have the same scope, aim, or purposes.

the conclusion that both legal instruments find application at the same time? If yes, how?[27]

B. The Overlap between the NIS Directive and the GDPR: More Detail

To better understand the need for integration in light of overlapping scope, we first need to examine the affected parties in both cases. GDPR applies to all undertakings that operate as data controllers or data processors, regardless of their nature or special features. The NIS Directive on the other hand applies only to operators of essential services (OES) and digital service providers (DSP). A possible overlap therefore would occur only if a hospital, for instance, as an OES, that is also a data controller, witnessed a security breach, which at the same time constituted a personal data breach. In other words, the Regulation does not cover security breaches that do not involve personal data violations, whereas the Directive does not affect undertakings that do not fall under these two categories (OES and DSP).

Once it is established that an undertaking operates under both capacities, the next question that needs to be answered is whether the security requirements imposed by the GDPR and the NIS Directive coincide, in the sense that an undertaking that falls under the scope of both instruments needs to apply all suggested security measures. *Should therefore the undertaking in question have an active cybersecurity policy and an active data protection policy even though they may overlap to some extent?* Answering this question is important in order to establish whether this undertaking is compliant under both regimes.

- Even when some security measures are in practice identical, the security requirements imposed by the GDPR should not be confused with the ones imposed by the Directive.[28]

[27] In practice this question breaks down into the following sub-questions: Do affected organizations by the NIS Directive need to comply with security requirements imposed by the GDPR for the protection of personal data as well? In case a security breach in the context of the NIS Directive is also a personal data breach according to the GDPR, should the player involved apply the notification process described in the Directive or the one of the Regulation or both at the same time? In the above case, which authority should be responsible to handle the case? Finally, when it comes to penalties for a breach that is both a NIS security incident and a GDPR personal data violation should a cumulative penalty be imposed or alternatively one for each breach?

[28] The security measures target the data processing itself (Art. 32 GDPR) and are designed to ensure the security of personal data, whereas the security requirements include technical and organisational measures which intend to protect network and information systems against the risks posed to their security. Furthermore, the fact that a violation of an obligation under the Directive leads to a violation of an obligation under the Regulation does not automatically mean that that the violated right is the same

- In the same context, notification of a security breach under NIS should not be confused with that of a personal data breach under GDPR.[29] It is possible that an incident, even though leading to a personal data breach, is not fulfilling the conditions of notification taken from the Directive.[30]
- Finally, the issue of penalties should be addressed accordingly. There are different processes and obligations that are violated and therefore the penalties provided by the two instruments should add up.

In our view, in the absence of case law and given the limited guidance found in the two legal instruments on this issue, the affected undertakings should comply with the requirements and processes indicated by both the GDPR and the NIS Directive. But that is too general and is not of a nature to hide coordination problems and concerns about whether, for example, double administrative sanctions can be issued for the same incident and whether security measures adopted under one regulatory tool (e.g. the GDPR) are sufficient to comply with the requirements stemming from the other one.[31]

Maria Grazia Porcedda has tilted this analysis to a higher level with her study of data breach notification duties that are incorporated not only in the NIS Directive and the GDPR but also in other cybersecurity (and data protection) related legislative instruments.[32] Porcedda observes that the definitions across

or that the rule of law actually being breached is the same. To the contrary, the legal right protected under the two documents is completely different, the Regulation protects the individuals' rights against the violation of their personal data, whereas the Directive protects network and information systems against cyber incidents. Protection of individuals rights, including that of personal data, occurs only incidentally and is not the direct purpose of the NIS Directive.

[29] The first refers to the obligation of the undertaking to notify any incidents having a significant impact on the continuity of the service they provide (Art. 14 NIS) whereas in the context of the GDPR this involves the notification of a personal data breach (Art. 33 GDPR).

[30] The practical complications of choosing one process and one authority against the other cannot be analysed here.

[31] Compare with the intervention of Zenzi De Graeve at the joint workshop on the EU cybersecurity law of 11 October 2019 organized by the Cyber and Data Security Lab (CDSL) and the Brussels Privacy Hub (BPH); see on her intervention Jasmontaitė-Zaniewicz, 'Mapping EU cybersecurity law and its future challenges', Minutes of the CDSL & BPH EU Cybersecurity Law Workshop (12 November 2019), https://cdsl.research.vub.be/en/minutes-of-the-cdsl-bph-eu-cybersecurity-law-workshop (last visited 26 May 2021).

[32] These include the e-Privacy Directive, Directive (EU) 2002/58, OJ 2002 L 201/37. This Directive has been amended by Directive (EU) 2006/24, OJ 2006 L 105/54 and Directive (EU) 2009/136, OJ 2009 L 337/11; the Framework Directive, Directive (EU) 2002/21, OJ 2002 L 108/33; the Electronic Identification and Assurance Services (eIDAS) Regulation, Regulation (EU) 910/2014, OJ 1999 L 257/73; and the PSD2, Directive (EU) 2015/2366, OJ 2015 L 337/35. In Porcedda, 'Patching the Patchwork: Appraising the EU Regulatory Framework on Cyber Security Breaches', 34(5) *Computer Law & Security* (2018) 1077 Porcedda proposes to group all these internal market instruments into two regimes. The e-Privacy Directive and the GDPR concern breaches affecting personal data, 'data breaches' for short; the remaining instruments concern 'incidents' or 'breaches of security' or 'loss of integrity' or 'security incidents' which do not necessarily affect personal data.

these laws vary, but that they have a common final objective—the protection of information and its confidentiality, integrity, and availability.[33] We end by observing that the complications of a possible overlap between the two instruments were partially and broadly addressed in the Commission's proposal for the NIS Directive, but disregarded in the process that followed.[34] As far as the GDPR is concerned, no specific reference to the two documents' relationship is made.

4. Drones Regulations: Superficial Referencing, No Integration (Case Study 2/Ex Post-GDPR)

A. Regulation (EU) 2018/1139 on Common Rules

Drones, unmanned aircraft systems (UAS) as industry and policy makers like to call them, are an interesting topic for understanding data protection and privacy discussions. They raise a lot of questions and beg for more detailed regulations.

The basic document is Regulation (EU) 2018/1139 on common rules in the field of civil aviation and establishing a European Union Aviation Safety Agency.[35] The regulation was published slightly after the entry into force of the GDPR on 22 August 2018 and aimed, inter alia, at creating a legal framework for the safe operations of drones in the EU by means of a risk-based approach. The preamble contains a vague reference to fundamental rights and makes some promises about future privacy safeguards to be introduced.[36] A closer look reveals that

[33] Her final recommendation, to consider a unified law to address the issue information security and encourage the development of a mutual learning mechanism, is worth coming back to at the end of our study which I will do.

[34] In this first draft released by the Commission, it was suggested that in the cases where personal data were compromised as a result of incidents, Member States should implement the obligation to notify security incidents in a way that minimizes the administrative burden in case the security incident is also a personal data breach in line with the Regulation. It was furthermore suggested that the European Union Agency for Cybersecurity (ENISA) could assist by developing information exchange mechanisms and templates avoiding the need for two notification templates (Recital 31 of the Proposal for a Directive). The Proposal also addressed the issue of the sanctions and mentioned that Member States should ensure that, when a security incident involves personal data, the sanctions foreseen should be consistent with the sanctions provided by the Regulation (Art. 17 of the Proposal). Nevertheless, the final draft of the Directive included none of these thoughts and was limited to mention in its Article 15(4) that: 'The competent authority shall work in close cooperation with data protection authorities when addressing incidents resulting in personal data breaches.'

[35] Regulation (EU) 2018/1139, OJ 2018 L 212/1.

[36] Preamble 31 Regulation (EU) 2018/1139: 'In view of the risks that unmanned aircraft can present for safety, privacy, protection of personal data, security or the environment, requirements should be laid down concerning the registration of unmanned aircraft and of operators of unmanned aircraft.'

the Regulation does not do anything extra, besides making this announcement. Towards the end of the Regulation there is a provision that urges Member States to 'carry out their tasks under this Regulation' in accordance with the GDPR.[37] All other references in the text to the GDPR are about pilot-data processing, not about protecting citizens against spying by drones.[38] In one of the Annexes to the Regulation ('Annex IX Essential requirements for unmanned aircraft') there is a bit more: an interesting suggestion (para. 1(3)) to consider the principles of privacy and protection of personal data by design and by default, and a rule to register operators of unmanned aircraft in accordance with the implementing acts referred to in Article 57, where they operate drones that present risks to privacy, protection of personal data, security, or the environment (para. 4(2)(b)).

B. The 2019 Commission Implementing Regulation (EU) 2019/947 on Rules and Procedures

So far, the EU has come up with two relevant post-GDPR texts in this topic. First there is the Commission Delegated Regulation (EU) 2019/945 of 12 March 2019 on unmanned aircraft systems and on third-country operators of unmanned aircraft systems.[39] This first regulation contains no data protection/ privacy relevant provisions and no reference to the GDPR.

Data protection fares better in the second instrument, the 2019 Commission Implementing Regulation 2019/947 on the rules and procedures for the operation of unmanned aircraft.[40]

[37] Article 132 Regulation (EU) 2018/1139: '(1) With regard to the processing of personal data within the framework of this Regulation, Member States shall carry out their tasks under this Regulation in accordance with the national laws, regulations or administrative provisions in accordance with Regulation (EU) 2016/679. (2) With regard to the processing of personal data within the framework of this Regulation, the Commission and the Agency shall carry out their tasks under this Regulation in accordance with Regulation (EC) No 45/2001.'

[38] The Preamble 28 insists that 'the rules regarding unmanned aircraft should contribute to achieving compliance with relevant rights guaranteed under Union law, and in particular the right to respect for private and family life, set out in Article 7 of the Charter of Fundamental Rights of the European Union, and with the right to protection of personal data, set out in Article 8 of that Charter and in Article 16 TFEU, and regulated by Regulation (EU) 2016/679 of the European Parliament and of the Council'. A subsequent paragraph where a duty to register drones is announced is interesting.

[39] Commission Delegated Regulation (EU) 2019/945, C/2019/1821, OJ 2019 L 152/1. This 42-article-long regulation contains a chapter on general provisions (chapter 1), followed by a chapter on UAS intended to be operated in the 'open' category (chapter 2) as opposed to drones operated in the 'certified' and 'specific' categories (chapter 3). In these chapters there are sections on product requirements, obligations of economic operators, conformity and notification of conformity assessment bodies and on Union market surveillance, control of products entering the Union market and Union safeguard procedure. Two last chapters deal with third country-UAS operators (chapter 4) and with final provisions (chapter 5).

[40] Commission Implementing Regulation (EU) 2019/947, C/2019/3824, OJ 2019 L 152/45.

This text has no chapters or sections, but simply lists 23 articles and an annex.

The following data-related provisions are of interest:

- *Registration*: registration-duties are imposed on operators, whose drones have sensors capturing personal data, unless such aircrafts are deemed toys[41] within the meaning of Directive 2009/48/EC ('products designed or intended, whether or not exclusively, for use in play by children under 14 years of age').[42]
- *Responsibility*: Operators are to be held responsible for compliance with, among others, privacy requirements or measures protecting against unlawful interference and unauthorized access.[43] If required, they must undertake personal data protection impact assessments in accordance with the GDPR.[44]
- *Geographical zone-determination*: Member States may determine geographical zones for 'safety, security, privacy or environmental reasons', and may among others, restrict or limit drone operations and access.[45]

In addition, there are two GDPR references.[46]

In neither of the two instruments is there a thorough integration of data protection principles as asked for by the GDPR and by Regulation (EU) 2018/1139.[47] Indeed, the above references to the GDPR do not necessarily enhance

[41] Art. 14(5)(a)(ii) Commission Implementing Regulation (EU) 2019/947; Recital 16 Commission Implementing Regulation (EU) 2019/947.

[42] Art. 2(1) Directive (EU) 2009/48, OJ 2019 L170/1.

[43] Art. 1(a) Commission Implementing Regulation (EU) 2019/947 OJ 2019 L 152/45 Annex, Part B, UAS.SPEC.050.

[44] Art. 1(a)(iv) Commission Implementing Regulation (EU) 2019/947, Annex, Part B, UAS.SPEC.050; Article 35 GDPR.

[45] Art. 15(1) Commission Implementing Regulation (EU) 2019/947.

[46] A first reference to the GDPR ~~in~~ is a footnote in Recital 19, suggesting that domestic registration systems comply with, among others, privacy and personal data related laws; and in the part of the Annex referring to responsibilities of operators, whose duty to establish procedures ensuring that all operations respect GDPR includes the requirement to carry out impact assessments. See Art. 1(a)(iv) Commission Implementing Regulation (EU) 2019/947, Annex, Part B, UAS.SPEC.050.

[47] Regarding discussions prior to their adoption, according to the European Union Aviation Safety Agency's (EASA) record, no GDPR-relevant debates took place. This could be because both instruments are delegated/implemented regulations; they do not follow the regular procedure; only technical issues are addressed by technicians/experts.

data protection. More attention could have been drawn, for instance, to technical data protection principles such as data protection by design.[48]

An additional role could be played by the European Union Aviation Safety Agency (EASA). In its important 2019 Opinion (aimed at offering cost-efficient rules for low-risk UAS), the Agency regrettably does not refer to personal data protection.[49] However, it has proposed a draft annex to Implementing Regulation 2019/947 with two declarations: an 'Operational declaration' and a 'Declaration of UAS operators that intend to provide practical skill training and assessment of remote pilots'.[50] In the latter, drone operators would declare that personal data 'will be processed for the purposes of the performance, management and follow-up of the oversight activities according to Regulation (EU) 2019/947'.[51]

5. Data Governance Act: Overlap, Obstinate Terminology (Case Study 3/Ex post-GDPR)

A. Background

In late 2020 a new, more ambitious post-GDPR legislation creation process started that relates directly to the data-driven digital economy, as part of the

[48] This could be done in the Delegated Regulation (EU) 2019/945, whose subject matter is laying down the demands regarding design and manufacture. *However, the Delegated Regulation (EU) 2019/945 makes no reference to the GDPR and includes no data-relevant provisions.*

[49] EASA, Opinion No 05/2019 on Standard scenarios for UAS operations in the 'specific' category (2019), https://www.easa.europa.eu/sites/default/files/dfu/Opinion%20No%2005-2019.pdf (last visited 5 February 2020).

[50] EASA, Draft Annex to draft Commission Implementing Regulation (EU) .../... amending Commission Implementing Regulation (EU) 2019/947 as regards the adoption of standard scenarios (2019), https://www.easa.europa.eu/sites/default/files/dfu/Draft%20Annex%20to%20Draft%20Com%20Impl%20Reg%20%28EU%29%20...-...%20amending%20Reg%202019-947.pdf or https://www.easa.europa.eu/document-library/opinions/opinion-052019 (last visited 5 February 2020).

[51] This Opinion has not yet been officially published; and the text of the proposed Annex is available as a draft document (without date, etc.). It is noted that the 'Operational declaration' is mentioned explicitly in the text and Annex of the Implementing Regulation 2019/947, but it does not have a ready template (as the one provided by the above Opinion); nor does it explicitly refer to personal data. See Article 2 Commission Implementing Regulation (EU) 2019/947, Annex, Part B, UAS.SPEC.020: 'A declaration of UAS operators shall contain (a) administrative information about the UAS operator; (b) a statement that the operation satisfies the operational requirement set out in point (1) and a standard scenario as defined in Appendix 1 to the Annex; (c) the commitment of the UAS operator to comply with the relevant mitigation measures required for the safety of the operation, including the associated instructions for the operation, for the design of the unmanned aircraft and the competency of involved personnel; (d) confirmation by the UAS operator that an appropriate insurance cover will be in place for every flight made under the declaration, if required by Union or national law.'

European Data Strategy.[52] Most of the discussion on the matter so far has focused on the proposals titled as the DSA[53] and the DMA.[54] However, there is a third component to this new wave of regulatory initiatives from the European Commission that rather slipped under the radar.[55] In spite of this, it might be the single most important piece of the new set of laws when it comes to regulating the data-driven society and in particular the 'big data-aspects': the DGA proposal.[56] Given its general applicability, it might provide some much necessary rules to address contemporary data practices in a comprehensive manner regardless of whether there are industry or sector-specific rules.

As such, it is worthy to ask how does the DGA relate to the data-driven economic development that the European Commission is trying to foster? Together with the Open Data Directive, the DGA aims to encourage open data and the re-use of data. The main ambitions of the DGA are to make public sector data further available beyond the Open Data Directive and to foster data sharing among businesses, against remuneration in any form. Also, the DGA tries to foster data use on altruistic grounds and the use of personal data with the help of a 'personal data-sharing intermediary', designed to help individuals exercise their rights under the GDPR.

The opening remarks of its explanatory memorandum explicitly indicate that the purpose of the DGA is to support the sector-specific legislation[57] on data access, use, and re-use with a common background upon which those *lex*

[52] Communication from the Commission to the European Parliament, the Council, the European Economic and Social Committee and the Committee of the Regions: A European strategy for data, 19.02.2020, COM(2020) 66 final.

[53] Proposal for a Regulation of the European Parliament and of the Council on a Single Market for Digital Services (Digital Services Act) and amending Directive 2000/31/EC, COM(2020) 852 final.

[54] Proposal for a Regulation of the European Parliament and of the Council on contestable and fair markets in the digital sector (Digital Markets Act) COM(2020) 842 final.

[55] In this respect, certain civil society organizations, such as European Digital Rights (EDRi), have put this matter on the table and include the DGA in the overall analysis of the current policy discussion landscape about the future of the European digital economy. See EDRi, 'EU alphabet soup of digital acts: DSA, DMA and DGA' (2020), https://edri.org/our-work/eu-alphabet-soup-of-digital-acts-dsa-dma-and-dga/ (last visited 5 March 2021).

[56] The European Data Strategy takes large data collection and data analytics for granted, as it repeatedly mentioned in that document, and as part of the data-driven economic future. A quick overview of both the DSA and the DMA proposals reveals to us that the data collection and exploitation by very large online platforms is a fact not questioned by either proposal. In fact, it would seem the European Commission desires to expand who can benefit from data-driven applications and allow small and medium enterprises to rely on such technological developments for commercial and economic success. In this respect, those business models developed around these data intensive practices are not put under the spotlight and questioned but rather are acknowledged as a fundamental part of our digital economy and, consequently, regulated and integrated even further into our society by general application regulations in the whole EU.

[57] In this respect, the explanatory memorandum as well as the footnotes 26 through 38 in the Recitals of the proposed regulation point to these sector-specific rules that should interact with the proposed DGA.

specialis on the matter can rest when in silence about certain issues or if they still have not been adopted as European regulations, such as in the case of the financial services industry.

As for the content of the DGA, it has eight chapters, structured in the typical format of European regulations, starting with a chapter on definitions and scope. After that, it follows the subject matter of the DGA: (i) re-use of data held by public bodies; (ii) data-sharing services; and (iii) data altruism. The remaining parts of the DGA tackle who are the competent authorities alongside the creation of the European Data Innovation Board as well as the granting of new powers to the Commission, much in a similar manner to what happens in the DSA and the DMA.[58]

B. Relation with GDPR: Different Definitions and Open Questions about Consent

A burning question in common between all these proposals is how they relate with the GDPR. Perhaps in the case of the DGA that question is even more pronounced as, in the words of the explanatory memorandum, '[t]he instrument aims to foster the availability of data for use by increasing trust in data intermediaries and by strengthening data-sharing mechanisms across the EU.' In this respect, the explanatory memorandum from the European Commission acknowledges that there is an interplay between the DGA proposal and the GDPR, which is then confirmed in the wording used in the actual regulation proposal, such as Article 1(2).[59] The question that could be raised in this respect is what this communion shall look like, in particular for two main reasons: (i) both pieces of legislation employ different terminology for the involved actors; and (ii) the scope of the DGA goes beyond what the GDPR has under its control. Therefore, the key area of discussion about the interplay between the envisaged DGA and the GDPR is how differences in definitions, in

[58] This last matter—the expansion of the powers of the European Commission—shall be addressed later as it is possible to identify a clear change in the enforcement regime foreshadowed in these new proposals.

[59] Art. 1(2) Data Governance Act: '*This Regulation is without prejudice to specific provisions in other Union legal acts regarding access to or re-use of certain categories of data, or requirements related to processing of personal or non-personal data.* Where a sector-specific Union legal act requires public sector bodies, providers of data sharing services or registered entities providing data altruism services to comply with specific additional technical, administrative, or organizational requirements, including through an authorization or certification regime, those provisions of that sector-specific Union legal act shall also apply.' (emphasis added)

particular around three concepts: data[60], data holder,[61] and data user,[62] have an impact on the application, the compliance, and the enforcement of both pieces of legislation.

The notion of 'data' as referenced in the current wording of the proposed DGA includes both non-personal and personal data.[63] The DGA would set a minimum set of duties and obligations for any data processing activity, regardless of this data being personal or non-personal. This approach provides a much-needed refresh to the debate around the (de)protection of non-personal data, since more and more of this kind of data can be grouped to arrive at personal data or, even more so, produce the same results on individuals without even setting foot in the personal data realm.[64]

To achieve this, the DGA further departs from the traditional terminology employed in the data protection arena regarding the parties involved in the data processing activities. In this sense, the DGA talks about data holders and data users. From a data protection perspective, on the one hand, a data holder can be either a data controller or even a data subject; on the other hand, a data user can only refer to a data controller.

There are three main activities for which rules are provided in the DGA: re-use of public data; data-sharing services; and data altruism. For this case study, the focus shall be placed on the latter two newly created institutes by the DGA.[65]

First, data-sharing services. When it comes to data-sharing services, the DGA stipulates that there are three activities covered in its provision: (a) intermediate between data holders and data users for the exchange of data through different means; (b) intermediate between data subjects and data users for the

[60] Art. 2(1) DGA: '... means any digital representation of acts, facts or information and any compilation of such acts, facts or information, including in the form of sound, visual or audiovisual recording'.

[61] Art. 2(5) DGA: '... means a legal person or data subject who, in accordance with applicable Union or national law, has the right to grant access to or to share certain personal or non-personal data under its control'.

[62] Art. 2(6) DGA: '... means a natural or legal person who has lawful access to certain personal or non-personal data and is authorized to use that data for commercial or non-commercial purposes'.

[63] This is because the purpose of the DGA is to provide a default regulatory framework for information use, re-use, and sharing, regardless of whether it is personal data or non-personal data. In this respect, the DGA can be applauded for acknowledging, even if it was not done on purpose, one of the most prominent debates around information and the border where it turns into personal data. See e.g. Bygrave and Tosoni, 'Article 4(1). Personal data', in C. Kuner, C. Docksey, and L. Bygrave (eds), *The EU General Data Protection Regulation (GDPR): A Commentary* (2020), at 103.

[64] In this respect, Purtova points out that the distinction between both regimes is pointless for an interconnected future populated by big data, Internet of Things (IoT) devices and intensive data-driven activities but instead the focus should be placed on providing legal protection in any scenario where an individual is involved and could be affected by harm. See Purtova, 'The Law of Everything. Broad Concept of Personal Data and Future of EU Data Protection Law', 10(1) *Law, Innovation and Technology* (2018) 40.

[65] The matter of re-use of public data needs to be read alongside the Open Data Directive, as well as the GDPR, and where much has already been written about.

exchange of data through different means for the purpose of exercising data rights provided for in the GDPR, mainly right to portability; and (c) provide data cooperatives services, i.e. negotiate on behalf of data subjects and certain data holders terms and conditions for the processing of personal data. Article 11 provides for the conditions that must be met to provide any of these three services.

The DGA provides that the operation of a data-sharing service must be notified to the competent authority in the relevant member state. When reviewing the wording used in the proposal text, it seems that the matter of an entity providing services in different jurisdictions is still under the same competent regulatory agency as it is provided for in the GDPR. As such, the question remains open as to whether this model would incur the same problems as the GDPR.[66]

Second, data altruism. The other new relevant institute created for the data-driven era is the figure of data altruism, which is defined as '... the consent by data subjects to process personal data pertaining to them, or permissions of other data holders to allow the use of their non-personal data without seeking a reward, for purposes of general interest, such as scientific research purposes or improving public services'.[67] It provides the possibility for data holders to make their data available for free or for a charge.

This concept of data altruism allows for a better understanding of the European Data Strategy envisaged by the European Commission, in particular when it comes to who,[68] and how one can make decisions regarding the use, re-use, and sharing of personal data. In this respect, consent plays a crucial role and the DGA proposal would seem to reject the application of any other legal basis for this kind of service. The question, as a consequence of selecting such a strict legal basis, is how the granularity demanded for having a legally valid consent can be achieved.[69] The GDPR has a very complex set of rules on

[66] Following the same spirit as the GDPR, registration before a national authority is not necessary to begin operations but instead it would seem that the lack of notification could constitute an illegal provision of service. The notification must disclose a certain amount of information regarding the service itself, as noted by Art. 10(5). Upon notification, the competent authority has a week to issue a standardized declaration; it is an open question if the data sharing service provider can effectively operate within that time window between the notification and the declaration.

[67] Art. 2(10) DGA.

[68] When it comes to the entity that provides the data altruism services, Art. 16 DGA states that it must be only a not-for-profit legal entity and completely independent from any for-profit entity. In contrast to data sharing service providers, the DGA mandates the registration of data altruism organizations before national competent authorities. In a similar fashion, the entity needs to disclose certain information about its operations and the competent authority has a 12-week period to grant the registration or deny it. Since the registration is necessary to provide the services, a data altruism organization cannot engage before such registration takes place.

[69] This is triggered because the wording used by the DGA would not require such a detailed description of the purpose for which the data will be used.

consent, with variables such as age, use of sensitive information or not, and purpose of the processing. It is striking to see that the DGA fails to clarify how data altruism should work in practice in the light of these multiple consent formats in the GDPR. The DGA, as a legal framework that pretends to set up a framework on data altruism but that is silent on these complex matters, does not deliver its promises. We will come back to this 'failure' of the DGA in our section on mimesis (section 7).

6. EU Regulation of AI: Integration (Case Study 4/Ex Post-GDPR)

A. The AI Ethical Aspects Resolution from the European Parliament

Over the last few years, the European institutions have expressed their interest in strengthening the regulation of AI technologies, addressing the call for a more transparent, robust, holistic, and coherent system for regulating the development and use of such technologies. This agenda is fuelled by the feeling that the GDPR and other laws in place remain sub-optimal on several fronts. It is not the place here to recall the history or the interplay between the different EU institutions with regard to AI policy making (from the Commission, over the high-level expert group on artificial intelligence [AI HLEG] to the Parliament and back to the Commission), neither can we go into detail about the concrete proposals. Key here is to understand the priority given to aligning, applying, and improving the rules and principles of data protection law as found in the GDPR, or at least considering them.

In this sense, the AI Ethical Aspects Resolution from the European Parliament provides for a good example.[70] It suggests that the Commission introduces a Regulation 'on ethical principles for the development, deployment and use of artificial intelligence, robotics and related technologies'. Read under a GDPR lens, the Parliament's recommendation essentially replicates the GDPR scheme (and even closely follows its structure). A new set of actors is introduced ('user', 'developer', and 'deployer', resembling GDPR's data subject, controller, and processor, respectively) in Article 4. Its principles, outlined

[70] Papakonstantinou and De Hert, 'Refusing to Award Legal Personality to AI: Why the European Parliament Got it Wrong', *European Law Blog* (25 November 2020), https://europeanlawblog.eu/2020/11/25/refusing-to-award-legal-personality-to-ai-why-the-european-parliament-got-it-wrong/ (last visited 26 May 2021).

in Article 5, very much follow the GDPR's ones ('safety, transparency, and accountability'). Unmissable GDPR-reminding ideas include 'risk assessments' in Article 14 (Data protection impact assessments in the GDPR), 'compliance assessment' in Article 15 (prior consultations in the GDPR), or the 'European Certificate of Ethical Compliance' (European Data Protection Seal in the GDPR). In addition, the Parliament recommends the establishment of 'national supervisory authorities' for monitoring all of the above (in Article 18); space for a European Data Protection Board (EDPB)-like institution is openly left in Article 20.

B. The Proposed 2021 Artificial Intelligence Act

The main outcome of the mentioned interest in strengthening the current legal framework is the proposed 2021 Artificial Intelligence Act (AIA).[71] Let us just give one example of the interesting GDPR interaction taken from this ambitious piece of work. Interesting in comparison with the GDPR is how this Act defines the key participants across the AI value chain. Looking at the definitions in Article 3, we learn that *development phase* and *use phase* are the two main phases in the AI lifecycle, whose key participants are *providers*[72] and *users*,[73] respectively. For our analysis it is relevant to note that the algorithmic issues and safeguards related to Article 22 GDPR only address the second stage of AI use.[74] The AIA proposal, on this important point, goes beyond the GDPR and states that already in the first stage of development appropriate human oversight measures should be identified and implemented by the provider (Recital 48):

[71] European Commission, Proposal for a Regulation of the European Parliament and of the Council laying down harmonized rules on Artificial Intelligence (Artificial Intelligence Act) and amending certain Union legislative acts, COM(2021) 206 final, 2021.

[72] Art. 3(2) 'provider' means a natural or legal person, public authority, agency or other body that develops an AI system or that has an AI system developed with a view to placing it on the market or putting it into service under its own name or trademark, whether for payment or free of charge.

[73] Art. 3(4) 'user' means any natural or legal person, public authority, agency or other body using an AI system under its authority, except where the AI system is used in the course of a personal non-professional activity.

[74] The first *development*-stage is indeed out of the GDPR scope when it comes to providing governance mechanisms for automated decision-making, just as this important stage remained beyond the scope of legal scholars' analysis and policy solutions (Lehr and Ohm, 'Playing with the Data: What Legal Scholars Should Learn About Machine Learning', 51 *U.C. Davis Law Rev* (2017) 653, at 655). According to Almada, 'a narrow interpretation that restricts intervention to the end stages would make it useless, but human intervention in the design stages may be more effective by proposing alternative models of the data that take such concerns into account' (Almada, 'Human Intervention in Automated Decision-Making: Toward the Construction of Contestable Systems', 17th International Conference on Artificial Intelligence and Law (ICAIL) (2019), 1, at 5).

(48) High-risk AI systems should be designed and developed in such a way that natural persons can oversee their functioning. For this purpose, appropriate human oversight measures should be identified by the provider of the system before its placing on the market or putting into service. In particular, where appropriate, such measures should guarantee that the system is subject to in-built operational constraints that cannot be overridden by the system itself and is responsive to the human operator, and that the natural persons to whom human oversight has been assigned have the necessary competence, training and authority to carry out that role.

These duties for the providers are further elaborated in Articles 13, 14, 16, and 29 of the AIA text. Providers shall ensure high-risk AI systems are compliant with the human oversight requirement.[75] To comply with this requirement, they must design and develop AI systems in a way that they can be effectively overseen by human agents during the use stage.[76] Before placing the AI system on the market, the providers either identify the appropriate measures to be implemented by the user, or identify and build them, when technically feasible into the system.[77] Such measures shall enable human agents—to whom human oversight is assigned—to understand the capacities and limitations of the system, to correctly interpret its outputs, or to interrupt the system, among others, in the use stage.[78]

To make AI oversight possible, one needs to add to these duties the transparency requirements laid down in Article 13 AIA[79] and the obligations for users of high-risk AI systems anchored in Article 29 AIA. This last provision, in a

[75] Art. 16(a) AIA.

[76] Art. 14(1) AIA. The Commission understands that the concept of human oversight focuses on the human agent interpreting and following or modifying the output at the use stage. This implies that 'oversight' as a requirement does not extend to concepts such as organizational oversight, although we can also qualify it as 'human' in a broad sense.

[77] Art. 14(2) AIA.

[78] Art. 14(4) AIA: The measures referred to in paragraph 3 shall enable the individuals to whom human oversight is assigned to do the following, as appropriate to the circumstances: '(a) fully understand the capacities and limitations of the high-risk AI system and be able to duly monitor its operation, so that signs of anomalies, dysfunctions and unexpected performance can be detected and addressed as soon as possible; (b) remain aware of the possible tendency of automatically relying or over-relying on the output produced by a high-risk AI system ('automation bias'), in particular for high-risk AI systems used to provide information or recommendations for decisions to be taken by natural persons; (c) be able to correctly interpret the high-risk AI system's output, taking into account in particular the characteristics of the system and the interpretation tools and methods available; (d) be able to decide, in any particular situation, not to use the high-risk AI system or otherwise disregard, override or reverse the output of the high-risk AI system; (e) be able to intervene on the operation of the high-risk AI system or interrupt the system through a "stop" button or a similar procedure.'

[79] These require that the oversight measures shall be facilitated to users in an accessible and comprehensible way (Art. 13(2) and 13(3)(d)).

nutshell, states that users shall utilize the information about human oversight measures to comply with their obligation to carry out a Data Protection Impact Assessment under Article 35 GDPR.[80]

Article 29 AIA shows a remarkable effort to bring the proposed regulation on AI into line with the GDPR.[81]

7. Mimesis, Consistency, and Distinct Regulatory Objectives

A. The Data Governance Act as an Example of GDPR Mimesis

From the four case studies above, we identify in at least three of them a 'ubiquitous' thread of mimesis with GDPR principles. In section 2, we contrasted *mimesis* as a more or less acceptable form of imitation, with *mimicry*, mockingly unacceptable imitation. But even mimesis in law can be controversial and, as shown below, can come at the expense of a lack of integration.[82] When looking at the previous sections, a light categorization of mimesis is possible on the following grounds: definitional mimesis, substantive mimesis, and symbolic mimesis. Let us illustrate this with our findings on the DGA (section 5 above).

First, definitional mimesis. We saw that different terminology is introduced, in the form of 'data holders', 'data users', 'data', or 'data sharing' (Article 2 DGA). It looks like the GDPR but not exactly, since this text talks about 'data subjects' (meaning individuals), and 'controllers' and 'processors' (meaning those doing the processing) interact through 'processing' of common or 'sensitive' 'personal information' (meaning any operation on personal data) (Article 4 GDPR). Is this a problem? Perhaps, but the DGA is (1) focused on certain data actors (public actors, data-sharing services, and data altruism entities:), (2) deals with very specific activities regarding data (re-use of data held by public bodies and data sharing), and, lastly, (3) applied to all data, a notion that includes both non-personal and personal data (Article 2.1 DGA).

[80] Art. 29(6) AIA.

[81] This effort is often absent in other relevant recent EU laws. See Papakonstantinou and De Hert, 'Post GDPR EU Laws and their GDPR Mimesis. DGA, DSA, DMA and the EU regulation of AI', *European Law Blog* (last visited 1 April 2021) at 3, https://europeanlawblog.eu/2021/04/01/post-gdpr-eu-laws-and-their-gdpr-mimesis-dga-dsa-dma-and-the-eu-regulation-of-ai/ (last visited 14 November 2022) The following section draws heavily on this blog.

[82] The theme of *GDPR mimesis* serves to enrich our discourse and respond to the question about how the EU considers GDPR principles and why it does so. The reasons for this EU lawmaking approach to technology are mapped out in the following sections to provide a realistic understanding of EU regulatory change.

Then there is substantive mimesis in the DGA. Recall that the DGA identifies a special set of principles to govern the provision of data-sharing services (Article 11 DGA), organizes a system of adequacy for data exports outside the EU (Article 30 DGA), and introduces new 'special' rights to assist individuals that want to engage in 'data altruism' (Article 19 DGA). Again, this should not be a problem. The GDPR can be seen as a basic set of rights and principles to protect personal data, but it can be justified in sectoral laws to advance the level of protection, like in this specific regulation that focuses on specific stakeholders and targets the sharing and use of personal and other data.

Finally, symbolic mimesis might be a more serious challenge. The DGA sets up a European Data Innovation Board that, at a closer look, is no more than an expert group advising the Commission to help regulate data-sharing practices in Europe (Article 26 DGA). All useful, of course, but the name of this instrument simply suggests too much in the light of the legal powers and competences of the European Data Protection Board set up by the GDPR or the Management Board of the EU Aviation Safety Agency set up by Regulation 2018/1139 (discussed previously in the section on drones). Not everything can be called a 'board' at the price of confusing the citizen.

B. Ample GDPR Mimesis, Little GDPR Integration

Is GDPR mimesis unavoidable? Our discussion of the drone regulations showed a strategy of very loose and general references, but no application or real engagement with data protection. That is questionable from an integration perspective (see below), but it can hardly be mimesis. Terms like lipreading and denial or avoidance seem more appropriate.

But the example of the NIS Directive discussed in section 3 shows that mimesis is not always applied. There are other, more recent examples. At the same time as releasing its DGA draft, in December 2020, the Commission also introduced two important proposals comprising the so-called Digital Services Act package:[83] the DSA[84] and the DMA.[85] Both texts are a counterexample of GDPR mimesis. Not a trace of the EU personal data protection scheme can be found in their texts. Why is that?

[83] European Commission, 'The Digital Services Act Package' (2021), https://ec.europa.eu/digital-single-market/en/digital-services-act-package (last visited 26 May 2021).
[84] Digital Services Act (n. 53).
[85] Digital Markets Act (n. 54).

The DSA and the DMA, as was the case with the GDPR, are not designed from scratch. Particularly the DSA furthers and expands Directive 2000/31/EC on certain legal aspects of information society services, in particular electronic commerce.[86] This e-Commerce Directive is an impressive text by its own merit that, similar to the 1995 Data Protection Directive, withstood for more than 20 years the internet revolution that took place in the meantime. In other words, the aim-setting of the DSA and the DMA is entirely different: they aim at regulating the provision of services over the internet. Their objective is to protect consumers and offer legal certainty to providers. They could well be the result of path dependency within the same policy cycle.

C. Is GDPR Mimesis such a Bad Thing After All?

Does it not make sense for EU legislators to copy a model that has demonstrably served its purposes well, placing the EU at the international forefront when it comes to protecting individuals from the unwanted consequences of technology? Yes and no. From a legal-technical point of view, complexity is increased. If all the above initiatives come through, the same company could be 'controller' or 'processor' under the GDPR, 'data holder' under the DGA, and 'provider' under AI regulation—not to bring into the picture any DSA or DMA characterization. But perhaps ours is an age of complexity, and simplicity in the digital era is long foregone. Notwithstanding any such pessimistic ideology, the fact remains that lawyers and state authorities will most likely have a particularly hard time juggling simultaneously over all the above capacities. Consistency, if it ever was an EU law objective at all, as most pertinently questioned by Brownsword,[87] would be substantially hampered.

Perhaps then the GDPR has formulated an EU model for technology regulation? A kind of acquis? While perhaps tempting from an EU law point of view, in line with the 'Brussels effect' identified by Bradford,[88] this finding may prove problematic. Would then the EU approach to technology essentially comprise a highly structuralist, bureaucratic approach composed of special roles, rights and principles, and the establishment of new state authorities?

Even under a straightforward, human creativity perspective, mimesis is a bad thing. One is allowed, and indeed compelled, to stand on the shoulders

[86] Directive (EU) 2000/31, OJ 2000 L 178/1.
[87] R. Brownsword, *Law, Technology and Society: Reimagining the Regulatory Environment* (2019) 155.
[88] A. Bradford, *The Brussels Effect: How the European Union Rules the World* (2020).

of giants but at some point, he or she must make his or her own contribution. Only then can they leave their mark. But in this we are not in creativity per se, but in law with its insistence on legal constraints, logic, and internal morality. Rules can be creative, but should be at least minimally clear and intelligible, free of contradictions, relatively constant, and possible to obey, among other things.[89]

Perhaps the most salient aspect of post-GDPR lawmaking is its refusal to integrate the new in the old. We are not discussing different terminology (see above), but coherence and substantive integration of old and new that should be spotlighted here. All post-GDPR laws state in their preamble that they are 'without prejudice to EU law and the GDPR in particular' or affirm 'in addition to their provisions, the GDPR provisions (also) need to be respected', but that does not bring us very far at all, on the contrary.

These disclaimers only make us more curious about how the GDPR and the post-GDPR laws integrate and interact concretely. That clarity is not given, even at the most elementary level. The GDPR requires for every processing a legal basis: any actor before processing personal data needs to identify a valid legal basis for that personal data processing activity and this can only be one the six legal bases for processing enumerated in Article 6 GDPR: consent; performance of a contract; legitimate interest; vital interest; legal requirement; public interest. One would expect from the DGA with its narrow scope (only three pillars or issues are dealt with) to detail and further clarify what kind of legal GDPR-basis applies in these three specific contexts, but that does not happen. The only exception would be the third 'pillar' (data altruism) as the DGA is explicit: this activity should be based around consent, and one cannot rely on any other possible legal GDPR-basis. Then again, no more information is given, while the GDPR is very elaborate on the ingredients of valid consent (given by a clear affirmative act, freely given, specific, informed, unambiguous, revocable . . .), distinguishes between consenting to processing of normal data (Article 7 GDPR), consenting of sensitive data (Article 9 GDPR), consenting by minors (Article 8 GDPR), and adds extra rules for international transfers of data. How does this play out in the context of data altruism (often involving very sensitive data, such as health data)? One would have expected more clarificatory work in the DGA as a *lex specialis* to the GDPR, but in vain. A useful clarification could have been cross-referencing with phrases like: 'Consent in the meaning of Article 8 GDPR is needed . . .'.

[89] L. Fuller, *The Morality of Law* (2nd ed., 1964).

Another example of unsatisfactory mimesis is the 2016 EU Police and Criminal Justice Data Protection Directive,[90] a 65-provision-long text that was published the same day (4 May 2016) as the GDPR. The latter clearly served as a basis and starting point for most of the provisions of the Directive. The Directive faithfully adheres to all terms, principles, and (most) of the rules from the GDPR but hesitates to go into the details about the processing work done by contemporary police and law enforcement. Big data relevant processing practices (web crawling, data mining, data matching, etc.) are simply ignored by the EU Directive. Moreover, ideas such as predictive policing are launched in the recitals and provisions of the Directive without any elaboration apart from the requirement that such processing operations need to be envisaged by law.

Let us now leave these case studies and return to our main inquiry: why is Europe missing its rendezvous with the GDPR and its data protection principles and rules? Why is it producing data protection laws of a general nature and initiating data-driven focused reform via other, more recent, laws? How can we explain the lack of integration in the post-GDPR laws?

8. Beliefs in Open Texture and Agencification (Factor 1)

A. The New Regulatory State Approach to Address Deficiencies in Lawmaking

The previous discussion with its insistence on the careful integration of laws cannot be disregarded with a general account about generality of international legal instruments.[91] A more ambitious expectation about integration by international regulators is not unreasonable per se. Especially the EU legal apparatus that seemed fit for the job of regulating at the European level in detail: the EU sought to replace diverse national laws mainly with *regulations*, single

[90] *See* De Hert and Papakonstantinou, 'The New Police and Criminal Justice Data Protection Directive. A First Analysis', 7(1) *New Journal of European Criminal Law* (2016) 7.

[91] So, we are not satisfied with a reminder about the limits of international or EU legal instruments and about the differences between EU regulations (the most centralizing of all instruments which are utilized to ensure uniformity) and directives (that need transposition, and leave Member States some discretion as to the form and methods used to transpose) and about conventions necessarily being vague. On this basis some would argue that silence on difficult integrative exercises or discretion is all that can be expected from international regulatory instruments, and we should bid farewell to our expectations and our trust in command and control via Strasbourg or Brussels using *hard law* instruments such as regulations, conventions, and directives, and counting on domestic courts (and sometimes European Courts) to make it all work.

European-wide pieces of legislation, that harmonize national provisions, linked to cycles of revisions and procedural provisions that would update the legislation in question in the light of technical progress. The latest proposals, as shown in sections 5 and 6, would seem inclined towards this approach to ensure those objectives as much as possible.

However, some commentators call this expectation and approach to regulation (applied in many areas of EU law) an 'old approach' characterized by major deficiencies: time-consuming, involving time-lags (outdated at the moment of implementation), and lacking flexibility needed for changing consumer behaviour and market innovation.[92] Like other international organizations, for example, the CoE, the EU was also confronted with another drawback of utilizing command-based techniques at the supranational level: it encountered more and more difficulties in achieving consensus in identifying collective policy goals and consensus in setting standards for achieving those goals.[93]

As a reaction, the EU became a 'new regulatory state' and did three interconnected things: it started to keep some of its hard laws rather open textured—even in its regulations—it relied for further guidance on the Court of Justice of the European Union (CJEU) (the Luxembourg Court endowed with more and more competences), *and* it relied on soft law and agency decision making. This new approach has been in vogue since the 1980s and is an obvious explanatory factor for the lack of integration and the use of vagueness in post-GDPR laws.

B. Agencification and the Reliance on Expert Systems in Data Protection Law

In particular, the role and strategic use of agencies, present in all possible institutional shapes and sizes, is remarkable.[94] Their role, next to court dispute

[92] 'It was considered time-consuming, given member-state sensitivities and decision-making rules that allowed for blockages, and it involved such a time-lag that by the time rules were adopted, they were already technically out of date. Other difficulties were that the regulations were too entrenched once passed, there was a degree of uniformity that reduced consumer choices and innovation, and the process made insufficient use of technical standardization and industrial norms—which led to duplications, delays, and inconsistencies' (R. Baldwin, M. Cave, and M. Lodge, *Understanding Regulation: Theory, Strategy, and Practice* (2nd ed., 2012) 392).

[93] 'As a result, supranational norms are often drafted in vague, aspirational or framework terms. Although these broad generalized statements of principle may conceal underlying political disagreement concerning their scope and content, they pose considerable difficulties for those responsible for their implementation. As domestic enforcement studies demonstrate, vague and indeterminate rules do not translate easily into hard, practical norms for guiding behaviour and identifying contraventions' (B. Morgan and K. Yeung, *An Introduction to Law and Regulation: Text and Materials* (2007) 323–324).

[94] Baldwin, Cave, and Lodge (n. 92) 397–398 with reference to Thatcher and Coen, 'Reshaping European Regulatory Space', 31(4) *West European Politics* (2008) 806. 'The agency landscape has not

resolutions systems, is crucial in view of the presence of supranational vague norms that conceal underlying political disagreement between states (see above). Legally binding court decisions might clarify these rules; but they may fail effectively to defuse underlying political disagreement and, therefore, call into question the legitimacy of these adjudicatory determinations.[95] This is where the agencies come in. As a network of expert actors operating on the basis of the same generally applicable standards, they can succeed in establishing global epistemic communities in specific policy sectors (like data protection) with shared knowledge, culture, and values that overcome disparities in national conditions, values, and practices.[96]

The prominence of agencies in the data protection field and the reliance on their guidance and the guidance by the CJEU can be highlighted with CJEU judgments such as *Patrick Breyer* and *ASNEF and FECEMD*, prohibiting states to clarify European data protection via national laws and creating a guidance monopoly for the European Court and data protection agencies.[97]

In our view, a first plausible explanatory factor for lack of integration is a consequence of the European regulatory approach and machinery relying heavily on agency expert knowledge, the pro-Europe activism of the CJEU, and soft power. Traditional European lawmaking via regulation and directives is now steered at the more general, while the more concrete norm building work and the more controversial or complex work is left over to less democratic decision making,[98] either by the agencies acting together or by the

stopped evolving and has taken different institutional shapes ranging from national regulators acting together, a mix of Commission and national regulatory staff, to purely "EU-level regulators" and the EU Commission acting as regulator.'

[95] Morgan and Yeung (n. 93), 323–324.

[96] Ibid. 324. with reference to C. Joerges and E. Vos (eds), *EU Committees: Social Regulation, Law and Politics* (1999): 'These epistemic communities have considerable potential to transcend local allegiances, especially where the appearance of universalistic, objective foundations for expert knowledge opens the possibility of depoliticising the rule-making process. It is therefore hardly surprising that international networks of experts have proliferated at the supranational level, accompanied by optimistic accounts of their potential role in global governance.'

[97] De Hert, 'Data Protection's Future without Democratic Bright Line Rules. Co-existing with Technologies in Europe after Breyer', 3(1) *European Data Protection Law Review* (2017) 20, with a discussion of Case C-582/14 *Patrick Breyer v Bundesrepublik Deutschland* (ECLI:EU:C:2016:779); Joined Cases C-468/10 and C-469/10 *Asociación Nacional de Establecimientos Financieros de Crédito (ASNEF) and Federación de Comercio Electrónico y Marketing Directo (FECEMD)* (ECLI:EU:C:2011:777). See also van der Sloot, 'Do Data Protection Rules Protect the Individual and Should They? An Assessment of the Proposed General Data Protection Regulation', 4(4) *International Data Privacy Law* (2014) 307, at 319–320: 'By undermining the diversity in national approaches, the democratic legitimacy of the right to data protection may be undermined as well'.

[98] Compare 'by charging an agency with the implementation of a general regulatory mandate, legislators ... avoid or at least disguise their responsibility for the consequences of the decisions ultimately made' (see Fiorina, 'Legislative Choice of Regulatory Forms', 39 *Public Choice* (1982) 33, at 47). In 1986 a more refined delegation mechanism was identified: delegation to agencies is pursued in areas of high

CJEU.[99] This translates into exercises of simple mimesis in post-GDPR laws and their lack of substantial integration of data protection rules and principles.

9. Beliefs in a Broader Mix of Regulatory Instruments and Institutions (Factor 2)

A. The GDPR Itself Requires a Broader Mix of Regulatory Approaches

In the introduction, I discussed a first approach towards post-GDPR law-making, especially among the data protection authorities in the period 2012–2016 regarding big data ('let it come and prove itself, no reason to change the principles now')? This attitude is still there and will probably inspire future reactions, at least from the institutional actors in data protection law, to any allegations (like the one in this chapter) about a missed regulatory *rendezvous* of the GDPR and the post-GDPR laws. To put it differently, one can probably expect a strong rejection by the data protection establishment of charges of under-regulation[100] and/or disconnection.[101] Some professionals from other circles (industry, academia) will join in,[102] especially those that criticize the limits of the hard and traditional supranational lawmaking (discussed in the previous section). *O, sancta simplicitas!*, they argue, traditional lawmaking is so imperfect and slow and regulatory detail is overrated. A more superior understanding of regulatory strategies is needed with an awareness of the existence of alternative regulatory instruments to complement vague (or sometimes too detailed) supranational norms and principles.

uncertainty, whereas a reliance on statute or enforcement through courts is pursued in case of certainty about the future. See Fiorina, 'Legislator Uncertainty, Legislative Control, and the Delegation of Legislative Power', 2 *Journal of Law, Economics and Organization* (1986) 33. See also Baldwin, Cave, and Lodge (n. 92) 56.

[99] The CoE machinery operates is a quite similar way, with treaties and conventions drafted in general terms, narrowed down in recommendations and other soft law guidance documents.

[100] On these charges, see Baldwin, Cave, and Lodge (n. 92) 69.

[101] On the concept of regulatory disconnection with regard to law and technology, see R. Brownsword and M. Goodwin, *Law and the Technologies of the Twenty-First Century: Text and Materials (Law in Context)* (2012) 398 and following.

[102] Sometimes it is without a good reason and the overall motor of critique is disbelief in regulatory interventions, disbelief in law. About 'futility', 'jeopardy', and 'perversity' as three rhetorical strategies commonly employed to resist progressive policy interventions, *see* Baldwin, Cave, and Lodge (n. 92) at 73, with a discussion of the work of Albert Hirschman who identified these strategies.

Command and control (use of legal authority and the command of law to pursue policy objectives) is indeed only one option. Next to soft law, there is self-regulation and there are other modes of delegating the regulatory function to bodies beyond the state via controlled certification schemes and audits of corporate risk management systems.[103]

Those who accept open texture in hard laws and agencification (see previous section) will often insist on the available alternatives to laws in the narrow sense. They will point at the optimal mixes of regulatory instruments and institutions made possible in and demanded for by the GDPR itself. This text is indeed a meeting point of different regulatory strategies: there are not only the very general but over-inclusive principles (that will apply to all that is yet to come, even big data), but where possible there are detailed rules, whereas data subjects' rights are further expanded, the enforcement mechanism is strengthened, and controllers are entrusted with duties to better inform data subjects via incentives.[104] Ideas such as certification, seals, and impact assessment are present and made possible by the GDPR.[105]

Open texture and detail, together, allow Europe to face new or specific data protection challenges and frame the data-driven economy without stifling it.[106] Post-GDPR laws should therefore be understood in a double perspective: standing on the shoulders of the GDPR they add some detail, but also some vaguer newer ideas. They can add vagueness to the vagueness/detail of the GDPR or add detail to the vagueness/detail. In its terminology, the DGA seems to add merely vagueness to the GDPR (section 5), but that would be an incomplete analysis. The stakeholder perspective (the Act contains specific

[103] Baldwin, Cave, and Lodge (n. 92) at 105 and following.

[104] De Hert, 'Data Protection as Bundles of Principles, General Rights, Concrete Subjective Rights and Rules. Piercing the Veil of Stability Surrounding the Principles of Data Protection', 3(2) *European Data Protection Law Review* (2017) 160. See also De Hert *et al.*, 'The proposed Regulation and the construction of a principles-driven system for individual data protection', 26(1&2) *Innovation: The European Journal of Social Science Research* (2013) 133. On law as threat and law as umpire, see Morgan and Yeung, (n. 93) at 5–6. On the basic capacities, other than command and acting directly, of states (to deploy wealth to influence conduct: to harness markets and channel competitive forces to particular ends; to inform, e.g. so as to empower consumers; to confer protected rights so as to create desired incentives and constraints: Baldwin, Cave, and Lodge (n. 92) at 105–106.

[105] See Kamara and De Hert, 'Data Protection Certification in the EU: Possibilities, Actors and Building Blocks in a reformed landscape', in R. Rodrigues and V. Papakonstantinou (eds), *Privacy and Data Protection Seals* (2018) 7.

[106] Malgieri and De Hert, 'Making the Most of New Laws: Reconciling Big Data Innovation and Personal Data Protection Within and Beyond the GDPR', in E. Degrave *et al.* (eds), *Law, Norms and Freedoms in Cyberspace—Droit, Norme et Libertés dans le Cybermonde: Liber Amicorum Yves Poullet* (2018) 525. See equally Forgó, Hänold, and Schütze, 'The Principle of Purpose Limitation and Big Data', in M. Corrales, M. Fenwick, and N. Forgó (eds), *New Technology, Big Data and the Law. Perspectives in Law, Business and Innovation* (2017) 17.

chapters on (i) public bodies; (ii) data-sharing services; and (iii) data altruism) is a valuable addition to the GDPR that is particularly weak in addressing actors by labelling them all 'controllers'. The Commission is enthusiastic and applauds this mix of regulatory instruments expanding GDPR protection (by including non-personal data) and clarifying GDPR protection (by voting laws on specific actors or problems). This approach would seem, according to the Commission, to be the way to foster data-driven innovations relying upon big data collection and data analytics.[107]

B. What to Think of this 'Enriched' Approach?

When a better understanding of regulatory alternatives to detailed laws boils down to defending open textured norms and to adding vagueness rather than detail to data protection law, we need not be too enthusiastic. It is hard for me to see a problem with more detail in data protection law. The choice of the GDPR to add very concrete rules and more elaborated rights to the basic set of data protection principles that go back to the 1970s and 1980s is not without justification. More detailed rules pose less considerable difficulties for those responsible for their implementation (see section 10 below) and fulfil human rights requirements such as transparency and foreseeability.

For some however recent reform has gone beyond the optimal mix by adding too much detail. Often heard in many, mainly oral, discussions, is that current data protection laws (especially the GDPR) are too long. A return to shorter texts with only the principles and some amendments would make these laws more resilient.[108] In these discussions, one hears strong echoes of well-known criticism on command-and-control strategies. Apart from the critique that many laws are the result of 'capture', by interest groups and civil society organizations, there are concerns about the limits of the reliance on legal rules of command-and-control strategies and its alleged propensity to produce too many *and* unnecessarily complex and inflexible rules, strangling either competition or civil liberties depending on the success of interest groups.[109]

[107] In this respect, the European Data Strategy takes the GDPR as the basis upon which further regulations can, and should, be enacted.

[108] See van der Sloot (n. 97) at 318–322.

[109] Baldwin, Cave, and Lodge (n. 92) at 108–109.

C. Detailed Laws Irritate

A more sophisticated and more fundamental sceptical stand is one that relies on systems theory thinkers such as Niklas Luhmann, Gunther Teubner, and Helmut Willke who perceive law, economy, politics, religion, sport, health, and family as subsystems with their own rationalities and insist on the problematic nature of the belief that legal norms can directly intervene in these other spheres.[110] Especially the lack of power of law to intrude in the economy has received a lot of attention. To have an impact in the economic subsystem, the law needs to translate its message to be understood but this is difficult and implies distortions and time delays. In that respect a shorter document with data protection principles might be a more effective way to tame big data economics.

Teubner's insistence on *irritations* is interesting. Attempts to intervene in subsystems, even with translation, are not necessarily successful because of the resistance of these subsystems to 'code' that is not theirs. Transplanting law and regulation in non-legal subsystems is at best creating 'irritation effects'. Other less desirable, but highly plausible, outcomes are mutual indifference (law is seen as irrelevant to the other subsystem) or colonization (either of the subsystem taken over by law, or of law being 'over-socialized' by the other subsystem).[111]

It would take more space to think through this analysis, but here is a first take.

On the one hand, it is very clear from political statements by EU political leaders that instruments like the DSA and the DMA (discussed in section 7) and other recent instruments such as Regulation 2019/1150, also known as the Platform-to-Business Regulation or P2B Regulation,[112] have the explicit aim to intervene in the market. The latter Regulation, for instance, seeks to bring fairness and transparency for businesses operating in the platform economy. It provides online businesses with a new set of rights that is intended to mitigate power imbalances between them and platforms. It is too early to assess the effectiveness of this agenda of the Ursula Von der Leyen Commission

[110] Morgan and Yeung (n. 93) at 69–74; Baldwin, Cave, and Lodge (n. 92) at 62–63 with a short discussion of G. Teubner, *Dilemmas of Law in the Welfare State* (1986); G. Teubner, *Law as an Autopoietic System*, (1993); Teubner, Nobles, and Schiff, 'The Autonomy of Law: An Introduction to Legal Autopoiesis', in D. Schiff and R. Nobles (eds), *Jurisprudence* (2003) 897; Luhmann, 'Law as a Social System', 83(1&2) *Northwestern University Law Review* (1989) at 136; Willke, *Systemtheorie III: Steuerungstheorie* (1995). See also Rottleuthner, 'Biological Metaphors in Legal Thought', in G. Teubner (ed.) *Autopoietic Law: A New Approach to Law and Society* (1988) 97.

[111] See Teubner, 'Das regulatorische Trilemma. Zur Diskussion um postinstrumentale Rechtsmodelle', 13(1) *Quaderni Fiorentini per la Storia del pensiero giuridico moderno* (1984) 109; Baldwin, Cave, and Lodge (n. 92) at 63.

[112] Regulation (EU) 2019/1150, OJ 2019 L 186/57.

that started working in December 2019. Irritations are to be expected, and scepticism over this approach is not unjustified: apparently the reliance on principles in the years before 2019 has not worked.

On the other hand, some post-GDPR laws are clearly designed to neutralize possible GDPR irritations to certain sectors. Instruments like the drone regulations (section 4) and the PSD2, that had no other intention than to please a series of actors (like the tech companies) by opening bank data to non-banking actors, aimed at building a bridge between the GDPR and sector-specific rules regarding data-intensive activities.[113]

Wrapping up our second factor, in our view, the optimal mix of regulatory instruments and institutions can account for the lack of substantive integration of GDPR principles in post-GDPR lawmaking.

10. Lack of Creative Legal Thinking about Data Protection Implications (Factor 3)

In this section I come back to the theme of rules and detail. As fundamental rights-trained lawyers, we are often amazed by the intensity of the *rules v. principles* discussion in legal and policy fora. It is almost a religious thing, especially the belief of some (most) in principles (abstract, non-eroded by private interests, rational, channelling to the public good), coupled to a certain disdain for rules (ordinary and vulgar, detailed, quickly outdated, replaceable, political, etc.). Like fundamental rights, principles can be bent, expanded, eroded, and replaced.[114] There is no fixed list, and their number is (also) prone to inflation. So, there is inflation of rights and principles, just like there is rule inflation.[115] Mobilizing the Luhmans and Teubners of this world in favour of data protection laws without rules, mainly spelling out the principles and no more, lacks profound substantiation.

[113] See our analysis, De Hert and Sajfert (n. 2) at 345–346.

[114] See what happened to the principle of data minimization in the Directive (see above). On the broadening of some principles and the quasi elimination of others (e.g. the principle of transparency) in data protection law, see van der Sloot (n. 97) at 311–314. On domestic police laws disregarding the purpose-specification principle, see Cannataci and Bonnici, 'The End of the Purpose-Specification Principle in Data Protection?', 24(1) *International Review of Law, Computers & Technology* (2010) 101.

[115] On 'regulatory ratchet', see chapter 7 in E. Bardach and R. Kagan, *Going by the Book: The Problem of Regulatory Unreasonableness* (1982). See also Baldwin, Cave, and Lodge (n. 92) at 108–109: 'Regulatory rules tend to grow rather than recede because revisions of regulations are infrequent; work on new rules tends to drive out attention to old ones; and failure to carry out pruning leads the thickets of rules to grow ever more dense.'

'New' rule-based devices, such as privacy impact assessments and privacy by design, might make translation, irritation, and proceduralization possible. More so, when they spell out bright-line rules, i.e. rules with concrete objective factors with no or limited margin for interpretation, regarding controversial matters ('the age of kids to go on the internet is x or y') they might be able to settle and stop confusion generated by these controversies. We briefly recall that complexity is one of Luhmann's other central themes, for whom reduction of complexity is one of the distinguishing features of (sub- or social-) systems.[116]

In past writings, I have therefore not hesitated to applaud the insertion of more and more concrete rules in data protection reform texts. Like principles, rules can pressure legislators to reduce discretions in favour of the 'rule of law'. Although some might regard this as an invitation to an excessive production of rules,[117] we think foreseeability of state actions and (other) infringements of fundamental rights is a worthy cause.

Of course, rules must be devised with care. In the area of police and law enforcement powers this boils down to finding the right balance between due process requirements and efficiency concerns. In the area of data governance, following our focus on the DGA, this boils down to achieving transparency, accountability, and participation in the governance of data, personal or not.[118] Baldwin *et al.* open their chapter on 'Explaining Regulatory Failure' with the observation that '[a]t the broadest level, regulatory failure can be explained by insufficient resources and by epistemological limitations ("failures of imagination")'.[119]

Part of the problem is indeed creativity. It takes creativity to understand the relation and interaction between regulatory modalities such as technology, markets, social norms, and laws. It takes creativity to understand a phenomenon such as data altruism and apparently it takes years to frame it. Profiling and machine learning might be other examples. Is Article 22 GDPR all we have to say about automated decisions and profiling? Is human intervention and the prohibition to use sensitive data provided for by this provision all that is needed to regulate profiling well?

[116] N. Luhmann, *Social Systems* (1995); Bednarz Jr., 'Complexity and Intersubjectivity: Towards the Theory of Niklas Luhmann', 7(1) *Human Studies* (1984) 55.

[117] Bardach and Kagan (n. 115). See also Baldwin, Cave, and Lodge (n. 92) at 108–109.

[118] Good governance can only be achieved if these three pillars are attended by the relevant policy maker: transparency, accountability, and participation. See De Hert, 'Globalisation, Crime And Governance: Transparency, Accountability and Participation as Principles for Global Criminal Law', in C. Brants and S. Karstedt (eds), *Transitional Justice and its Public Spheres: Engagement, Legitimacy and Contestation* (2017) 91.

[119] Baldwin, Cave, and Lodge (n. 92) at 72–73.

Similar questions regarding the DGA: does it provide any new form of governance or is it just another patch to the flawed current business models based around advertising? Are the providers of data-sharing services any different from what we already have? Can data altruism organizations provide an alternative for fostering responsible data sharing to enable big data innovations without all the negative traits that they are currently producing? The fact that the DGA escapes the constraints of the definitions provided for by the GDPR and acknowledges that non-personal data also plays a crucial role in the development of data-driven businesses should already be applauded for providing an alternative to explore and try new paths, in spite of the criticism that certain regulators, such as the European Data Protection Supervisor (EDPS) and the European Data Protection Board (EDPB),[120] have already raised. In her excellent *Advanced Introduction to Privacy Law*, written based on a thorough understanding of the history of privacy, Megan Richardson contemplates the necessity to see new ideas on privacy protection developed. Sometimes these ideas are the result of a crisis, sometimes they are not and present themselves in a routine way and may grow over time.[121] Using the work of Michel Callon, she points at processes of adjustment and readjustment as opposed to 'grand steps' that characterize modern regulation.[122]

[120] EDPB and EDPS, 'EDPB and EDPS Joint Opinion 03/2021 on the Proposal for a regulation of the European Parliament and of the Council on European data governance (Data Governance Act)', https://edpb.europa.eu/system/files/2021-03/edpb-edps_joint_opinion_dga_en.pdf (last visited 26 May 2021).

[121] M. Richardson, *Advanced Introduction to Privacy Law* (2020) 85. On the other hand, some legal changes seem to have happened in a fairly routine way, as for instance with the passing of the Human Rights Act in the United Kingdom, prompting inter alia a new tort of misuse of private information which has then been turned (along with data protection standards) into a legal tool to address contemporary issues. The long-gestated EU GDPR 2016 can be placed in the same category albeit on a much bigger scale. Indeed, quite often there is nothing that can be identified as a 'crisis', as such: rather it is just that with the benefit of experience of new technologies, practices, and norms it becomes clear that new ideas are needed about how laws should be framed and applied in this environment. Or, as Lawrence Lessig put it in 1999, talking about the internet's open architecture as a threat to liberty, 'we are coming to understand a new powerful regulator in cyberspace, and we don't yet understand how best to control it'—and yet the threat to liberty was '[n]ot new in the sense that no theorist has conceived of it before. Others have. But new in the sense of newly urgent'.

[122] Ibid. 35. with reference to Callon et al., 'The Management and Evaluation of Technological Programs and the Dynamics of Techno-Economic Networks: The Case of AFME', 21(3) *Research Policy* (1992) 215, at 215: 'We can use Lessig's analysis to imagine the effect of regulatory modalities on privacy subjects who may be constrained or enabled in their pursuit of privacy by the combination of technology, markets, social norms and law. This may occur in a range of ways, bearing in mind that, as Lessig says, the modalities do not only govern directly but also indirectly. For instance, privacy laws may be geared to influencing not just behaviour but social norms, technologies and/or market practices (and conversely the laws will also be subjected to influences from these other modalities). Moreover, the process of adjustment and readjustment will likely be an ongoing one. Or as Lessig puts it in *Code: Version 2.0* quoting Polk Wagner, 'the interaction among these modalities is dynamic, <requiring consideration of not only ... legal adjustments, but also predicting the responsive effects these changes will stimulate>, with the legal regulator seeking an <equilibrium> among the modalities. Thus, we can posit a dynamic feedback loop in which technological changes are followed by adjustments in markets, social norms

Wrapping up our third explanatory factor, we summarize that information and time limitations can partly account for the lack of guidance and creativity in the GDPR and other text regarding integrating data protection into novel data practices. That explanation might be benevolent to the regulator of the past but is not reason to sit still with a text of 2016. Like for the case of data-driven practices, for some their effects are becoming apparent now and guidance is needed now.[123]

11. Closing Remarks: Careful Crafting and Understanding Regulatory Modalities

In this longer study I looked at post-GDPR laws and the mess they create with regard to data protection law. My focus on the preservation in post-GDPR laws of the spirit and letter of the data protection law as incorporated in the GDPR has brought me to a critical diagnosis about mimesis as a recurrent practice without the noble art of legal integration. We are often *not* helped. We are sometimes even sent to the desert with small rhetorical tricks like 'nothing in this law is meant to derogate from the GDPR', leaving the citizen and norm addressee with many questions about the data protection practicalities, like what kind of consent is needed for data altruism in the DGA (section 5 and 7) and how many notification obligations I have in case of a security breach (section 3).

What emerges from the examined post-GDPR laws in our case studies is that the regulatory approach of EU lawmaking agents shows patterns of GDPR mimesis and a lack of substantive integration of those principles. I would

and legal standards—examples of what French sociologist Michel Callon and his co-authors describe as <iterations>, movements to and for, negotiations and compromises of all sorts". The language suggests that changes will typically be more in the way of "iterations" than grand steps, that is, involving small incremental adjustments.'

[123] 'Consequently, when designing big data regulations, it seems advisable for governments to develop future-proof policies that follow and, where possible, anticipate this trend. If regulators only begin to regulate this phenomenon five or ten years from now, many of the projects will have already started. The negative impact may already have materialized, and it will be difficult to adjust and alter projects and developments that have already flourished. It should also be remembered that good, clear regulation can contribute to innovation and the use of big data. Since the current framework applying to new big data projects is not always clear, some government agencies and private companies are reluctant to use new technologies for fear of violating the law. New regulation could provide more clarity.' van der Sloot and van Schendel, 'Ten Questions for Future Regulation of Big Data', 7(2) *Journal of Intellectual Property, Information Technology and Electronic Commerce Law* (2016) 110, at 116. More nuanced on the regulatory void situation created by technological development, see Brownsword and Goodwin (n. 101) at 371 and following.

reserve the term *mimicry* for those laws that mock data protection, such as the drone regulations (section 4). The element of ridiculing suggested by the term *mimicry* is warranted because ridiculing is what these laws do: not taking the GDPR and its content seriously. *Mimesis*, the other term, is then reserved for many other post-GDPR laws with data protection relevance discussed in this chapter. Whether it is definitional, substantive, or symbolic, it should be approached with suspicion. Only in cases where a real added value is envisaged, some mimesis is acceptable. In all other cases it is imitating a set of rules and principles with a high moral legitimacy, hoping that some of that bling would also work on other things. General disclaimers about the importance of the GDPR do not do the job and the argument that the DGA is also applicable to non-personal data (contrary to the GDPR) does not justify the lack of effort to integrate well.

Regulation should not be about bling, but about careful crafting and understanding regulatory modalities, without necessarily having the ambition for giant steps. Some of that care would be demonstrated by a concern for coherence and integration. In our discussion of the NIS Directive, we quoted Maria Grazia Porcedda who found notification duties in several EU laws all with the same objective to create more information or data security (section 3). Her final recommendation, to consider a unified law to address the issue of information security and encourage the development of a mutual learning mechanism, is worth recalling in the conclusion of this study.[124] The EU has no criminal law code, no commercial code, no data protection code, none of the kind. So, codification is hard to realize, and the idea of integration will have to be pursued differently. In the case at hand here, adding provisions to the GDPR, hardening certain rules that need hardening and ensuring explicit cross-references to other post-GDPR laws, must be considered. A reverse exercise is to spell out in detail in all post-GDPR laws what GDPR provisions they impact and how this data protection impact should be understood in an unambiguous way.

Approaches based on open texture and EU-wide agencification, as well as approaches based on mixing EU laws with other regulatory modalities combined with simple facts about the lack of legal creativity were discussed in the three last sections to contextualize post-GDPR lawmaking, and to a certain extent, justify or topologically understand its attitude towards the boundaries of data protection law. Sociological insights about irritations (Teubner) and the slow speed legal insight (Michel Callon) indeed help to create a more realistic understanding of regulatory change. If there are no good ideas about regulating

[124] Porcedda (n. 32) at 1090–1098.

privacy aspects of drones about yet, then mimesis and promises about compliance with the GDPR might be all we have. My short, but benevolent discussion of AI reform (section 6) testifies for the capacity of the legal community to integrate well and to innovate legally, when all conditions are favourable.[125]

This said, there are reasons to understand the historical movement of the past years. With these three explanatory factors I drifted away from my previous research where, influenced by Bourdieu, I went after the questions of: Who are the actors involved in regulatory change (who is the state)? And why and how do they push for certain regulatory outcomes? However, as this contribution is part of a broader reflection on the boundaries of law, let us come back to the actor perspective in our concluding paragraphs. What are the relevant facts at stake in this post-GDPR lawmaking period? One basic document, the GDPR, serves as a generic framework and a plurality of subsequent laws that apply this framework to (new) stakeholders, (new) political objectives (fairness of the market), and new developments in technology and societal practices (data altruism).

Each time, with every directorate launching a new proposal on a certain aspect of the data-driven society, the GDPR is translated towards interpretations (templates, procedures, information notices, etc.) by a different set of actors that shape personal data protection. Of course, all legal provisions, however clearly voiced they may be, require interpretation by lawyers, judges, experts, or developers, shaped by and shaping social contexts. *Mimicri* and meaningless *mimesis* is guaranteed when these actors operating outside the data protection context are not motivated or challenged to apply a genuine data protection exercise.[126]

[125] In my first drafts I added other explanatory models based on path dependency, and the co-existence of critical junctures, but I decided not to include them and to invite critical readers to add their own explanations for regulatory developments with regard to data protection.

[126] Breuer and Pierson, in their comparative analysis of smart city projects in two countries, reach a similar outcome: cities become smart without genuine data protection compliance whenever data protection experts or data protection savvy citizens are absent around the policy table. Data protection in policy and application contexts is always in a state of 'interpretative flexibility': semantic variations, or different interpretations, exist and groups compete to convince others. These actors interact with 'non-human actors' such as technologies and other artefacts (patents, contracts, other legislation, etc.) that together define and shape the respective ecosystems. See Breuer and Pierson, 'The right to the city and data protection for developing citizen-centric digital cities', 24(6) *Information, Communication & Society* (2021) 797; Pinch and Bijker, 'The Social Construction of Facts and Artefacts: or How the Sociology of Science and the Sociology of Technology might Benefit Each Other', *Social Studies of Science* 14(3) (1984) 399-441; Callon, 'Techno-economic Networks and Irreversibility', *The Sociological Review* 38.1_suppl (1990), 132–161; Law, 'Actor Network Theory and Material Semiotics, version of 25th April 2007', Companion to Social Theory (2007); and Lievrouw, 'Materiality and Media in Communication and Technology Studies: An Unfinished Project' in T. Gillespie, P.J. Boczkowski and K.A. Foot (eds) '*Media Technologies: Essays on Communication, Materiality, and Society* (2014) 21–51.

This calls for a specific, topological understanding of post-GDPR lawmaking at EU level. The sheer fact that the digital is now everywhere and that almost every EU-directorate has a portfolio affecting data protection demands heightened concerns about integration and rent-seeking by interest groups within their familiar ecosystems far away from the state officials that traditionally discuss data protection (DG JUST, EDPS, or EDBP). Interventions of data protection expert bodies like the EDPS or the EDBP in the legislative process, should therefore be singled out as of constitutional importance and should require more explicit attention, for instance, in the Recitals of EU laws. This and other ideas will make more meaningful coordination with the GDPR as a boundary setting instrument and subsequent laws possible.

In a past blog, my colleague Papakonstantinou wrote a particularly powerful concluding paragraph that I slightly reformulated and it sounded like this:

> The GDPR is an immensely successful legal instrument that has a life and history of its own. EU personal data protection is currently busy tilting the planet towards stronger protection of the privacy of individuals under technological deluge. This seat is therefore taken. Any new EU regulatory initiatives will have to create a story of its own or better integrate in the consolidated GDPR mother story, and this, not by faking its appearance but by clarifying explicitly its implications for the new regulatory layer.[127]

[127] Papakonstantinou and De Hert (n. 81).

5

Beyond Originator Control of Personal Data in EU Interoperable Information Systems: Towards Data Originalism

*Mariavittoria Catanzariti and Deirdre Curtin**

1. Introduction

The EU is nowadays synonymous with the General Data Protection Regulation (GDPR)[1] when it comes to personal data protection and, as De Hert has pointed out in Chapter 4, also several other pieces of regulation, although different in scope, follow the same trajectory in mimetic fashion. The law and practice of personal data sharing is a much less visible and less understood phenomenon but here too we can see the emergence of institutional practices and regulation in particular in the Area of Freedom, Security and Justice (AFSJ) and, more recently, much more generally in the new Data Governance Act.[2] The focus of our chapter is not on rights—individual or otherwise—but rather on seeing how, in data-driven Europe, public administrations process and access personal information in a systemic manner that affects individuals in their daily lives and in law in a variety of ways—in a manner quite divorced from the GDPR and certain of its core understandings.

Our chapter attempts to grapple with the complexities not only of the still relatively new Interoperability Regulations but also the many other distinct regulations that govern agencies and their access to shared information. This throws up legal questions on ownership or otherwise of personal data but also questions the ability of those who 'originate' data into the system to, in practice,

* The authors wish to thank Marco Lasmar Almada for research assistance. Thanks to all participants in the online workshop 'Data at the Boundaries of Law' held at the European University Institute in April 2021, and special thanks to Tommaso Fia and Marco Lasmar Almada for their generous and helpful comments on an earlier version of this paper.

[1] Regulation (EU) 2016/179, OJ 2016 L 119/1.

[2] Regulation (EU) 2022/868 (Data Governance Act), OJ 2022 L 152/1.

Mariavittoria Catanzariti and Deirdre Curtin, *Beyond Originator Control of Personal Data in EU Interoperable Information Systems: Towards Data Originalism* In: *Data at the Boundaries of European Law*. Edited by: Deirdre Curtin and Mariavittoria Catanzariti, Oxford University Press. © Mariavittoria Catanzariti and Deirdre Curtin 2023.
DOI: 10.1093/oso/9780198874195.003.0005

impose controls on how it is shared further, with whom, and according to what conditions it can be used.[3] This is not simply a matter of qualifying originators[4] as controllers or processers, as the GDPR would do, but of looking at processes of data sharing more from an institutional and technical perspective of sharers and users and not only as the objects (persons) of the data in question. In so doing we aim to clarify the role that security principles play in practice as well as the opaque nature of the power that is exercised by a whole variety of public actors and executives in accessing, sharing, and using personal data, in particular in and around the domain of law enforcement.

State use of automated information collection systems has gradually succeeded more traditional and ad hoc ways of collecting, storing, and processing personal information. Automation as a term comes from the word automatic and refers to the technology by which a process or procedure is performed with minimum human assistance.[5] The key feature of an automated administrative system is the capacity to build in and automate administrative decision logic into a computer system.[6] The contemporary administrative state is not replaced by modern information and communication technologies but core parts of the traditional administrative state have been automated with a significant impact on both institutions and their accountability.[7] At the level of the EU, we find the same phenomenon and it has grown exponentially.

Automation goes hand in hand with what has become known over time as interoperability. Interoperability is a technical feature that connects systems through data sharing.[8] It has been increasingly developed in many EU regulatory sectors from integrated public services supplied by public administrations

[3] The principle of originator control (ORCON), largely used in intelligence information sharing, 'requires recipients to gain originator's approval for re-dissemination of disseminated digital object'. We borrowed the definition provided by Park and Sandhu, 'Originator Control in Usage Control', *Proceedings Third International Workshop on Policies for Distributed Systems and Networks* (2002).

[4] By originators we refer to those entities, Member States or Union Agencies, under whose authority certain conditions of data sharing have been created that are applicable to the entire interoperable process.

[5] Wikipedia, 'Automation' (2021), https://en.wikipedia.org/wiki/Automation (last visited 17 December 2021).

[6] Finck, 'Automated Decision-Making and Administrative Law', in P. Cane, H. C. H. Hofmann, E. C. Ip, and P. L. Lindseth (eds), *The Oxford Handbook of Comparative Administrative Law* (2020) 656.

[7] Curtin, 'The EU Automated State Disassembled', in E. Fisher, J. King, and A. Young (eds), *The Foundations and Future of Public Law: Essays in Honour of Paul Craig* (2020) 233.

[8] According to the definition by J. Palfrey and U. Gasser, *Interop: The Promise and Perils of Highly Interconnected Systems* (2012) 5), and the 'Standard Glossary of Software Engineering Terminology' (IEEE 610) of the Institute of Electrical and Electronics Engineers, interoperability is the 'ability to transfer and render useful data and other information across systems, applications, or components'. For a general overview of data sharing, see De Gregorio and Ranchordas, 'Breaking Down Information Silos with Big Data: A Legal Analysis of Data Sharing', in J. Cannataci, V. Falce, and O. Pollicino (eds), *New Legal Challenges of Big Data* (2020) 204.

to digital service markets.[9] For the purpose of this chapter, this term refers to the ability of different information systems—in EU justice and home affairs—to communicate, exchange data, and use the information that has been exchanged.[10] Interoperability of information systems implies not only full availability of but also the interconnections between the functionalities of interoperable components operating transversally and contextually on databases. It does not mean the creation of 'an enormous database where everything is interconnected'.[11] It refers rather to the ability of information systems to exchange (personal) data and to enable the sharing of information.[12] It implies that the data stored in different databases by a national authority or EU body can become searchable and accessible to some EU authorities (providing specific arrangements have been made) or to national authorities in other Member States who may rely on that data in their own national context.[13] From the very beginning, interoperability, especially in the context of the EU, has been presented as a technical matter, a matter of protocols and interfaces.[14] Its legitimacy in political and legal terms has been downplayed, perhaps even ignored. Yet, as De Hert and Gutwirth put it more than a decade ago on this very subject: 'there is a lot of wisdom in taking seriously the political dimension of technical things'.[15]

The idea behind our chapter is that interoperable data is data originated by a specific body or actor, which makes that data available for interoperable use (originator) but once that data becomes interoperable, its status changes: data is then shared and no longer exclusively under the control of the body or actor that had included it in one of the six databases. We aim to explore what sort of data is originated and then shared, whether or not that data is always under the control of the originator, whether the originator loses control over

[9] European Commission, *New Interoperability Framework* (2017); Kerber and Schweitzer, 'Interoperability in the Digital Economy', 8 *Journal of Intellectual Property, Information Technology and Electronic Commerce Law* (2017) 39.

[10] J. Ballaschk, Interoperability of Intelligence Networks in the European Union: An Analysis of the Policy of Interoperability in the EU's Area of Freedom, Security and Justice and Its Compatibility with the Right to Data Protection (2015) (PhD thesis on file at the University of Copenhagen) 51; European Commission, *High-level Expert Group on Information Systems and Interoperability: Final Report* (2017).

[11] J. King, 'Commissioner King's Remarks on Interoperability' (2017), https://web.archive.org/web/20200308141441/https://ec.europa.eu/commission/commissioners/2014-2019/king/announcements/commissioner-kings-remarks-interoperability-presentation-final-hleg-report-libe-committee-european_en (last visited 17 December 2021).

[12] European Commission, *High Level Expert Group on Information Systems and Interoperability: Scoping Paper* (2016).

[13] European Data Protection Supervisor, *Reflection Paper on the Interoperability of Information Systems in the Area of Freedom, Security and Justice* (2017) 6.

[14] De Hert and Gutwirth, 'Interoperability of Police Databases within the EU: An Accountable Political Choice?', 20 *International Review of Law, Computers and Technology* (2006) 21.

[15] Ibid. 32.

data once it shares it or whether the originator retains some power on the further usage of that shared data. The claim of this chapter is that the effective right of individuals affected by migration and security databases to reverse a decision unlawfully based on incorrect data or data wrongly attributed to them by interoperable components may depend on the rules of data sharing. As far as these rules are transparent—not only regarding data access but also data usage, conditions of onward use, and, above all, who decides on what and how—individuals may enjoy better data protection safeguards addressing why certain data has been used to achieve a certain decision.

The puzzle is that originators freely decide to share data but once they share data, it is unclear whether they enjoy a certain degree of discretion to impose their own rules and limits on the sharing. This inevitably affects the access and onward use by others because we do not know if originators have the power to decide which kind of use their 'original' data should be subject to. There are gaps in this sense in the new Interoperability Regulations establishing a framework for interoperability between specific new EU information systems in the field of police and judicial cooperation, asylum, and migration[16] and in the field of borders and visas.[17] These Regulations entered into force but the Commission has not determined yet the date when the European Search Portal is to start operations by means of an implementing act, and we have no practice yet.

Lack of specificity and transparency produces grey zones in which there are legal gaps (for example, whether an originator can do something with shared data that another subject cannot) where it is not clear which rules apply to data sharing, formulated by whom, applicable to whom, and in what circumstances. In other words, while the new regulations taken as a whole claim to elaborate a precise and complete system of how data sharing is technically put in place, they do not indicate where the balance of power in sharing personal data lies. Given this lack of clarity, we seek to reflect in a systematic and deeper manner on the impact of the recently-established EU interoperable architecture on the way in which data originates, is shared, and is then further aggregated to create identities of affected individuals. There are two more specific issues that this chapter also raises. First, it is not clear whether interoperability implies access to data by the users of interoperable components[18] without having to fulfil

[16] Regulation (EU) 2019/818, OJ 2019 L 135/85.

[17] Regulation (EU) 2019/817, OJ 2019 L 135/27.

[18] These users can be different officers depending on which interoperable component they have access to. The use of the European Search Portal is reserved to Member States authorities and Union Agencies having access at least to one of the EU information systems, to Europol data and Interpol data and to the common-identity repository and the multiple-identity-detector (Art. 7 Interoperability Regulations).

any (extra) conditions. As pointed out by the Fundamental Rights Agency, 'in Article 9 the wording "in accordance with the user profile and access rights" is connected to the search launched by the officer instead of being related to the response he or she receives. The last sentence of Article 9 (6) seems to suggest that "where necessary" the officer could have access to additional information beyond what the officer is authorized to see.' The unclear wording of Article 9 could lead to different interpretations, and to its implementation in a way that is not in accordance with the principle of purpose limitation of data in the GDPR.[19]

Second, the interoperable sharing of data that originates with national authorities for purposes other than those underlying the contexts in which the data is being shared (in the respective legal instruments related to the databases in question) may inevitably affect the rights of persons related to the use of data and to what extent this is instrumental in making decisions regarding visa, asylum applications, or residence permits. As a way of exploring these issues, our chapter investigates the practice of interoperability from a specific angle, whether and how what we term the originalism of personal data in the context of EU interoperability affects data access and data use for three different categories of actors: national authorities, EU authorities, and finally individuals, in particular third-country nationals. We use the term 'originalism' in a very loose fashion that does not draw on other very different contexts.[20] We use it to pinpoint the role of data originators in establishing their sharing regime, what can be accessed or not, and under which conditions. Apparently similar to the 'originator control' (ORCON) principle, a principle of information sharing that is based on the originator's power to set up the terms of dissemination and authorize further usage,[21] in our view data originalism has the

The use of the Common Identity Repository is reserved to police authorities (Art. 20(1) Interoperability Regulations). The access to the Multiple Identity Detector is reserved to visa authorities, migration authorities, and ETIAS Central Unit and SIRENE Bureau of the Member State creating and updating a SIS alert (Art. 26(1) Interoperability Regulations).

[19] See Fundamental Rights Agency, *Interoperability and fundamental rights implications. Opinion 1/2018* (2018) 4, https://fra.europa.eu/sites/default/files/fra_uploads/fra-2018-opinion-01-2018-interoperability_en.pdf: 'To ensure compliance with the principle of purpose limitation, the EU legislator should adjust the wording of Art. 9 (1) to make clearer that a search launched by an officer only queries the systems he or she is authorised to access. In addition, the last sentence of Art. 9 (6) should be deleted.'

[20] Used to describe theories based on the original understanding of the US Constitution at the time it was adopted. See further, R. W. Bennet and L. B. Solum, *Constitutional Originalism: A Debate* (2011); S. G. Calabresi (ed.), *Originalism. A Quarter-Century of Debate* (2007).

[21] This principle is largely used in the field of classified information sharing in the EU, see Decision of the Bureau of the European Parliament of 15 April 2013, OJ 2013 C 96/1; Commission Decision (EU, Euratom) 2019/1961 of 17 October 2019, OJ 2019 L 311/1. On examples of dissemination requirements,

advantage that it focuses on the source of information, namely data, in a twofold manner. Only users holding certain data can launch a query, but the data available through the access to interoperable components can be data originated by different users. This means that data originated in the databases will not necessarily be interoperable, because only data present in the databases and also belonging to users who query the interoperable components may become interoperable.

With the term 'originalism', we aim to shed light on the interplay between the original legal status of shared personal data and the effects of data sharing over time in the interoperability context. In this way we delve into the technical and legal details in a manner that we hope fills a gap in the literature and sheds more light on the important political dimension and the broader implications of a seemingly limited technical debate.

In the context of data-driven Europe, this analysis urges us to reflect on the various layers of transparency that are at the core of interoperability logic. However, in an operational context, such as the interoperability of information systems, this means decoding transparency in a certain sense, since the system is already technically designed to ensure transparency. This reveals, in practice, the tendency of some data originators to behave as if they are data owners. We aim to provide legal and operational arguments to reject the idea of applying ownership in the personal data context and to propose an alternative framework to address issues of personal data usage by public authorities. We argue that certain prerogatives on data usage and data access should be made transparent to the users of interoperable components as well as to individuals whose data is processed. This objective braids together the conceptual threads of data originalism as a framework that limits the powers of originators to misuse personal data.

Our chapter is structured as follows: Section 2 introduces interoperability of migration and security information systems in the EU; Section 3 discusses a shift of paradigm from no interconnection between information that is integrated into databases to the interoperability of information systems that makes this interconnection effective; Section 4 introduces and explains the relevance of the notion of data originalism in the context of interoperability and why it does not overlap with the concept of originator control; Section 5 identifies the rationales that could pull together the concepts of data ownership and data originalism, discussing the main reasons a right in personal data cannot be

see Jin and Ahn, 'Role-based Access Management for Ad-hoc Collaborative Sharing', Proceedings of the 11th ACM Symposium on Access Control Models and Technologies (2006).

considered as a proprietary right and why this is relevant for data sharing; finally, Section 6 tries to elaborate on interoperability as a model of data unownability where integrated data is in origin personal but at the same time shared by other actors.

2. Locating Interoperable Information Systems in the EU

One of the defining characteristics of the (traditional) European administrative space is the complexity of the EU's mechanisms for gathering, processing, and distributing information.[22] In recent years, automation at the supranational level has evolved from rather informal beginnings in particular in the AFSJ to an intricate array of separately constituted databases. The web of databases not only increased through separate arrangements with national authorities of one kind or another but also through their many interconnections, as Vavoula has well documented.[23] Many different arrangements existed—and continue to exist—that link not only the national databases with supranational ones but also the supranational databases to each other, and at times (for certain actors, e.g. Europol) also to third parties or states. Over time, a fragmented system of relations was put in place governing relations between different state authorities at different governance levels in the EU and involving (personal) data collected for different purposes and shared with a growing number of actors.

Interoperability is an ambitious and widespread policy objective at the European level that—up until a few years ago—had taken shape in scattered bits and pieces and had not been the subject of much legal or institutional analysis outside of data protection.[24] However, the adoption of specific EU legislation regulating the principle of interoperability in a specific context meant that the supranational and the national were formally linked. In May 2019, the EU legislator adopted two important regulations establishing a framework for interoperability between specific new-EU information systems in the field of police and judicial cooperation, asylum, and migration,[25] and in the field of

[22] Hofmann, 'Seven Challenges for EU Administrative Law', in K. de Graaf, J. Jans, A. Prechal, and R. Widdershoven (eds), *European Administrative Law: Top-Down and Bottom-up* (2009) 37, at 53.

[23] N. Vavoula, *Immigration and Privacy in the Law of the European Union: The Case of Information Systems* (2022).

[24] F. Boehm, *Information Sharing and Data Protection in the Area of Freedom, Security and Justice, towards Harmonized Data Protection Principles for Information Exchange at EU-Level* (2012) 7. But see on migration management, Mitsilegas, 'The Borders Paradox: The Surveillance of Movement in a Union without Internal Frontiers' in H. Lindahl (ed.), *A Right to Inclusion and Exclusion? Normative Fault Lines of the EU's Area of Freedom, Security and Justice* (2015) 55.

[25] Regulation (EU) 2019/818 (n. 16).

borders and visa.[26] At the same time, the existing—fragmented—rules on collection, sharing, access, and use remained in place. The new regulations came in addition to the existing largely tertiary rules and provided secondary rules for specific new databases.[27] In fact, their ambition is to keep sectoral legal regimes of single databases autonomous, while providing an organic framework that connects their functionalities. It is obvious that interoperability of information systems is thus not only to be understood as technical but also as legal.

The rationale of both sets of rules—secondary and tertiary—is that border guards, customs authorities, police officers, and judicial authorities in the Member States need easier access to personal data for operational reasons to carry out their AFSJ-related tasks.[28] Information sharing in the new secondary legislation is integrated into six databases[29] that are made interoperable through 'interoperable components':[30] a European search portal, a shared biometric matching service, a common identity repository (CIR), and a multiple identity detector. The interoperable components also cover Europol data, but only to the extent of enabling Europol data to be queried simultaneously with these other EU information systems. The main objectives of interoperability in this system are to safeguard security at Member State level and in the AFSJ, ensure effectiveness of border management, and to fight against illegal migration and serious crimes. These objectives will be realized through the identification of persons,[31] requiring processing of a huge amount of personal data in the EU information systems that may rely on 'different or incomplete identities'.[32] To give an example, we can imagine that information on previous convictions handed down against third-country nationals by criminal courts in the EU (ECRIS-TCN) is matched with alerts on persons (refusals of entry or stay, EU arrest warrant, missing persons, judicial procedure assistance, discreet and specific checks—and objects—including lost, stolen and invalidated identity or travel documents), or with fingerprint data of asylum applicants and

[26] Regulation (EU) 2019/817 (n. 17).

[27] See the interesting debate between Hart and Dworkin based on two seminal works by these authors: H. L. A. Hart, *The Concept of Law* (2012); R. Dworkin, 'The Model of Rules', 35(1) *University of Chicago Law Review* (1967), 14.

[28] Vavoula, 'Interoperability of EU Information Systems in a "Panopticon" Union: A Leap Towards Maximised Use of Third-Country Nationals' Data or a Step Backwards in the Protection of Fundamental Rights?', in V. Mitsilegas and N. Vavoula (eds), *Surveillance and Privacy in the Digital Age. European, Transatlantic and Global Perspectives* (2021).

[29] The Entry/Exit System (EES), the Visa Information System (VIS), the European Travel Information and Authorisation System (ETIAS), Eurodac, the Schengen Information System (SIS), and the European Criminal Records Information System for third-country nationals (ECRIS-TCN).

[30] Art. 1 Regulations (EU) 2019/817 and 2019/818 (hereinafter 'the Interoperability Regulations').

[31] Ibid. Art. 2(2)(a).

[32] Ibid. Recital 22 and Art. 3.

third-country nationals who have crossed the external borders irregularly or who are illegally staying in a Member State (Eurodac). This data set puts together bits and pieces of personal identities, as recently also acknowledged by the Proposal for the Artificial Intelligence Regulation (AI Act).[33] It classifies AI systems in the area of migration, asylum and border control management as high-risk AI systems[34] because they affect people who are often in a particularly vulnerable position and who are dependent on the outcome of the actions of the competent public authorities.[35]

Many technical issues remain unclear due to the complexity and the lack of practice in the field. The profiles of interoperable users[36] do not include any indication of a requirement on the originator (the national or European authority) to impose rules and limits on the data being shared. Moreover, the Regulation stipulates that the use of the European search portal 'shall be reserved to the Member State authorities and Union agencies having access to at least one of the EU information systems'[37] and that their scope applies to 'persons in respect of whom personal data may be processed in the EU information systems'.[38] This legal framework sheds light on the symmetric logic that informs interoperable information systems according to which access to interoperable data belongs to those authorities that may process data included in the single databases, but its general character does not clarify the role of data originators with respect to those authorities and their mutual relationships. For example, in 2021 eu-LISA published the list of designated authorities that have access to data recorded in Eurodac;[39]however, it is not clear whether those designated authorities can also use interoperable components.

It is not merely a matter of transparency of the rules, if any,[40] but also of a more structural type of transparency of the system as a whole (as opposed to any kind of operational transparency).[41] Is there any EU actor that can step

[33] European Commission, COM/2021/206 final.

[34] Recital 39 Proposal for the Artificial Intelligence Regulation, European Commission, COM/2021/206 final.

[35] On the marginalization of vulnerable data subjects, see Malgieri and Niklas, 'Vulnerable Data Subjects', 37 *Computer Law & Security Review* (2020).

[36] Art. 8 Interoperability Regulations.

[37] Ibid. Art. 7(1).

[38] Art. 3(2) Regulation (EU) 2019/817 and Art. 3(3) Regulation (EU) 2019/818.

[39] eu-LISA, 'List of designated authorities that have access to data recorded in the Central System of Eurodac pursuant to Art. 27(2) of the Regulation (EU) No 603/2013, for the purpose laid down in Art. 1(1) of the same Regulation' (2021).

[40] See Section 3.

[41] See an extensive conceptualization of transparency in studies on access to official documents, Curtin and Leino, 'In Search of Transparency for EU Law-Making: Trialogues on the Cusp of Dawn', 54(5) *Common Market Law Review* (2017) 1673; D. Curtin and P. Leino-Sandberg, *Openness, Transparency and the Right of Access to Documents in the EU* (2016).

into the breach? Can for example, eu-LISA—the EU agency responsible for the operational management of large-scale IT systems—require originators to formulate (transparent) legal rules applying conditions on how shared data is made accessible? The interplay between the ambition of operational transparency of data sharing and the legal gaps emerging from the informality of practices aimed to fill those gaps invites us to reflect upon a model of data-driven interoperability that aligns the technical performance with responsibility for its single steps. This implies engaging with the substantial layers of transparency in data sharing that would ascribe responsibilities for all the steps required to build up a data sharing process, and not only for data breaches that are traceable operationally. This approach, if combined with a realistic recognition of the powers of data originators in granting access to designated subjects, can neutralize the detrimental effects of data misuse on individuals whose data may be accessed and used or whose access can be denied or limited.

3. From Systemic Opacity to Transparent Interoperability

Interoperable information systems in the context of the AFSJ are, in a significant sense, the cutting edge of the EU's system of administrative governance—truly an 'administration of information'.[42] The sophisticated informational cooperation implied in data sharing indicates novel frontiers in European governance in a way that potentially at any rate shifts existing boundaries in terms of law and practice.[43] It effectively links up different databases existing in the Member States and at the European level through the mechanism of interoperability. Bridging the 'information gaps' between these databases,[44] interoperable information systems have the ambition of overcoming the fragmentation of information that is used and shared often multiple times. The plurality of public actors that use (algorithmic) data operationally (for example, national border control officers and immigration officials, police and customs enforcement authorities, as well as a number of EU agencies) profoundly shapes the nature of information sharing. It blurs automation and discretion or at the very least makes it (very) fuzzy. Once information systems are joined up and made

[42] H. Hofmann, G. Rowe, and A. Türk, *Administrative Law and Policy of the European Union* (2011) 411.

[43] See Brito Bastos and Curtin, 'Interoperable Information Sharing and the Five Novel Frontiers of EU Governance: A Special Issue', 26(1) *European Public Law* (2020) 59.

[44] Vavoula, 'Interoperability of EU Information Systems: The Deathblow to the Rights to Privacy and Personal Data Protection of Third-Country Nationals?' 26(1) *European Public Law* (2020) 131, at 134.

interoperable, the basic principle of *purpose limitation* enshrined in data protection law at Article 8(2) of the Charter and Article 5(2) GDPR—according to which data shall be 'collected for specified, explicit and legitimate purposes and not further processed in a manner that is incompatible with those purposes'—is at risk of not being applied in practice as data is shared and further processed.[45] It follows that data gathering and data usage are in practice divorced from the purposes for which they were originally collected or shared. This reality of linked-up data, which is factually disconnected from the purpose for which it was gathered, should at the very least in our view be technologically transparent. The type of transparency that is envisaged is partial and is only designed to reveal which actors can access interoperable data but does not envisage making the content of such data itself accessible as operational secrecy can be reasonably claimed in sensitive decision-making.

In fact, what interoperability makes evident is that the principle of transparency has different implications when applied to the technical functioning of operational tools or merely as a legal principle inspiring data processing. Keeping logs of access to interoperable components, for instance, is far from being a transparent form of governance if nobody knows what those logs mean and if they only offer retrospective analysis of the probable behaviour of users within the interoperable environment.[46] The slippery threshold between technological transparency, as a means of giving authorities full control over individual identities, and legal transparency, as a protective legal principle giving individuals access to their data when used in decision-making affecting them, is not always clear. This is especially the case when the goals of legal tools, such as the Interoperability Regulations, depend upon their technical feasibility and the concept of transparency becomes rather a 'functionality of the system' that is inherent in the technical performance rather than a substantial requirement.

What could transparent interoperability mean in practice? Would it only cover the recording of data matching between databases or would it entail the actual tracking of data usage? The CIR, for example, creates an individual file for each person that is registered in each of the six databases.[47] Imagine, however, that one or more of these files contains mistakes. If this mistaken

[45] Vavoula, 'Consultation of EU Immigration Databases for Law Enforcement Purposes: A Privacy and Data Protection Assessment', 22(2) *European Journal of Migration and Law* (2020) 139; for an analysis of the first wave of centralized databases based on purpose limitation principle, see Vavoula, 'Databases for Non-EU nationals and the Right to Private Life: Towards a System of Generalized Surveillance of Movement?', in F. Bignami (ed.), *EU Law in Populist Times: Crises and Prospects* (2020) 227, at 231–232.

[46] See Curtin and de Goede, Chapter 6, this volume.

[47] Art. 17 Interoperability Regulations.

information leads to a match—that is, to the 'existence of a correspondence as a result of an automated comparison between personal data recorded or being recorded in an information system or database'[48]—a third-country national who lawfully entered a Member State could be wrongly suspected of a crime because of inaccurate or wrong data. The result could be that a preventive measure is imposed on a third-country national depriving her of her liberty. In what sense could access to her data included in the CIR be useful to the exercise of her rights to reverse an administrative decision based on the processing of that data? Should she be allowed to know only those users who accessed her data during the time period in question or should she also have the right to know what those users have done with that data?

These questions suggest an inner core of opacity since interoperability in practice challenges the fact that EU competences, largely based on law enforcement cooperation, exclude, as a matter of general principle, cooperation between (domestic) security services and (foreign) intelligence services.[49] If, for example, police authorities identify an individual and subsequently exclude them from the EU territory relying on random identity checks at national level (using data matching with interoperable components as now stipulated by the Interoperability Regulations[50]) this has multiple individual and systemic effects. It not only obviously affects the rights and interests of the targeted individuals but it also represents a frontier in terms of our traditional understandings of the basis of 'shared' administration in the legal and political system of the EU, broadly considered as a functional integration of national and Union executives and administrations.[51] It in fact affects the trust among law enforcement and policing institutions as well as the broader issue of equality of national authorities.[52]

Law enforcement and migration are areas where this is paradigmatic. If, in theory, nation states shall be granted equal conditions in data access, in practice the interoperability legal framework establishes that these conditions rely on the data that nation states themselves have with which to launch a query.

[48] Ibid. Art. 4(18).

[49] Arts 4 TEU and Arts 72, 73, and 88 TFEU.

[50] See Art. 20 Interoperability Regulations.

[51] See Hofmann and Türk, 'The Development of Integrated Administration in the EU and Its Consequences', 13 *European Law Journal* (2007) 253; Vavoula (n. 44) 146; P. Craig, *EU Administrative Law* (2018) 80. See also on the concept of European composite administration O. Jansen and B. Schöndorf-Haubold (eds), *The European Composite Administration* (2011).

[52] Aden, 'Information Sharing, Secrecy and Trust Among Law Enforcement and Secret Service Institutions in the European Union', 41(4) *West European Politics* (2018) 981, at 991–993; Brouwer, 'Interoperability and Interstate Trust: A Perilous Combination for Fundamental Rights', *Verfassungsblog* (2019), https://verfassungsblog.de/interoperability-of-databases-and-interstate-trust-a-perilous-combination-for-fundamental-rights/ (last visited 25 February 2022).

If police authorities query the CIR with the data of a person and the results indicate that this data is stored in this interoperable component, then these authorities shall have access to this data[53] and may use it in practice to issue an arrest mandate for this person. This person—who is more likely to be an undocumented migrant, an unaccompanied minor, or an asylum seeker—does not have any knowledge (or indeed any means of having that knowledge) that her data has been accessed by police through the EU-wide CIR nor will she know who provided that data originally. On top of that, she may not speak the same language as the border authorities so even basic communication will be a challenge. In addition, at times the identification procedure issued by border authorities may be based on incorrect biometric data and will need to be manually verified by the authority of the country where the third-country national applies for a short-stay visa or a residence permit. Should those data be inaccurate or wrong and refer to another person, which authority is then responsible in the event of data misuse? What shall such an authority do in practice in order to avoid detrimental effects for individuals deriving from data use in further administrative proceedings affecting them? Is the authority responsible for the manual verification of data or does the responsibility lie with the originator of incomplete/uncorrected data?

Beyond the framing of transparency, interoperability in fact obscures different layers of power relationships that derive from data control. What Bignami calls 'spillover from borders to policing and criminal justice'[54] has its drawback on the lack of effective participation of individuals in the administrative proceedings regarding them that rely on data processing. This is particularly significant if we consider that these individuals will mainly be, in practice, non-EU third-country nationals.[55] For example, the regulation governing the European Travel Information and Authorisation System (ETIAS)[56] stipulates that visa authorities shall consult the Entry/Exit System (EES) when examining visa applications and adopting decisions relating to those applications, including decisions to annul, revoke, or extend the period of validity of an issued visa.[57] What's more, the border or immigration authorities are to have access to fingerprint and facial image databases to identify any third-country

[53] Art. 20 Interoperability Regulations.

[54] Bignami, 'Introduction. EU Law in Populist Times: Crises and Prospect', in F. Bignami (ed.), *EU Law in Populist Times: Crises and Prospect* (2020) 14.

[55] Groenendijk, 'Nothing New Under the Sun? Interoperability of EU Justice and Home Databases', *Un-Owned Personal Data Blog Forum*, https://migrationpolicycentre.eu/interoperability-eu-justice-databases/.

[56] Regulation (EU) 2018/1240, OJ 2018 L 236/1 (hereinafter 'ETIAS Regulation').

[57] Ibid. Art. 24.

national who may have been registered previously in the EES under a different identity.[58]

One of the most relevant variables affecting power relationships is the asymmetry in data usage by those users who originate data to share with specific other 'users'. The data protection rights of third-country nationals are strongly curtailed as the Interoperability Regulations only in fact provide information rights, right of access, rectification, or erasure.[59] The real issue is that the data subjects should know if their data is included within interoperable components and also who originated their personal data in that form in order to fully exercise their information rights. On top of that, not all data stored in the databases can be accessed by users of interoperable information systems. They can only access data from authorities that have it in their possession (or matched with other data in their possession). If, for example, the EES originates some data that is then stored in the CIR, how could a national authority in practice launch a query of the CIR without having the same matching data to input into the query? These seemingly purely technical questions reveal serious underlying issues in terms of relevance of data used because only matched data can be used to launch a query, but it is hard—if not impossible—for individuals to know if there is also other data included in the databases that national authorities do not have, and therefore cannot be made interoperable. Moreover, at least in terms of individual identification through the matching of personal data, this complex architecture reveals important shortcomings that could prejudice the effective rights of third-country nationals. It may happen in fact that incomplete data is not used by the same authority that included it in the databases, but by other users, either by respecting or otherwise the indications provided by data originators but not necessarily visibly.

Personal data integrated in the databases by national officers can become further searchable and accessible to some other EU agencies (providing specific arrangements have been made with them) or to national authorities in other Member States which may want to rely on that data in their own national context.[60] Once a query in the European search portal is launched, a few actors—the four interoperable components, the six databases, Europol, and Interpol—provide the data they hold.[61] If data is provided in the interoperable

[58] Ibid. Art. 27.

[59] Arts 47 and 48 Interoperability Regulations.

[60] European Data Protection Supervisor (n. 13) 6. Brouwer, 'Large-Scale Databases and Interoperability in Migration and Border Policies: The Non-Discriminatory Approach of Data Protection', 26(1) *European Public Law* (2020) 71.

[61] Art. 9 Interoperability Regulations.

components, the reply to the query has to also indicate to which information system or database that data belongs. In this sense data moves beyond various governance borders—territorial, functional, interindividual—in such a fluid way that it is not always easy to identify the originator. It entails different layers of data sharing—at the same time technical, legal, operational, institutional, and informal. Depending on the effective power of the data originators, information can be manipulated, changed, or labelled differently but also logged in certain ways and shared at various levels to which different terms of sharing apply. In the daily practice of data sharing,[62] it seems that once some actors, in particular law enforcement authorities, appropriate data, they effectively posture in their relationships with other parties as if they were the data originators, in order to prevent data access and further use by other actors. In doing so, they can exert discretion in the manner they dispose of data through data exchanges with their power to grant or refuse data access to individuals or other authorities.

What does this mean in practice in the context of data sharing for law enforcement purposes? Does it only mean that decisions that are based on allegedly wrong identifications cannot be easily reversed or does it imply control during the whole process of data usage underpinning individual identification? If it is understood as individual control during the whole process, what can the affected individuals do to combat a choice not to make data available nor to communicate to data subjects the use of their data nor for which purposes?[63]Moreover, are we sure that technological transparency is the solution to limit discretion in granting access or denying access to data?

Interoperability opens a Pandora's box that goes far beyond technological concerns. Crucial values and legal principles—such as the non-discrimination of third-country nationals with respect to EU citizens or data protection safeguards—in addition to the general formal compliance with fundamental rights[64]are in practice negated. This happens within the context of administrative proceedings within a cumbersome technological architecture so that it is difficult to distinguish the separate phases in the process of information sharing. The challenge behind the concept and application of interoperability

[62] Milieu, 'Study on the Practice of Direct Exchanges of Personal Data between Europol and Private Parties' (2020), https://www.statewatch.org/media/1493/eu-com-europol-private-parties-data-exchange-study-full.pdf (last visited 18 December 2021). See also Galli, 'Interoperable Law Enforcement Cooperation Challenges in the EU Area of Freedom, Security and Justice', *EUI Working Paper RSCAS 2019/15* (2019), https://cadmus.eui.eu/bitstream/handle/1814/61045/RSCAS201915.pdf?sequence=1&isAllowed=y, last visited 20 September 2021.

[63] Curtin, 'Second Order Secrecy and Europe's Legality Mosaics', 41(4) *West European Politics* (2018) 846, at 857.

[64] Art. 5 Interoperability Regulations.

is to ensure the immediate and integral transparency of the full process of information sharing, and not merely data included in a users query to interoperable components at the disposal of those users. The next section aims to shed light on how these technical mechanisms enabling interoperability may be strictly dependent on the manner in which data was first included in the original databases.

4. From Originator Control to Interoperable Data Originalism?

The ORCON principle is widely used in the field of information sharing, in particular by the intelligence community globally, when exchanging classified information. This is a designation that is given to certain types of information (knowledge that can be communicated in any form) to protect against unauthorized disclosure.[65] It follows that recipients of such information need the originators' approval prior to sharing the information. Also the extraction of information by automated systems and its sharing can be thus controlled by the originators of the information or data, who 'maintain knowledge, supervision and control of the distribution of ORCON information beyond its original dissemination'.[66] This principle has been over the years integrated into existing EU law at various levels.[67] Information sharing regimes established in the legal instruments of the interoperable databases as well as Europol are largely based

[65] In the field of information security originators are entitled the power to control the usage and further dissemination of information, see Park and Sandhu, 'Originator Control in Usage Control', *Proceedings Third International Workshop on Policies for Distributed Systems and Networks* (2002); Thomas and Sandhu, 'Towards a Multi-dimensional Characterization of Dissemination Control', *Proceedings of the Fifth IEEE International Workshop on Policies for Distributed Systems and Networks* (2004); Janicke, Sarrab, and Aldabbas, 'Controlling Data Dissemination', in J. Garcia-Alfaro, G. Navarro-Arribas, N. Cuppens-Boulahia, and S. de Capitani di Vimercati (eds), *Data Privacy Management and Autonomous Spontaneus Security, Vol. 7122. Lecture Notes in Computer Science* (2012), at 303; Kelbert, 'Data Usage Control for the Cloud', *Proceedings of the 13th IEEE/ACM International Symposium on Cluster, Cloud and Grid Computing* (2013), at 156. In the field of digital rights management technology usability obstacles depend on licenses' policies that hinder interoperability. In this way the protection of contents and rights management issues are necessarily connected in a digital environment and can be compatible only within an interoperable environment. See Iannella, 'Open Digital Rights Language', (ODRL) Version 1.1., Open Digital Rights Language (ODRL) Version 1.1. (2002), http://www.w3.org/TR/odrl/; 'Digital Rights Management (DRM) Architectures', in D-Lib Magazine 7.6 (2001).

[66] Intelligence Community Policy Guidance 710.1, https://fas.org/irp/dni/icd/icpg710-1.pdf, p. 2 (last visited 20 September 2021).

[67] See, for example, Art. 4(5) of the Commission Regulation 1029/2001, OJ 2001 L 144/1: 'A Member State may request the institution not to disclose a document originating from that Member State without its prior agreement'. See Curtin, 'Keeping Government Secrecy Safe: Beyond a Whack-a-Mole', Max Weber Lecture 2011/7 (2011) 8–9, https://cadmus.eui.eu/bitstream/handle/1814/18641/MWPLS Curtin201107rev.pdf?sequence=3 (last visited 18 September 2021); Curtin, 'Overseeing Secrets in the EU: A Democratic Perspective', 52(3) *Journal of Common Market Studies* (2014) 684.

on this principle. For example, Europol may process information for a purpose other than the one for which it has been provided only if authorized by the provider of information who, at the moment of sharing, can also indicate restriction to data access or data use.[68] The provider of information can be a Member State, a Union body, a third country, or an international organization, but if it is a Member State, it has the power to access all personal data stored by Europol for cross-checking of suspects or analysis of a strategic or thematic nature. The Eurodac Regulation also provides that in the case of international protection, only Member States of origin can have access to data they have transmitted to the Central System of Eurodac but not to those of other Member States.[69] Access to data stored in ETIAS is generally allowed to border authorities only to obtain the travel authorization status of a traveller present at an external border crossing point and only under strict requirements,[70] while it is allowed to immigration authorities only to obtain the travel authorization status of a traveller present on the territory of the Member State.[71] Detailed rules in the EES govern entering, amending, consulting, and erasing data[72] in the same way that rules in the Schengen Information System (SIS) govern accessing and reviewing alerts.[73]

The principle of originator control has also recently been included in the Data Governance Act precisely in the field of personal data sharing, although this instrument relates to personal data stored by public sector bodies and does not apply to data protected for reasons of national security, defence, or public security.[74] Article 2 defines 'data holders' as legal persons or data subjects who 'have the right to grant access to or to share certain personal or non-personal data under its control'; 'data users' as natural or legal persons who 'have lawful access to certain personal or non-personal data and are authorized to use that data for commercial or non-commercial purposes'; 'data sharing' as the 'provision by a data holder of data to a data user for the purpose of joint or individual use of the shared data, based on voluntary agreements, directly or through an intermediary'. It follows from this provision that data holders can both grant access under specific requirements or fully share data. Depending on the option they choose, the status of the data will be different in the sense

[68] Art. 19, Regulation (EU) 2016/794, consolidated version amended by Regulation (EU) 2022/991 of the European Parliament and of the Council of 8 June 2022, OJ 2016 L 135/53 (hereinafter 'Europol Regulation').

[69] Art. 27 Regulation (EU) 2013/603, OJ 2013 L 180/1 (hereinafter 'Eurodac Regulation').

[70] Art. 13(2) ETIAS Regulation.

[71] Art. 13(4) ETIAS Regulation.

[72] Art. 9 Regulation (EU) 2017/2226, OJ 2017 L 327/20 (hereinafter 'EES Regulation').

[73] Art. 44 Regulation (EU) 2018/1862, OJ 2018 L 312/56 (hereinafter 'SIS Regulation').

[74] Art. 3(2)(d) Data Governance Act.

that originators may or may no longer play any role. The new definition included in this proposal is very helpful in the wider context of interoperability.

Rules of data sharing are most relevant for the functioning of interoperable information systems, in particular the alignment of technical and legal feasibility of operational instruments. The way in which originators set clear rules of access to personal data may play a significant role in preventing the appropriation of data and its possible misuse. These rules might also include specification of the meaning to be given to certain data or some interpretation guidelines provided by originators for those users who reuse data that has already been used for certain purposes. The concept of the reuse of data, even if it is not expressly included, is central to the interoperable logic. Interoperability implies data re-use, but re-use cannot be fully controlled unless only technically by keeping logs as a way to conduct a purely retrospective analysis.[75] Depending on how reuse is operationalized, it can systemize the practice of sharing and (re)use of shared data in administrative proceedings that affect the rights and interests of third-country nationals. One of the key issues in the Data Governance Act is the concept and limits of data reuse.[76] It provides, in Article 5, that public sector bodies are allowed to grant or refuse access to data reuse and must make publicly available the conditions imposed for such reuse in relation to the type of data and the purposes of its reuse. Among the conditions that can be set up, public sector bodies can also impose obligations that guarantee additional safeguards upon reuse. Another complementary piece of legislation, the proposal for a regulation on harmonized rules on fair access to and use of data (the Data Act), also provides specific obligations for data holders to share data with public sector bodies and EU institutions, agencies or bodies based on exceptional needs, such as a public emergency, upon specific demonstration of an exceptional need.[77]

In the context of interoperability, the act of data sharing establishes multiple power relationships and related responsibilities. According to the originator control principle, originators have the power to share or not and to impose conditions. However, once data is shared within interoperable components, shaping identities through personal data that is subject to multipurposed processing is something that data originators can do but individuals cannot. Personal data shared as interoperable information aims to 'build identities', by

[75] Arts 10, 16, 24, and 36 Interoperability Regulations.

[76] Art. 5 Regulation (EU) 2022/868, OJ 2022 L 152/1 (Data Governance Act).

[77] Arts. 14, 15 and 17(b) European Commission, Regulation of the European Parliament and of the Council on harmonized rules on fair access to and use of data (Data Act), COM/2022/68 final (Data Act).

ensuring the correct identification of persons.[78] Individuals are *de jure* granted the right to the protection of personal data but not the right to 'own their identity' in the sense of setting rules on the access and usage of data related to them. This prerogative belongs to those authorities who share data into databases and allows other interoperable actors to access that same data. Building identities through the identification of persons may be the result of a discretionary activity by authorities who are willing to input data into interoperable databases. Or they may be prevented from sharing data or share data only with actors they want to grant discretionary access to. Finally, they may choose not to share the personal data or multiprocessed data at all. If we look for example at the ECRIS-TCN Regulation, what emerges is a complete shift from individual control to originator control of the data imposed by the Member States in the context of criminal records. Pursuant to Article 9 of this regulation, Member States may modify or erase the data that they have input into ECRIS-TCN, but individuals may not do so. Only the liability regime of most databases includes individuals and Member States among the subjects who may suffer material or non-material damage as a result of an unlawful processing operation and who may seek compensation from the responsible Member State or eu-LISA.[79] This implies that the margin of individual control during proceedings affecting them is really not existing, while the only remedy is to seek damages once the right to access, erasure, rectification is denied.[80]

Once data is shared, it no longer belongs to the originator in the sense that the originator cannot decide to revoke the 'shared status' of data nor can it control its further use. However, data originators who choose to share data can still elaborate the technical and legal rules under which that data has been shared. For example, such rules could require that data usage is limited to the original meaning that originators attribute to data. Our analysis aims to assess whether the power of data originators to authorize uses even for non-classified information enables them to set usage conditions: for example, to (a) grant or deny access to data; (b) use data without interference by third parties; (c) grant access to data under certain conditions (for example, limiting its further use); and (d) provide unequivocally the meaning according to which data is to be interpreted and used. These putative conditions can be met by setting rules

[78] Art. 2(2)(a) Interoperability Regulations.

[79] Art. 20 Regulation (EU) 2019/816, OJ 2019 L 135/2 (ECRIS-TCN Regulation), Art. 63 Regulation (EU) 2018/1240, OJ 2018 L 236/1 (ETIAS Regulation), Art. 72 Regulation (EU) 2018/1862, consolidated text as amended by Regulation (EU) 2022/1190, OJ L 2018 312/57

(SIS Regulation), and Art. 33 Regulation (EC) 767/2008, consolidated version 3.8.2022, OJ 2008 L 218/60 (VIS Regulation).

[80] Arts 25 and 27 ECRIS-TCN Regulation.

for dissemination and usage, such as those provided for in dissemination controls: pre-approval, according to which 'the originator may identify a user, set of users, or type of use for this information or may pre-approve new users as a result of requests made on behalf of new recipients'; and further dissemination that 'may only occur as a result of originator permission or pre-approval'.[81]

We argue that interoperability, if fully achieved, shall in effect dismantle the arbitrary element of the principle of originator control or else coexist with it. The latter can only happen if the rules of sharing set up by data originators are transparently shared at the same time as the information to be shared.

Data originalism in the context of the interoperability of personal data presupposes the origin of data as *shared information* under conditions laid down by the data originators. This assumption has been elaborated from initial textual references included in both Regulations. Article 18 of the Interoperability Regulations states that the CIR—one of the four interoperable components—stores data '*logically separated according to the information system from which the data have originated*'[82] and that for each set of data it '*shall include a reference to the EU information systems to which data belong*'.[83] Nonetheless, interoperability of information sharing does not imply for data originators an obligation to share, with the result that data that are made interoperable may not be all relevant data needed to ground a decision. This is in particular the case with regard to national and EU law enforcement authorities and their frequent use of migration and borders data to combat crimes.[84] In fact, the consultation of interoperable components is generally limited to double-checking those data that are used to start a query in those components, unless there 'are reasonable grounds to believe that consultation of EU information systems will contribute to the prevention, detection or investigation of terrorist offences and other serious criminal offences'.[85] In this case the designated authorities and Europol may request information of the CIR and not just double-check matching data.

Given that the aims and the operation of interoperable information systems should take into account the need to balance respect for fundamental rights, their functioning in practice could, we argue, vary a lot depending on whether interoperable users might only be aware of the existence of information through the so-called system of 'flagged hits' or they might have direct

[81] Office of the Director of National Intelligence, *Intelligence Community Policy Guideline 710.1* (2012) 7.

[82] Emphasis added.

[83] Emphasis added.

[84] V. Mitsilegas, 'The Preventive Turn in European Security Policy: Towards a Rule of Law Crisis?' in F. Bignami (ed.), *EU Law in Populist Times* (2019) 301.

[85] Art. 22 Interoperability Regulations.

access to information. In terms of actual practices, some agencies, such as Europol, and some databases, such as Eurodac (but also SIS 2), for example, adopted the ORCON principle following the first option (a system of flagged hits). Member States who originated the data must first be notified of a 'hit' by another Member State and only then will they decide whether or not to disclose the contents of the information in question. The choice between full disclosure or partial disclosure of hits can profoundly influence the authorities' conduct in investigations and the fairness of procedures. If the actual content is not disclosed, the hits provide only hints regardless of the actual contents. The discretion of originator authorities to disclose or otherwise the actual contents can differ among the authorities. These authorities can, at their discretion, impose non-disclosure obligations for certain data or practice secrecy informally, thus altering the balance between information management and reciprocal scrutiny. The choice between these two alternatives can determine the different degrees of efficiency in practice of the interoperable systems. Similarly, the issue of interoperable data transfers to third parties cannot be maintained with a mere technical prohibition of such transfers, but it will additionally be necessary to create substantive remedies in the event of a breach.[86] In this sense, provisions imposing professional secrecy and a duty of confidentiality on the persons or bodies required to work with interoperable data[87] are at best partial and not sufficient in practice.

At the level of actual practice, the concept of originalism includes both the act of creation of data as information that can—or cannot—be shared according to the specific conditions that are imposed by the data originators as well as the subsequent power to set up specific rules governing sharing. It produces a usage regime of sorts for data that is intended to be applied in accordance with the aims at the time the data was originally put in the system. In this sense, data originators are those who have, in a manner of speaking, a right of disposal over the data they have created.

In line with this concept of originalism as the right to originate information, there are at least two different challenges arising from the practice of data sharing. If we refer to a power in practice to impose rules on access to/use/onward use of data, we rely on what individuals (as data subjects) and authorities who input data into databases (as data originators) can effectively do with the data as a particular form of de facto control. This may resemble the concept

[86] Art. 50 Interoperability Regulations; E. Brouwer, *Digital Borders and Real Rights: Effective Remedies for Third-Country Nationals in the Schengen Information System* (2008).
[87] Art. 43 Interoperability Regulations.

of data ownership only factually if we take into account the broader or narrower degree of disposal powers that originators may have. If we instead rely on full legal control over data transmissibility (*de jure* entitlement), it is relevant whether the discretion of authorities in granting access to data may imply total exclusion of other parties from data disposal.

The operational functioning of interoperability emphasizes the relevance of data originalism as it depends upon the rules set up by those who share data when this data is made interoperable. Interoperability is therefore far from being a transparent neutral architecture where data is automatically shared, and power relationships are deactivated. On the contrary, data sharing always shows the *ability*[88] to overcome the tensions between the power of information and the role played by the actors involved. Data originators can also use their power of sharing of the data they handle in such a way as not to undermine rights of third parties.

Why is originalism then relevant for the practice of information sharing? The specific conditions laid down by national authorities inherent in the act of data origination makes interoperable information sharing either a mere technical means to manage borders and enhance internal security or a tool for preventing originators and in particular law enforcement authorities from exercising too much discretion in data sharing and handling data as if they owned the data on an ongoing basis.

Tracing all interoperable steps would imply: (1) tracking all that happens to data once it is originated and is made interoperable; and (2) also sharing the terms and conditions of sharing set up by originators, as they flow with the data. In this way, each user can be aware of these terms. In practice this entails reducing secrecy in data sharing and enhancing its transparency.[89] If rules set up by originators are known, data sharing becomes normatively transparent and not only in principle or technically. In this sense Article 22 of the Interoperability Regulations seems ambiguous when it states that the reply to queries indicating that certain personal data are present in any of the EU information systems shall be used only for the purposes of submitting a request for full access of data. In other words, this means that queries of data coming from originators and access to data for designated authorities and Europol are strictly interlinked and usually one to one. They will be more likely the same subjects and there is not much control of the accuracy and the correspondence

[88] Interoperability is defined as the 'ability of information systems to exchange data and to enable the sharing of information': https://ec.europa.eu/commission/presscorner/detail/en/MEMO175241 (last visited 20 June 2021).

[89] Curtin (n. 63).

of that data by third parties that may be potentially interested or involved in the process.

A major underlying challenge for interoperability is the necessity to elaborate a horizontal framework within which users, for example, law enforcement authorities, are compelled to cooperate once data is shared. This framework is deeply altered if data is not shared or only shared under certain conditions imposed by originators. If instead it were to be recognized that a responsible role for originators of data is to elaborate transparent rules of data usage once data is made interoperable, this would avoid deadlock. It would follow that neither Member States vis-à-vis other Member States, nor Member States vis-à-vis agencies, for example, Europol, European Border and Coast Guard Agency or eu-LISA, nor third-country nationals vis-à-vis Member States or the authority responsible for the ex post manual verification of identities[90] could behave as if they 'owned' the data.

Interoperability arguably offers a framework enabling this concept of originalism to be compatible under certain conditions with the fact that personal data are not in fact owned by anyone. It in effect facilitates a mechanism to share data that does not involve incremental steps, while at the same time they are made accessible both to interoperable actors and individuals. The variables inherent in this assumption are basically (1) the way in which personal data is used by authorities to deliver administrative decisions affecting individuals, and (2) the transitioning legal position of individuals that is determined by the fact that data moves across interoperable databases changing meaning as well as potentially the purposes of processing.[91]

On the first point, the discretionary nature of administrative decisions is amplified by the blurring of purposes of the data processed by different actors. It is then likely that administrative acts regarding migrants can be justified on the grounds found in data on them and processed in another database. This implies that data usage is opaque if originators do not elaborate transparent rules for sharing.

On the second point, the fact is that individual identities only result in 'datafied' flags, logs and bytes relating, for example, to their biometric data or fingerprints. This may heavily impact the meaning of that data if they are used to determine the legal status of third-country nationals as migrants or asylum seekers, or suspect persons. The way in which matching data is automatically

[90] Art. 29 Interoperability Regulations.

[91] Brouwer, 'Legality and Data Protection Law: The Forgotten Purpose of Purpose Limitation', in L. Besselink, F. Pennings, and S. Prechal (eds), *The Eclipse of the Legality Principle in the European Union* (2011) 273.

operationalized through interoperability, affects the rights *in fieri* of these persons, in the sense that their rights can change based on inaccurate or accurate data on them.[92] The changing status of information may involve different ways of sharing data: data can either be shared among some parties—for example, Member States, and then input into common databases, or it can be originally input into databases as raw data, for example, fragmented information, and reaggregated in view of the purposes pursued by the database in question. Data shared originally in this way (and intrinsically un-owned as a result) cannot be subject to any further specification of disposal by any of the interoperable users nor by originators. This would make it possible for individuals whose data is processed to exactly know why and how some administrative proceedings affecting them are based on that data. This may also avoid individual stigmatization following from the same interpretation of that data in a repeated and not motivated way.

5. Why Data Originalism Challenges Data Ownership

The role of data originators in potentially authorizing all relevant actions related to the subsequent sharing of data[93] needs to be considered in the context of the broader debate on machine-generated personal and non-personal data ownership that has recently featured on the EU agenda.[94] The boundaries of originalism that implies the setting of rules on data usage and preventing the misuse of data by third parties who are not compliant with the originators' rules, lie in the necessity to limit the right of disposal of data by third parties.[95] This is the power data originators enjoy when sharing data and originating it in databases. There are some more comprehensive accounts of what originators rights can consist of: for example, in the field of data espionage and phishing, German Criminal Law enables originators to dispose of clusters of

[92] Art. 37 Interoperability Regulations.

[93] See Curtin (n. 63) 849.

[94] See European Commission, *Building a European Data Economy*, COM (2017) 9 final. As correctly pointed out by J. Drexl, *Data Access and Control in the Era of Connected Devices* (2018) 3: 'The discussion on "who owns the data" runs the risk of ignoring the preliminary question of whether there is a justification for recognising ownership in data. The frequently stated economic value of data does not provide such justification. Quite the contrary, data as information goods are non-rival and, therefore, will not be exhausted by their use. This means that social welfare will in principle be maximized by guaranteeing full access to data. This explains why unrestricted data access should be considered the default rule, while introduction of exclusive rights is in need of a special justification. This analysis is supported by the constitutional principle of freedom of information and the public interest in access to data.'

[95] There is an indication in the profiles created by eu-LISA of the users and types of queries: Art. 8 Interoperability Regulations.

data as goods or they may stipulate agreements on the process of collection, recording, and organization of the data in question preventing access to third parties.[96] Conversely, in the context of interoperability, the public infrastructure that operationalizes data sharing is under the management of eu-LISA and not owned by the originators of data that are input into interoperable components. This also clarifies the policy options presented to support free flows of data.[97] Alternatives are unrestricted access regimes that ensure certain levels of exclusivity.[98] The previous version of Europol Regulation is in fact the only European legal instrument that expressly mentioned the word 'ownership'. It distinguishes ownership of data from the protection of personal data, making it clear that a property right to personal data is not part of the EU legal framework. Furthermore, it poses the issue in terms of access: 'To respect the ownership of data and the protection of personal data, Member States, Union bodies, third countries and international organisations should be able to determine the purpose or purposes for which Europol may process the data they provide and to restrict access rights.'[99]

In this sense, the notion of data originalism comes close to the debate on data ownership if we consider what aspects of this concept are related to a de facto power on the usage regime of the data in question.[100] When exploring this debate it may nonetheless be helpful to understand if and how certain models aimed at granting rights to information can be applied in the context of information sharing. From a methodological perspective, this does not imply a comparative analysis of data ownership in property law and public law, as the purposes are indeed not comparable. It instead entails investigating how a sort of functional equivalence of doctrinal and operational results achieved in the debate on data ownership might be helpful to understand certain linked phenomena in other contexts, such as the one specifically related to the origination of data in the interoperable information systems.

Originators have the power to establish a bundle of defensive rights over data 'to protect the right holder (i.e. themselves) against impairment by third

[96] Boerding *et al.*, 'Data Ownership. A Property Rights Approach from a European Perspective', 11 *Journal of Civil Law Studies* (2018) 323, at 333, 357, and 358.

[97] M. Fink, *Frontex and Human Rights. Responsibility in 'Multi-Actor Situations' under the ECHR and EU Public Liability Law* (2018) at 196–232 (liability for fundamental rights' violations); see also J. Lodge, *Biometrics: A Challenge for Privacy or Public Policy—Certified Identity and Uncertainties* (2007) at 193–206.

[98] F. Mezzanotte, 'The Role of Consent and the Licensing Scheme', in S. Lohsse, R. Schulze, and D. Staudenmayer (eds), *Trading Data in the Digital Economy: Legal Concepts and Tools* (2017) 159.

[99] Recital 26 Europol Regulation (before the amendment of Regulation (EU) 2022/991).

[100] The connection between the concepts of 'sovereignty' and 'property' explains more clearly the idea of a de facto power: Cohen, 'Property and Sovereignty', 13(1) *Cornell Law Review* (1927) 8.

parties'[101]—such as access, dissemination, reuse, exclusion, but also interpretation of the meaning of data, but this power needs to be contextualized within in the context of information sharing.[102] Powers related to data sharing for public purposes, such as those mentioned in the interoperability framework, cannot be compared to property rules as they have different aims and protect different interests. Interoperability thus needs other framing principles to address the limits to the powers related to information sharing rules: horizontal transparency, sharing of purpose limitation principles of single information systems, mutual trust between Member States and interoperable users, etc. In fact, the aim of data originalism within the interoperable context is quite the opposite of a proprietary paradigm: interoperable data is originally shared and therefore not owned by anyone, although it previously 'belonged' to single information systems. Interoperability, therefore, at least in principle, should comply with the principle of free flow of personal information according to which individuals shall be entitled to full oversight mechanisms over their data while originators have the duty to ensure lawful processing but also to be responsible about the impact the data sharing implies as well as its meaning.

Examples of how the originator control principle can impact on originators' duties in practice are to be found in specific AFSJ legal instruments. The Europol Regulation is, for example, based on the ORCON principle, according to which the information shall not be shared without an explicit authorization by the provider.[103] However, Europol may directly transfer personal data: to a Union body, as far as such transfer is necessary for the performance of its tasks or those of the recipient Union body;[104] to third-country authorities or international organizations, according to an adequacy decision of the Commission or an international or cooperation agreement.[105] Article 23 of the Eurodac Regulation expressly qualifies data originators as responsible for ensuring that fingerprints are taken, transmitted, recorded, stored, corrected,

[101] Boerding *et al.* (n. 96) 362. In the field of IP law an example of defensive right is the one of '*shared data with limited access*', defined by Julia Baloup as '(i) any technical or business information that is accumulated in a reasonable amount by electronic or magnetic means (ii) provided to specified persons on a regular basis and (iii) managed by electronic or magnetic means'. See Baloup, 'The European Strategy for Data: EU to Design a Defensive Mechanism to foster B2B Data Sharing?', *CITIP Blog* (2021), https://www.law.kuleuven.be/citip/blog/the-european-strategy-for-data/ (last visited 16 June 2021).

[102] European Commission, 'Commission Staff Working Document on the free flow of data and emerging issues of the European data economy Accompanying the document Communication Building a European data economy', SWD/2017/02 final (2017) 33. See also, on the different but linked concept of 'default entitlement', Malgieri, '"Ownership" of Customer (Big) Data in the European Union: Quasi-Property as Comparative Solution?' 20(5) *Journal of Internet Law* (2016) 2.

[103] Art. 22 Europol Regulation. See n. 3.

[104] Ibid. Art. 24.

[105] Ibid. Art. 25.

erased, and processed lawfully. Finally, the liability regime of the ECRIS-TCN Regulation[106] applies to material or immaterial damages as a result of unlawful processing by Member States or eu-LISA. Ownership plays no role. Nonetheless the fact that data is not 'owned' in any real sense does not prevent its misuse if limits are not set up by the original holders of that data. Tracing all queries to interoperable components and keeping logs of them[107] does not give any account of the way in which data is shared, but only of the way in which data is accessed. The interoperability framework utilizes terms such as 'to belong' or 'data holder'[108] in quite an imprecise way whereas data transparency only results in a partial theoretical principle only showing queries and replies to queries[109] and disregarding how—in which modalities and in what form—data has been originally shared.

The impression may well be then that there is always a sort of hidden 'data owner' behind the curtain pulling the levers in secrecy and that interoperability as it functions (now?) only ensures transparency by making accessible subsequent queries to these data. The implications of data originalism on the mechanisms of control over data sharing and individual rights can usefully be explored in the context of the debate on data ownership within the context of the European Data Strategy. In the field of law enforcement and border management, the context is obviously very different to that of the European digital single market where there is a considerable debate on granting property rights over non-personal and personal machine-generated data[110]—the so-called data producer's right[111]—as prized economic assets.[112]

On the one hand, individuals do not need to exclude others to be granted certain protection, but only need to control what other parties do with their data. On the other hand, users of interoperable components are not bound among themselves by a hierarchical principle, which means that EU and national authorities are not in a position to exclude other interoperable users from data access but only generally third countries.[113] In practice, a framework

[106] Art. 20 Regulation (EU) ECRIS-TCN Regulation.

[107] Arts 16, 24, and 26 Interoperability Regulations.

[108] This terminology is now also included in the Data Governance Act, where Art. 1 defines a data holder as 'a legal person or data subject who, in accordance with applicable Union or national law, has the right to grant access to or to share certain personal or non-personal data under its control'.

[109] Arts 9 and 22 Interoperability Regulations.

[110] European Commission (n. 94) 9.

[111] Stepanov, 'Introducing a Property Right over Data in the EU: the Data Producer's Right—an Evaluation', 34(1) *International Review of Law, Computers & Technology* (2020) 65.

[112] See Burri, 'The Governance of Data and Data Flows in Trade Agreements: The Pitfalls of Legal Adaptation', 51 *UC Davies Law Review* (2017) 65; T. Pertot, M. Schmidt-Kessel, and F. Padovini (eds), *Rechte an Daten* (2020).

[113] According to Art. 50 Interoperability Regulations, data transfers to third countries, international organizations and private parties are not allowed.

that assumes data originalism as the opposite of data ownership may represent a useful framework for interoperability, as interoperability could become an instrument to deny the exclusive use of information by originator authorities in horizontal relationships. Behaving as data owners in order to limit the data access of others may hamper the purposes laid down by the interoperability legal framework. In fact, the emphasis put on data protection safeguards of third-country nationals by Article 5 of the Interoperability Regulations clashes with the specific regime of single interoperable databases. The material scope of the ETIAS, ECRIS, and SIS databases generally exclude the application of GDPR and the Law Enforcement Directive for all data that are processed by Member States' designated authorities and Europol for the purposes of the prevention, detection, and investigation of terrorist offences or of other serious criminal offences falling under their respective competences.[114] It is relevant not only from a methodological point of view, but also as a matter of substance to explain the limits of the proprietary paradigm in relation to personal data for the reasons that we now briefly explain in the following sub-sections.

A. Different Concepts of Property Rights

Ownership evokes completely different ideas in the different European legal traditions. Whereas, for example, civil traditions build on a notion of property, based on absolute and in theory permanent powers and prerogatives of the owner, common law traditions focus on the temporal dimensions of property, which can be limited in time.[115] In the common law approach, property rights can be attached to any tradeable goods on the basis of delivery, consensus, and possessory lien.[116] Some civil law countries, such as Germany, only recognize ownership over tangible items, preventing in principle its application to immaterial goods such as data, unless it has a legal basis, such as the right to dispose of objects at one's own discretion and the exclusion of others from any influence. Other countries, such as France, include immaterial goods as well as debts and obligations as objects of property rights.[117] In the strict meaning, ownership refers to a specific exclusive right over something (*res*), which includes

[114] Arts 1(2) and 49 ETIAS Regulation; Arts 1(2) and 49 EES Regulation; Art. 66 SIS Regulation.

[115] Graziadei, 'Transfer of Property Inter Vivos', in M. Graziadei and L. Smith (eds), *Comparative Property Law—Global Perspectives* (2017) 71. 'Property' in English law is a set of rules that enables legal owners to *share* the benefits of their assets with third parties by way of different types of derivative interests, whether those derivative interests are possession, security interests, or trust interests.

[116] Boerding *et al.* (n. 96) 337, 338.

[117] Y. Emerich (2017), *Droit commune des biens: perspective transsystématique* (2017).

any form of own disposal and excludes any form of use by third parties. Most legal systems exclude the notion of ownership for intangible goods, such as digital data, as the right of disposal in an absolute manner is only applied to physical goods.[118] German legal traditions assume a precise notion of ownership, as generally owning a specific good implies that nobody else can own that good at the same time; that not everything is 'ownable' but only certain goods that are generally tangible; that only a limited number of property rights exist (*numerus clausus*) and, even according to a legal basis, new property rights can be created only if they fit within that limited number.[119] In a strict meaning, ownership refers to a specific exclusive right over something (*res*), which includes any form of own disposal and excludes any form of use by third parties. Regarding the notion of digital property, the main arguments stress that factual control is relevant when referred to tangible resources. The non-rivalrous nature of immaterial entities instead implies that they are non-consumable goods enabling more than one person to enjoy them at the same time.[120]

B. Data Protection as a Non-Proprietary Paradigm

The right to data protection has never been defined as data ownership, rather as the right to control one's own data flows for ensuring informational self-determination.[121] In the context of the EU, there seems to be considerable reluctance to accept that there can be a property right to data, as there are no legal provisions expressly stating the right to own information.[122] Protection of personal data is expressly indicated in Recital 4 GDPR as a non-absolute right that shall be balanced with conflicting fundamental rights, such as the right to information or freedom of expression, in accordance with the principle of proportionality. The right to control the use of information by third parties protects data subjects against certain uses (and not all uses) by third parties. Neither does the economic interest in the use of personal data—now

[118] For a detailed analysis across EU countries, see M. Barbero *et al.*, *Study on Emerging Issues of Data Ownership, Interoperability, (Re-)usability and Access to Data, and Liability* (2017).

[119] Van Erp, 'Ownership of Data and the Numerus Clausus of Legal Objects', in S. Murphy and P. Kenna (eds), *eConveyancing and title registration in Ireland* (2019) 125.

[120] Joseph Drexl (n. 94) 30: 'The economic reasons for this are equally clear: information as a public good can be used by everybody without exhausting the information as a resource'.

[121] Wenderhost, 'On Elephants in the Room and Paper Tigers: How to Reconcile Data Protection and Data Economy', in S. Lohsse, R. Schulze, and D. Staudenmayer (eds), *Trading Data in the Digital Economy: Legal Concepts and Tools* (2017) 327.

[122] Drexl (n. 9) 61; Hugenholtz, 'Data Property in the System of Intellectual Property Law: Welcome Guest or Misfit', in S. Lohsse, R. Schulze, and D. Staudenmayer (eds), *Trading Data in the Digital Economy: Legal Concepts and Tools* (2017) 75.

recognized by the Digital Contents Directive as counter performance for a service provided by internet platform operators—justify a property right on data on the sole basis of the economic use of personal data.[123] Generally, the applicable legal framework of interoperability is GDPR,[124] according to which data usage unequivocally means processing of personal data, whereas in the field of property rights the use of tangible objects and the power of their disposal has multiple meanings (trade, exchange, reuse, misuse, exclusive possession, personal use, income from the use). Fundamental rights, such as data protection, are inclusive rights applicable to natural persons regardless of the subjective status of 'owner'. In this sense, it is arguable that property rights are irrelevant to fundamental rights' protection, not only because the underlying logic of safeguarding personal data is not the economic exploitation of information goods, but also because fundamental rights protection does not need vested property to be autonomous. Moreover, the right of data subjects to withdraw consent in any phase of data processing or to erase data would make possible schemes of licensing/long-term use of data/granting data access rights unstable and uncertain, which is exactly the opposite of absolute and perpetual property rights. That is the reason why some scholars argue for a form of non-waivable data access rights.[125]

The main arguments to reject data protection as ownership are: (1) consent for data processing cannot be considered a legal basis for the transfer of data property because in the field of data protection consent is an act with a unilateral structure that does not need any ratification or acceptance (although it is usually completed following a specific request from the counterpart) which functionally implements the right of 'informational self-determination'. It is possible at any time to withdraw consent. (2) Data portability rights avoid a possible lock-in effect of data property. Pursuant to Article 20 GDPR, the data subject shall have the right to receive the personal data concerning him or her, which he or she has provided to a controller, in a structured, commonly used and machine-readable format and have the right to transmit those data to another controller without hindrance from the controller to whom the personal data was originally provided. That right applies where the data subject provided the personal data on the basis of her consent, or the processing is necessary for the performance of a contract and in addition where the processing is

[123] Directive (EU) 2019/770, OJ 2019 L 136/1. See Drexl (n. 9) 64.
[124] Recital 53 Interoperability Regulations states it expressly.
[125] Drexl (n. 9) 4, 33, 60-67.

carried out by automated means. It also includes the right of the data subject to have the personal data transmitted directly from one controller to another, where technically feasible. However, it shall not apply to processing necessary for the performance of a task carried out in the public interest or in the exercise of official authority vested in the controller. Finally, data portability shall not compromise rights and freedoms of others as well as the right to rectification or erasure of personal data.

In the European context it is not obvious to think in terms of commercial appropriation of personal data, because the idea of giving an economic value to attributes of personality is considered to offend against dignity.[126] There are two main arguments behind this idea: the right to personal data protection is a personality right that cannot be 'ownable'; it is also a fundamental right that is not compatible with any other exclusive right over data.[127] Individuals' right to data protection means that they have the right to control their data flows, for example, information related to them. They do not own data containing that information.[128] In fact, data protection, not property law, protects the meaning of that information (semantic layer) as the potential knowledge regarding individuals,[129] while intellectual property law generally restricts the remit of property rights to the syntactic layers of data as codified information (e.g. not the content) excluding human understandable information.[130] Only code can be protected as property, never information.[131] Personal data as information content is protected as 'information related to identified or identifiable natural persons' from misuses of ways in which third parties treat data.[132]

[126] Whitman, 'The Two Western Cultures of Privacy: Dignity Versus Liberty', 113 *Yale Law Journal* (2004) 1151.

[127] Against this backdrop see Purtova, 'The illusion of Personal Data as No One's Property: Reframing the Data Protection Discourse', 7(1) *Law, Innovation and Technology* (2015) 83, at 86, 87: 'maintaining that personal data is res nullius or nobody' s property and it is naturally in the "public domain" is an illusion not viable in the information-driven economy'. She argues that 'private property in personal data vs personal data in public domain' does not reflect the current state of data processing practices'. See also Yu and Zhao, 'Dualism in data protection: Balancing the right to personal data and the data property right', 35(5) *Computer Law & Security Review* (2019).

[128] Drexl, 'Designing Competitive Markets for Industrial Data. Between Propertisation and Access', 8 *Journal of Intellectual Property, Information Technology and Electronic Commerce Law* (2017) 257, at 267: 'Protection of personal data is neither vested in the natural person for economic purposes, nor is it an absolute right. Personal data protection does not allocate economic value'.

[129] Drexl (n. 9) 62.

[130] Kerber, 'Rights on Data: The EU Communication "Building a European Data Economy" from an Economic Perspective', in S. Lohsse, R. Schulze, and D. Staudenmayer (eds), *Trading Data in the Digital Economy: Legal Concepts and Tools* (2017) 114.

[131] Hoeren, 'Big Data and the Ownership in Data: Recent Developments in Europe', 36(12) *European Intellectual Property Review* (2014) 751.

[132] Mezzanotte (n. 98) 163.

C. Data Originalism as a de facto Power

In the field of law enforcement, any public interest in sharing data is hardly justifiable as a property right. The practice of information sharing is based on the usage control by which authorization decisions of the provider state allow or deny the recipient state access to certain information. In other words, recipients of information need to gain the originator's authorization to get access and reuse information.[133] It may well be, as Barbero pointed out,[134] that there is in fact hardly any difference between ownership and access. This is because the right to manage data involves several public actors who may compete with each other and with individuals in the enjoyment of rights to data access, data portability, data transfer, data erasure, and data sharing. What is at stake is how data is *used*, for what ends, and by whom. All these issues stem from the possibility to grant access to data, on what this possibility relies, and what it implies precisely for data sharing.

With regard to data sharing, the focus is how a certain bundle of data is made interoperable through the release or the disclosure, following the consent of the interoperable initiator—that is, the providing party who input the interoperable data in the first place, often police authorities. The distinction between non-disclosure of information to third parties for security reasons and exclusion of third parties from full disposal of information have different grounds that are not comparable. In the context of interoperable information sharing, exclusion may imply that data originators exclude third parties from taking notice of the stored information, while granting an exclusive right over data can mean the right to exclusively reproduce and copy data (a sort of right modelled on data portability)[135] or to benefit from the outcome of data processing or to transfer single competences to others. The prevention of unauthorized access may imply a connection to property rights[136] as far as data originators might be considered the original authors of data, because they can make the data available in a database. If considered as a type of self-sovereign control over data, originators can be assimilated to factual owners/holders of a power of authorization according to which they can attach usage control policies to restrict access and use.

[133] Park and Sandhu (n. 3).
[134] Barbero *et al.* (n. 118) 386.
[135] The right to data portability provided by Art. 20 GDPR is not provided by the Law Enforcement Directive (Directive (EU) 2016/680, OJ 2016 L 119/89).
[136] Boerding *et al.* (n. 96) 333.

A de facto power similar to that of an owner might also include the duty to ensure the maintenance of the interoperability infrastructure, specifically the technical management for the purposes of the proper functioning of information systems. De facto holders—such as for example the operators of data sharing platforms, and arguably eu-LISA for interoperable information systems, involved in the process of encoding data—have a legitimate interest in getting access to data and to preserve data involving, for instance, confidentiality requirements.[137] Nonetheless, it is not clear whether they need to be conceptually distinguished from data originators, such as authorities or individuals, who input data in the system. In property law, the owner of a good or product generally has the power to prevent third parties from disposing of goods but also the responsibility for the maintenance of data. In the case of interoperability, there seems to be a different rationale. In fact, the duty to ensure the operational functioning of the system—abstractly similar to a warranty against defects and misuses offered by the owner—and the exclusive right of disposal of personal data for purposes of border management would belong to different authorities, the former to eu-LISA while the latter to originators.[138] Within interoperable information systems, the use of the data is traceable, for example, through a logging mechanism that the data originator can view upon any authorized access. A rules-based authorization concept and access logging that can be viewed can be set up by data originators. In other words, if we consider data originators as data holders, with the right to grant access to or to share certain personal data under their control, we can arguably point out that data originators are all data holders, but data holders are not necessarily data originators. In the context of personal data access for law enforcement purposes, data is regarded as a thing that can be accessed to enable further action. Data originators who input and share data in an interoperable system can ultimately: (1) claim legitimate limits to access by other interoperable actors performing as if they were exerting an exclusive right over the data, and (2) prevent third-country nationals from activating any form of control over their own data, or other possible safeguards, as they cannot resort to national remedies on the basis of citizenship but only through special forms of international protection. Data holders, such as eu-LISA can for example set up technical requirements for ensuring the accuracy of shared data and ensure

[137] Mezzanotte (n. 98) 169. Drexl (n. 9).

[138] Fia, 'An Alternative to Data Ownership: Managing Access to Non-Personal Data through the Commons', 21(1) *Global Jurist* (2020).

that the shared status of data remains as such and it is not revocable by data originators.

D. Data Originalism versus *sui generis* Database Protection

The possible applications of data originalism to databases and information systems can be developed building on some similar rights provided in the field of IP rights on databases. We can assume that interoperable users could be entitled to rights over the contents of databases, shared with other interoperable users. However, within IP law, the creation of a new IP right on data could only be justified if it creates an economic incentive based on an added value as a whole data collection and not as an amount of single data.[139] This economic incentive has to be considered in the light of the production of data;[140] if it facilitates the use and trade of data; and if it is provided by law. To better explain the implications of the so-called 'right to data',[141] it would be useful to remember a recognized principle of intellectual property according to which knowledge, once it is communicated and then becomes public, cannot be not subject to any right.[142] The Database Directive[143] (96/9/EC) defines two different regimes that are exceptions to this general principle: copyright, dedicated to databases that 'by reason of the selection or arrangement of their contents ... constitute the author's own intellectual creation';[144] and *sui generis* right, that assigns to 'the maker of a database which shows that there has been qualitatively and/or quantitatively a substantial investment in either the obtaining, verification or presentation of the contents' the right 'to prevent extraction and/or re-utilization of the whole or of a substantial part, evaluated qualitatively and/or quantitatively, of the contents of that database'.[145]

In this sense, the *Horseracing* case[146] is informative—even in the different contexts of IP law and law enforcement—as its reasoning distinguishes

[139] Zech, 'Information as Property', 6(3) *Journal of Intellectual Property, Information Technology and Electronic Commerce Law* (2015) 192.

[140] Wandtke, 'Ökonomischer Wert von Persönlichen Daten', 1 *Multimedia und Recht* (2017) 6.

[141] Wiebe, 'Schutz von Maschinendaten durch das sui-generis Schutzrecht für Datenbanken', *Gewerblicher Rechtsschutz und Urheberrecht* (2017) 338.

[142] The dissenting opinion by Justice Brandeis in the case *International News Service v Associated Press* (1918) reads as follows: 'The general rule of law is, that the noblest of human productions—knowledge, truths ascertained, conceptions and ideas—after voluntary communication to others, are free as the air to common use.'

[143] Directive 96/9/EC, OJ 1996 L 77/20 (hereinafter 'Database Directive').

[144] Ibid. Art. 3.

[145] Art. 7 Database Directive. See also Mezzanotte (n. 98) 165.

[146] Case C-203/02, *The British Horseracing Board Ltd and Others v William Hill Organization Ltd.* (EU: C:2004:695).

between pre-existing data and created data. This can potentially be helpful *mutatis mutandis* in the context of interoperability where—once data is integrated into the system—it receives another designation as 'shared data', in the sense of no longer being at the exclusive disposal of the originator. This judgment points out that the 'purpose of the protection by the *sui generis* right provided for by the directive is to promote the establishment of storage and processing systems for existing information and not the creation of materials capable of being collected subsequently in a database'[147] and that 'the protection of the *sui generis* right provided for by Article 7(1) of the Database Directive gives the maker of a database the option of preventing the unauthorized extraction and/or re-utilization of all or a substantial part of the contents of that database'[148] This means that, even in the different context of IP law, a *sui generis* right, as such, is not applicable to 'new data' but only to pre-existing ones. Interoperable data can then be considered originated as shared in the sense of having a new designation when input into the system, so that the right of the data originator is limited to prevent unauthorized use of them.

The main options of copyright and *sui generis* data do not extend to data per se as information included in databases. Recital 45 of the Database Directive stipulates that the 'right to prevent unauthorized extraction and/or re-utilization does not in any way constitute an extension of copyright protection to mere facts or data'. Furthermore, copyright provides relevant protection only for original databases that have a creative value in originating a data collection. Protection of data compilations that result from creative selection and arrangement (copyright) or substantive investment (*sui generis* database right). Nevertheless, the directive does not extend the protection to the content of databases.[149] These reflections may help to understand that, in an interoperable system, if we reflect in terms of ownership, it is arguably feasible to refer to the ownership of databases and 'interoperable production' in the sense of the original use of such data for an interoperable purpose, irrespective of what has been done before the act of sharing, but not in terms of ownership of data.[150] While property rights of databases do not extend to data, as they are not per se a creative production,[151] such analysis does not protect the individual subject

147 Ibid. para. 31.

148 Ibid. para. 44.

149 Art. 3(2) Database Directive. On this topic, see Falce, 'Copyrights on Data and Competition Policy in the Single Market Strategy', 5(1) *Antitrust & Public Policies* (2018) 32.

150 According to the European Commission (Communication COM(2018) 232 final (2018) 6): 'One of the main conclusions in the evaluation is that the *sui generis* right does not systematically cover big data situations and single-source databases, thus does not prevent problematic cases where certain right-holders could claim indirect property rights of digital data.'

151 Hugenholtz (n. 122) 75–100.

from the collection of the data nor from its aggregation, but instead protects the holder of the aggregated database from *its* use by preventing third parties from access to the compilation either in whole or in part.

Given this framework, the conceptualization of a *sui generis* right to database in the context of EU information sharing meets two unsurmountable obstacles: on the one hand, the economic exploitation of the collection; on the other hand, the substantial investment that in the logic of IP should be remunerated by revenues. However, as a way of reasoning on models prompted by the law in similar cases (discipline of databases), but in different contexts (IP and public law), and with different rationales (commercial exploitation of a creation, and immigration and border controls) the reflections on the *sui generis* right to databases open interesting paths.

Contextualizing these findings in the field of interoperability, one can argue in practice the following:

1) Data originators may claim a *sui generis* right over databases because of the creative value inherent to a collection of pre-existing data (namely data belonging to them), provided that national authorities and eu-LISA have made substantial investments in setting up interoperable components. This right does not extend to the actual content of the interoperable databases, for example, interoperable shared data.
2) As this right does not extend to data per se, it is arguable that the contents of databases shared by interoperable actors are 'un-owned' and therefore can freely flow within the system.
3) On the contrary, interoperable users may be as a result protected from misuse and unauthorized appropriation of substantial parts of data collection by third parties on the basis of the *sui generis* right over database granted to data originators.

The recent Data Act contributes to clarify the scope of a *sui generis* right to databases in the context of data sharing by excluding its application 'to databases containing data obtained from or generated by the use of a product or a related service'.[152]

However, the other EU legal instruments—such as the ePrivacy Directive,[153] the GDPR, the Regulation on a Framework for the Free Flow of non-personal data,[154] the EU's laws on intellectual property, and the Trade Secrets

[152] Art. 35, Data Act.
[153] Directive 2002/58/EC, OJ 2002 L 201/37.
[154] Regulation (EU) 2018/1807, OJ 2018 L 303/59.

Directive[155]— do not include any legal provisions indicating possible ownership of data outside the protection of personal data, or the protection of trade secrets or software.

In this sense we conclude that data stored within interoperable systems cannot be covered by a property right, neither in the form of personal data nor in the form of a *sui generis* right on personal data collection. They are thus un-owned. Interoperability in fact dismantles the idea of unilateral control over data *de jure* as far as users and individuals are capable of knowing the history of the data use.[156]

6. The Originalism of Data Sharing for Un-owned Data

As we have seen, the storage and exchange of information has become a defining element of European integration, taking place thanks to data sharing in the context of fragmented institutional structures of EU databases. The fuel for this process of data sharing—personal data flows integrated into an interoperable information system—engages, on the one hand, the rights and interests of individuals, in particular of third-country nationals whose personal data will be stored and further processed for multiple purposes; on the other, the discretionary power of authorities in granting access to the sharing of such data.

Although acknowledging a property right in data could in theory be useful to guarantee exclusive rights to the relevant stakeholders involved in data sharing—both national authorities or EU agencies, for borders and security management, as well as the third-country national data subjects—this in practice could not be tailored to the composite and multifaceted architecture of interoperability. In fact, it would significantly weaken the rationale of interoperability that primarily aims to foster cooperation among states and agencies in a peer-to-peer framework in order to counteract identity frauds. Third-country nationals are often obliged to hand over their data even if they only applied for a visa or other permits/authorizations. They will not have a choice. A property right will not add anything to their situation as they have no commercial or legal powers vis-à-vis states and agencies. Moreover, the fact that third-country nationals are equal to other parties in not exercising a property right over their data is the pre-requisite for their equal protection before the

[155] Directive (EU) 2016/943, OJ 2016 L 157/1.

[156] Hilty, 'Big Data: Ownership and Use in the Digital Age', in X. Seuba, C. Geiger, and J. Pénin (eds), *Intellectual Property and Digital Trade in the Age of Artificial Intelligence and Big Data* (2018) 85.

law, which is ultimately based on fundamental rights protection under the EU Charter of Fundamental Rights. Conversely, a property right over data would also not be ideal for authorities or agencies that access data and share them for interoperable purposes. One of the reasons is that consent provided by individuals for interoperable data processing (a specific legal basis of data processing in data protection law) is not technically equivalent to a legal transfer of property rights to data to public authorities. Transfer of property rights to data either needs to be combined with a contractual agreement or must be totally independent of consent. This means that in any case, logically, any abstract entitlement of authorities or agencies over property rights on data presupposes an original entitlement of individuals whose data is subsequently shared and re-used.

If data originalism is considered as the act of creation of the shared status of information—provided that handing it over or sharing it is incompatible with the property regime of personal data—interoperability could also become an instrument to limit the discretionary use of data by originators.

The hypothesis of data originalism as a descriptive term of un-owned data, is then particularly fruitful to offer an interpretative framework in which the meaning of data access can imply a set of other rights. It offers a promising path towards a framework that recognizes how different legal regimes surrounding interoperability—such as data protection, law enforcement, fundamental rights protection, and international protection of third-country nationals—can however be negated in practice by the discretionary data usage by data originators. Understanding interoperable data originalism as 'designation of shared data' intended to enable originators to only exercise defensive rights on data they originate—a sort of veto access and usage on shared data—preserves the underlying logic of data protection not only *de jure*, but also de facto, because data originally un-owned cannot subsequently be appropriated. Interoperability appears in this light as a relevant benchmark where the identification of persons should be integrated in a complex structure of data usage rules and effective legal remedies against data misuse. It in fact adds relevant substantive grounds also from the perspective of public law, since personal data is not only un-owned because it is subject to fundamental rights' protection[157] but also because this data directly originates as 'shared data' in interoperable systems.

The interoperable designation of data as 'shared data' (and thus un-owned/un-ownable), is a guarantee also for individuals as their data is inherent to their

[157] Art. 8 Charter of Fundamental Rights.

personality rights and it would therefore not be necessary to create for them property rights in order to ensure better legal protection. On the contrary, the creation of a property right over personal data may legitimize those trends that use the protection of fundamental rights in only a rhetorical way and not with a real legal purpose. After all, data protection and privacy are clearly recognized as fundamental rights even in the Interoperability Regulations. Based on this premise, the purpose pursued by the interoperability legal framework in addressing 'identity fraud' requires personal identity to be built upon fragmented pieces of information that are shared, handed over, disaggregated and reaggregated in a partial and sometimes biased way. This may strongly jeopardize third-country nationals' rights, that is, those individuals who would be most affected by the illegitimate use of data.

The legal framework encompassing interoperable information systems and single databases is suggestive of the fact that personal data must be considered inherently un-ownable, although factually appropriated. Interoperability of EU information systems thus calls for a normative agenda that limits appropriating powers of data originators in view of their actual discretionary powers. However, the core of information sharing is represented by the meaning the right of access may assume differently over time and in the content of the derivative rights of giving, not-giving, or ending access. Both of the Interoperability Regulations impose strict requirements for access to the CIR for identification by police authorities[158] and for the detection of multiple identities by authorities responsible of manual verification of identities,[159] as well as for the access to multiple identity detectors by single databases.[160] Additionally, the ETIAS Regulation provides the requirements for access to data for identification[161] and sets up the conditions for access to data recorded in the ETIAS Central System by designated authorities of Member States,[162] while the EES Regulation stipulates that border authorities shall have access to the EES in order to verify the identity and previous registration of third-country nationals only for limited purposes.[163]

Originalism as applied to interoperable data can arguably have a positive meaning, namely that personal data is originated in interoperable systems as shared data with all the safeguards related to the regime of personal data

[158] Art. 20 Interoperability Regulations.
[159] Ibid. Art. 21.
[160] Ibid. Art. 26.
[161] Art. 27 ETIAS Regulation.
[162] Ibid. Art. 52.
[163] Art. 23 Regulation (EU) 2017/2226 (as amended by Regulation (EU) 2021/1152), OJ 2017 L 327/21 (Entry/Exit System—EES Regulation).

protection. Originalism in this sense resists against any attempt to create de facto ownership by authorities who appropriate data and make use of them first. The rationale of data protection safeguards is in line with this understanding, as neither individuals nor anybody else own information related to them but rather are only in a position to entirely control the information flows related to them.

7. Conclusions

This chapter has shown how the complexity of the architecture underlying interoperability requires legal solutions that look at the reality of the practice of data sharing. The tension between the inherent secrecy or informality of sharing practices for the sake of security and the technical transparency of interoperable operations, by means of keeping logs of all data processing operations within interoperable components, is not entirely addressed by the existing legal framework. This reflects the impossibility of addressing the operational aspects of interoperability with a mere legal design. The reality shows that data sharing relies considerably on power relationships among authorities and thus requires rules of sharing and usage in order to prevent misuses or appropriation of data.

What the law can do is instead elaborate legal concepts that better reflect reality. Its role is to provide a normative framework where the different actors' interests are brought together based on the underlying rationales of specific legal institutions. These rationales help us to strike a balance between conflicting interests, such as security and border management, on the one hand, and fundamental rights and non-discrimination of third-country nationals, on the other.

In our view, unpacking the concept of data originalism has been helpful in order to uncover a grey zone related to the originator control principle, according to which recipients shall receive originators' approval to disseminate information. According to this principle, data originators can give access or not to what they want or not to share. However, the rules according to which data access is granted by originators is not always accessible. We conclude that data is originally un-owned because it is personal data with the attached safeguards of data protection law and fundamental rights protection. It is additionally un-owned in an original sense that once it is made interoperable, its designation as shared data means that it cannot be appropriated by any user or originator.

We have seen for example how the idea of 'ownership' as applied to interoperable data requires modifications in the manner in which it is legally anchored. The general debate on a data economy strategy reveals an existing trend of considering the framework of data ownership more in the sense of defensive rights.[164] These rights can be modelled on the idea of protecting information from external misuse or from a mismatch between data processing and usage purposes. It can result in, for example, injunctions against further exploitation, exclusion from commercialization of services and products built on the basis of misused data, compensation for damages for unauthorized use of data, denial of access to third parties. This understanding is the closest one to our idea of data originalism according to which data originators are entitled to, in essence, protective rights of information that they process as first or that they share as first (after processing).

As a first cut, the challenge of this approach is represented in the transposition of ideas commonly occurring in the field of private law adapted to the public purposes of judicial cooperation in the fight against crime and borders control. However, our reflection on the way that data ownership could be understood more as a substantive rationale rather than as an applicable legal category is not only a theoretical exercise. It seeks in fact to be a way of identifying the legal implications of the technological architecture of interoperable information systems. Regulatory tasks for interoperable data originators should be similar to the idea of defensive rights that allow originators to set up rules of data usage/data access without exceeding the limits of their limited right. This implies that terms of data usage (tailored as a sort of licensed data usage) set up by data originators should, for example, be notified to all interoperable users and above all individuals whose data are processed in such a transparent way. This could prevent misuses in data usage that are otherwise increased by the informal and secret modalities of data sharing outside the interoperable framework in the Interoperability Regulations or by a partial disclosure of data. In practical terms, the agenda for originators includes liability rules for sharing but also conditions under which data is shared. Interstate fiduciary duties based on sincere cooperation between public administrations should be the means to reconnect liability rules for data misuse

[164] On basis of rights *in rem* that include the right to license data usage (a set of rights enforceable against any party independent of contractual relations thus preventing further use of data by third parties who have no right to use the data, including the right to claim damages for unauthorized access to and use of data) or a set of purely defensive rights, the general opinion is that the right should be only protected at the syntactic level (code and data) and not at the semantic one (information incorporated in the code). See European Commission (n. 102) 33.

to the effectiveness of data sharing. However, lack of trust cannot be replaced simplistically by operational standards of interoperability. It must rather make the conditions under which data sharing has occurred transparent and try to reconstruct a history of all data that has been used to identify a certain individual. This means that the cycle of data sharing starts from the original creation of the data, as well as from the original meaning attributed to that data. The cycle then continues through transparent terms and conditions of sharing to its final usage. Beyond the concept of data originalism lies a rule-making challenge that may also represent a valuable and unprecedented opportunity for the European Union.

6

Bits, Bytes, Searches, and Hits: Logging-in Accountability for EU Data-led Security

*Deirdre Curtin and Marieke de Goede**

1. Introduction

The EU security model for fighting terrorism and organized crime, cybersecurity, countering terrorism financing, and border security depends in large measure on cross-border (intra-EU and external EU) information exchange and the creation, operation, and interconnection of specialized databases, with acronyms such as SIS, VIS, ETIAS, EU-PNR, TFTP, IRU and others.[1] The EU Security Union works through a paradigm of 'preventive justice' that is heavily reliant on 'the collection of personal data and the cooption of the private sector'.[2] Data-led security is crucial to current EU policies and practices of security integration, in particular through the building and interoperability of databases. In this context, the model of EU data-led security poses profound challenges to democratic control and to the normative principles of legal protection and accountability. Under the guise of supposedly value-neutral and apolitical support for information sharing, the technological solutions inherent in database interoperability reflect deeper policy choices

* The authors wish to thank Asma Balfiqih and Sarah Tas for research assistance and help with compiling the figures and tables in this chapter. Thanks to all participants in the online workshop 'Data at the Boundaries of Law' held at the European University Institute in April 2021, and special thanks to Niovi Vavoula and Mariavittoria Catanzariti for their generous and helpful comments on an earlier version of this paper.

Prof de Goede's work on this paper received funding from the European Research Council (ERC) under the European Union's Horizon 2020 research and innovation program (research project 'FOLLOW: Following the Money from Transaction to Trial', Grant No. ERC-2015-CoG 682317).

[1] SIS (Schengen Information System), VIS (Visa Information System), ETIAS (European Travel Information and Authorization System), EU-PNR (EU passenger name record), TFTP (Terrorist Finance Tracking Program), and IRU (Internet Referral Unit). Commission Communication 673 final on The EU Internal Security Strategy in Action: Five steps towards a more secure Europe (2010).

[2] S. Carrera and V. Mitsilegas (eds), *Constitutionalising the Security Union: Effectiveness, Rule of Law and Rights in Countering Terrorism and Crime* (2017), at 12; E. Fahey and D. Curtin (eds), *A Transatlantic Community of Law: Legal Perspectives on the Relationship between the EU and US Legal Orders* (2014); M. de Goede, *Speculative Security: The Politics of Pursuing Terrorist Monies* (2012).

Deirdre Curtin and Marieke de Goede, *Bits, Bytes, Searches, and Hits: Logging-in Accountability for EU Data-led Security* In: *Data at the Boundaries of European Law.* Edited by: Deirdre Curtin and Mariavittoria Catanzariti, Oxford University Press.
DOI: 10.1093/oso/9780198874195.003.0006

that have a significant impact on individuals' fundamental rights.[3] Our normative view is that adequate mechanisms of accountability for data-led security are indispensable in democratic governance: they allow citizens, parliaments, and many other fora to assess and pass judgment on the actions of government as well as private actors engaged in the public domain.[4] Yet the question of how accountability mechanisms could or should look in the context of 'data at the boundaries of law' is a particularly challenging one as we explain in this chapter. In the broader agenda of generating 'data justice', accountability for algorithmic decisions in general and data-led security in particular, is a pressing puzzle that has given rise to a large and growing literature.[5] Meanwhile, actual data-led security practices in Europe and elsewhere are developing apace and are creating novel forms and ad hoc arrangements of accountability that will generate new standards by default.

This chapter maps and analyses the concrete mechanisms and practices that are taking shape in EU data-led security, and assesses to what extent these are—what we call—'logged-into' actual data practices. EU data-led security is giving rise to hybrid accountability arrangements and single institutions, as well as pivotal EU agencies with various specific databases under their management.[6] Novel data-led security programmes are creating limited oversight and accountability structures that work to generate new standards. The purpose of this chapter is to explore and analyse these structures and standards from the perspective of their encounter with data. The most specific and in many ways most far-reaching creation that could provide a future model for accountability in other areas is in the field of external relations. In June 2012, the Directorate-General for Migration and Home Affairs (DG Home) of the European Commission recruited for an entirely new position: a deputy overseer to work inside the US Treasury in Washington. The role of the deputy overseer is to assist 'in the oversight and monitoring mission' of the EU as

[3] Rijpma, 'Brave New Borders: The EU's Use of New Technologies for the Management of Migration and Asylum', in M. Cremona (ed.), *New Technologies and EU Law* (2017) 197, at 203; Galli, *Interoperable Law Enforcement: Cooperation Challenges in the Area of Freedom, Security, and Justice*, 15 EUI Working Paper RSCAS (2019), at 3.

[4] Bovens, Goodin, and Schillemans, 'Public Accountability', in M. Bovens, R. E. Goodin, and T. Schillemans (eds), *The Oxford Handbook of Public Accountability* (2014), 1.

[5] Taylor, 'What Is Data Justice? The Case for Connecting Digital Rights and Freedoms Globally', *Big Data & Society* (2017) 1; Amoore and Raley, 'Securing with Algorithms: Knowledge, Decision, Sovereignty', 48 *Security Dialogue* (2016) 1; Kosta, 'Algorithmic State Surveillance: Challenging the Notion of Agency in Human Rights', *Regulation and Governance* (2020) 1.

[6] Sullivan and de Goede, 'Between Law and the Exception: The UN 1267 Ombudsperson as a Hybrid Model of Legal Expertise', 26(4) *Leiden Journal of International Law* (2013) 833; Sullivan, 'Transnational Legal Assemblages and Global Security Law: Topologies and Temporalities of the List,' *Transnational Legal Theory* (2014), 5(1): 81–127.

agreed in Article 12 of the 'EU-US Terrorism Financing Tracking Agreement on the Processing and Transfer of Financial Messaging Data' (TFTP Treaty). This Agreement enables and regulates the transfer of financial transaction (SWIFT) data from the EU to the US in the context of counterterrorism. The TFTP Treaty established the role of an EU overseer to work inside the CIA and monitor the operation of the programme in the context of the Treaty stipulations. The remit of the overseer and his deputy is to 'review, analyze and verify the legitimacy of data searches' that are carried out by the US Treasury in the context of the TFTP. The overseer and his deputy are allowed to block searches if they judge them to be not compliant with Agreement provisions. According to the vacancy text, suitable candidates for the deputy overseer position were expected to have 'well-proven professional experience in counterterrorism' and eligibility for US security clearance.[7]

The creation of the overseer and deputy overseer positions illustrates the challenges of accountability in EU data-led security politics that are also transatlantic in nature and involve the creation of new and in-between oversight bodies that have access to the data used in security decision-making. The TFTP Overseer positions form an entirely new part of EU governance architectures that is understudied and little known. They are generally seen as an important EU achievement in the context of what was previously a secret and unaccountable US security programme. They have been negotiated as part of an international relations exercise and not as internal EU governance with full involvement of the European Parliament. Nonetheless, these new positions are innovative and may even contain the seeds of something that could possibly be transplanted more broadly within the EU, as our chapter will argue. An overseer with security clearance can closely observe the ways in which data are handled, shared, and analysed, and can be logged-into the data-driven nature of security analysis and decisions as part of the public administration. An overseer presumably has access to all data immediately with the power to actually block searches before they happen or are ongoing.

However, there is much that is unknown about how the TFTP overseers actually operate in practice within the TFTP, and much that can be challenged about their practices. The secrecy surrounding their identity and the procedures of data sharing and analysis is striking when compared to staff in other EU oversight institutions, such as the EU Ombudsman or the European Data

[7] Selection of temporary staff for Directorate-General Home Affaires (HOME) COM/TA/HOME/12/AD8, https://www.mzv.cz/file/827535/Vacancy_note_TA_2A___EN.pdf (last visited 16 December 2021).

Protection Supervisor (EDPS), who operate in very visible and well-regulated ways.[8] The TFTP overseers work *inside* the US Treasury and in close collaboration with Treasury and CIA officials. Despite being the very face of EU accountability in relation to the TFTP, secrecy reigns even with regard to entirely non-operational facts, such as the actual identities of the overseer and his deputy, which have never been in the public domain. The requirement that they have substantial experience in counterterrorism, rather than, for example, in data protection, influences their expertise and their practical orientation. In this sense, the overseers are fully part of the security structure of the TFTP (and of the US government)—whereby personal financial transactions data are shared transatlantically and algorithmically mined—but they seem to remain rather isolated and 'logged-out' of wider structures of accountability towards a European public.

The TFTP overseer is external in terms of EU governance and accountability structures, and this is unusual although it has now been the case for a decade. Other data-led security regulatory initiatives also focus on imposing obligations on external actors, including private actors. TERREG, for example, authorizes social media service providers to police and remove terrorist-related utterances from their platforms. This raises distinct accountability challenges but ones that can presumably—within limits—be supervised by EU institutions. Newer data-led security initiatives create new databases (for example, ETIAS, European Criminal Records Information System—Third Country Nationals [ECRIS-TCN]) that are interoperable with various existing actors and other databases—as a matter only of EU governance—and rely on existing EU institutions in terms of accountability, in particular on one increasingly important EU agency in this field, eu-LISA.

This chapter analyses the ad hoc practices and processes of accountability that are developing in relation to the actors and instruments in (a number of) EU security programmes, and assesses their 'loggedness' in relation to data. Our aim is twofold. First, we offer a mapping exercise in relation to accountability practices for a selection of established and emerging database configurations in the EU security realm. Second, in a manner not previously done in the literature, we assess the extent to which the selected mechanisms are 'logged-in' to the work of data analysis that they are expected to give account of (as opposed to logged-out or not connected). The term 'logging' is pivotal in

[8] V. Abazi, *Official Secrets and Oversight in the EU: Law and Practices of Classified Information* (2019); de Goede, 'The SWIFT Affair and the Global Politics of European Security', 50 (2) *Journal of Common Market Studies* (2012), 214-230.

this context as it refers to the practice of creating a record, reporting, noting, or registering information in the present that may be used to retrace current or past decisions in the future. Key to the practice of logging is that it uses a standardized format, on the basis that it is not presently known what actions, decisions, or factors are needed to account for a future emergency or control. Like with a ship's logbook, logging can help establish the causality of events in retrospect.

In this chapter, we show that logged-out accountability is typified by: (1) transfer of reporting, transparency and accountability to the private sector or to public security authorities; (2) an emphasis on public reporting and narrative justification on the actors' *own terms*, trumping independent investigation and request for information; and (3) a lack of ways in which accountability fora can actually be assembled, to look at, for example, concrete complaints or causes of harm. The term 'logged-out' suggests our hypothesis that the form of accountability, which is planned or in operation, risks being out-of-the-loop and possibly below par. The ideal practice, one that is aligned to the nature of the data as object, is that the accountability mechanisms and practices are 'logged-in'.

Our departure point on giving meaning to the concept of accountability is the well-known definition that describes accountability as 'a relationship between an actor and a forum, in which the actor has an obligation to explain and to justify his or her conduct, the forum can pose questions and pass judgment, and the actor may face consequences'.[9] We start by examining how all elements of this definition—actor, conduct, and forum—are challenged in data-led security. Our chapter then develops a theoretical approach that moves beyond understanding accountability as a normative principle to seeing it as a concrete mechanism and practice, that we call rendering 'account-able'.[10] Subsequently, the chapter maps and analyses how accountability mechanisms have taken shape in relation to four different EU data-led security programmes (and the actors behind them). This mapping enables us to draw conclusions concerning the characteristics of what we describe as 'logged-out accountability', and to reflect on what a fuller, more meaningful 'logged-in' accountability in relation to data-led security could and should look like both in terms of institutions

[9] Bovens, Curtin, and 't Hart, 'Studying the Real World of EU Accountability: Framework and Design', in M. Bovens, D. Curtin, and P. 't Hart, *The Real World of EU Accountability: What Deficit?* (2010) 31, at 35.

[10] Bovens, 'Two Concepts of Accountability: Accountability as a Virtue and as a Mechanism', 33 *West European Politics* (2010) 946, at 951. The term account-able draws on the work of Daniel Neyland, 'Bearing Account-able Witness to the Ethical Algorithmic System', 41(1) *Science, Technology, & Human Values* (2016).

and digital practices. One promising avenue we consider in more detail is the notion of an EU-overseer in the field of data-led security who is independent, specifically created, and logged-into the data-led environment in which the office would exercise a supervisory role.

2. EU Data-led Security: In Uncharted Administrative Territory

The rise of both interoperable and algorithmic governance presents unprecedented challenges to preserving, let alone strengthening, the practices of accountability we have inherited from past generations of administrative and constitutional lawyers. This section discusses the challenges that data-led security poses to established notions of accountability. It charts why and how the focus on database interoperability, that is so prominent in contemporary EU security, poses particular questions of accountability.

Database interoperability is crucial to EU data-led security. It enables the (partial) connection of different actors and (pre-existing) databases in decentralized ways.[11] Such interconnections can be realized across different jurisdictions, different institutions, and across public–private spaces. In each concrete case, interoperability is based on specific techno-juridical arrangements that allow (pre-existing) databases to connect and communicate.[12] Thus, database interoperability is redrawing many pre-existing constitutional and political boundaries of EU governance and the place of national authorities, EU institutions, and data subjects in it.[13] EU authorities—paradigmatically, eu-LISA—may appear in a mediating role, as they perform tasks auxiliary to the exchange of personal data by Member States' authorities, such as developing the technological infrastructure required to facilitate data exchanges. Other EU agencies such as Europol and Frontex manage to put themselves more prominently on the map of interoperable systems by gaining ever-increasing

[11] Curtin, '"Accountable Independence" of the European Central Bank: Seeing the Logics of Transparency', 23 *European Law Journal: Review of European Law in Context* (2017) 28; Carrera and Mitsilegas (n. 2).

[12] M. Gutheil *et al.*, *Interoperability of Justice and Home Affairs Systems*, Study for the LIBE Committee, European Parliament (2018); Galli, 'Interoperable Database: New Cooperation Dynamics in the EU AFSJ?', 26(1) *European Public Law* (2020) 109; Brouwer, 'Large-Scale Databases and Interoperability in Migration and Border Policies: The Non- Discriminatory Approach of Data Protection', 26(1) *European Public Law* (2020) 71; Aden, 'Interoperability Between EU Policing and Migration Databases: Risks for Privacy', 26(1) *European Public Law* (2020) 93; Leese, 'Fixing State Vision: Interoperability, Biometrics, and Identity Management in the EU,' *Geopolitics*, 27:1 (2022), 113–133.

[13] Curtin and Brito Bastos, 'Interoperable Information Sharing and the Five Novel Frontiers of EU Governance: A Special Issue', 26(1) *European Public Law* (2020) 59.

access to data shared by others and for broader purposes.[14] Moreover, interoperability produces a form of networked administration characterized by the sharing of sensitive personal data within domains—such as security and border management—that are themselves politically sensitive. In this light, it becomes evident that the EU's bet on technological solutions in security is enhancing European administrative power in that area.[15] This is true both of the various agencies involved but also of the Commission which has increased considerably its power to legislate (for example, on ETIAS) through delegated and implementing acts.[16]

However, enhanced power requires enhanced safeguards of public accountability and it is not clear that they are sufficiently in place and sufficiently adapted to match the data-led nature of security cooperation. As Harlow and Rawlings aptly put it, the bureaucratic use of artificial intelligence (AI) in particular is 'moving us fast into uncharted administrative territory, one in which prior achievements in terms of rights protection and the good governance triad of transparency, accountability and participation may be restricted, even reversed'.[17] Interoperability relies on AI and algorithmic matching in many crucial respects but can also take place more mechanically.[18] For example, sharing information across decentralized databases in security programmes is often done on the basis of algorithmic matching of records or specific search terms.

The challenges to practising accountability in relation to EU data-led and interoperable security are substantial, for at least three reasons. First, there are challenges of secrecy and the availability of information. Without information to hold the power wielder to account, citizens and non-citizens cannot hope to attain accountability for the actual decision taken which may be of a transient

[14] Quintel, 'Interoperable Data Exchanges within Different Data Protection Regimes: The Case of Europol and the European Border Coast Guard Agency', 26(1) *European Public Law* (2020) 205.

[15] D. Bigo *et al.*, *The EU Counter-Terrorism Policy Responses to the Attacks in Paris: Towards an EU Security and Liberty Agenda* (2015); D. Bigo *et al.*, *Mass Surveillance of Personal Data by EU Member States and its Compatibility with EU Law* (2013); E. Guild, *EU Counter-Terrorism Action: A Fault Line between Law and Politics?* (2010).

[16] Art. 89 ETIAS Regulation (EU) 2018/1240 OJ L 236/1, e.g. the Commission delegated Regulation (EU) 2019/946 on the allocation of funding from the general budget of the Union to cover the costs for the development of ETIAS (2019) or the Commission delegated Regulation (EU) 2021/916 establishing a ETIAS as regards the predetermined list of job groups used in the application form (2021); S. Alegre, J. Jeandesboz, and N. Vavoula, *European Travel Information and Authorisation System (ETIAS): Border Management, Fundamental Rights and Data Protection* (2017), at 27.

[17] Harlow and Rawlings, 'Proceduralism and Automation: Challenges to the Values of Administrative Law', in E. Fisher, J. King, and A. Young (eds), *The Foundations and Future of Public Law: Essays in Honour of Paul Craig* (2020) 275, at 297; Ulbricht and Yeung, 'Algorithmic Regulation: A Maturing Concept for Investigating Regulation of and through Algorithms', 16(1) *Regulation & Governance* (2021), 3; Yeung, 'Algorithmic Regulation: A Critical Interrogation', 12(4) *Regulation & Governance* (2018), 505.

[18] C. Dumbrava, *Artificial Intelligence at EU Borders—Overview of Applications and Key Issues* (2021).

nature, for example, exclusion from the territory of a Member State/EU. In many cases, such decisions (for example, exclusion from a territory) will not lead to a full judicial hearing where the data relied on is scrutinized at the national level.[19] This is of course tricky in the context of police cooperation as the data in question are not usually shared outside policing networks, not even for the purposes of public accountability. At the supranational level, when data are retained in databases and subsequently shared, there are inevitably operations that are invisible not only to outsiders but also to insiders. Secrecy is fostered by data protection laws and the legal requirement of not sharing personal data and this may operate as an accountability inhibitor in a more substantive sense.

The second challenge to practising accountability in EU data-led security is the complex and multilevel landscape of EU security governance, involving different layers of EU institutions on the one hand and Member States on the other. Moreover, EU security governance involves complex webs of transatlantic cooperation and information sharing, as well as processes of 'agentification'.[20] Thus, the setting of data-led police and security cooperation is profoundly multilevel and this is of direct influence on the possibility of accountability. Information sharing takes place in a setting where the information asymmetry is systemic and particularly accentuated, also in terms of the participants within the conclave of governance, let alone when it comes to the possibility of external accountability. The very nature of the subject matter is fragmented and invisible: shared personal data by police and other associated authorities in a non-national setting. In this arena, executives anyway enjoy a wide strategic and operational discretion where 'normal' accountability mechanisms do not traditionally apply.[21] The position of third-country nationals whose data is contained in EU databases and shared is particularly weak.[22] The strong executive governance impacts on the conceptualization and implementation of accountability practices in the Area of Freedom, Security and Justice (AFSJ) that need to be adapted to the actual ownership of data and exercise of power to be effective. In this context, 'post hoc accountability', in the form of explanation and justification 'in retrospect', is becoming a key mode of (democratic) control and legitimation.[23]

[19] E. Brouwer, *Digital Borders and Real Rights: Effective Remedies for Third-Country Nationals in the Schengen Information System* (2008), at 289.

[20] Busuioc and Curtin, 'The Politics of Information in EU Internal Security: Information-Sharing by European Agencies', in T. Blom and S. Vanhoonacker (eds), *The Politics of Information* (2014).

[21] C. Moser, *Accountability in EU Security and Defence: The Law and Practice of Peacebuilding* (2020), at 119.

[22] Vavoula, 'Interoperability of EU Information Systems: The Deathblow to the Rights of Privacy and Personal Data Protection of Third-Country Nationals?', 26(1) *European Public Law* (2020) 131.

[23] D. Curtin, P. Mair, and Y. Papadopoulos (eds), *Accountability and European Governance* (2012).

Third, and perhaps most importantly, the fact that EU data-led security works in large measure through database interoperability (as discussed above), means that anchor points for accountability need to be located in complex public–private networks of cooperation and data sharing.[24] Interoperability exacerbates a number of issues including perceived mutual trust in national administrations and trust in technologies.[25] It aggravates the obscurity and difficult accountability that results from the fragmented character of composite administration, where the EU administration enjoys status of a 'second order' administration that is only answerable to other administrations, if at all.[26] It becomes hard to pinpoint at exactly what level of administration mistakes are made. It is also close to impossible for the public or for institutions not involved in the interoperable (law enforcement) networks to demand access and understand how the processing of data results in concrete security decisions.[27] As the intelligence networks in AFSJ contain both personal and non-personal data this implies for the individuals whose data is being shared within interoperable networks and databases that they lose control over their own personal data. The fact is that the data in question are largely collected by the administrative authorities of the Member States using a variety of methods and sources, including information that may have been in many instances collected originally by private parties.

3. Accountability as Mechanism and Practice: Logging-in Overseers

As the example of the TFTP overseers and databases discussed in our introduction shows, EU data-led security is creating novel mechanisms and devices of accountability in a relatively fragmentary fashion. Even if existing concepts and structures of accountability are challenged through data-led security and its reliance on interoperability, new ad hoc practices are emerging. The translation of ideal-typical accountability into concrete practices is the result of complex processes of negotiation in a multilevel setting. The overseer positions have, for example, been designed in a unique and path-dependent process of

[24] Curtin and Brito Bastos (n. 13).

[25] Vavoula, 'Information Sharing in the Dublin System: Remedies for Asylum Seekers In-Between Gaps in Judicial Protection and Interstate Trust', 22(3) *German Law Journal* (2021) 391.

[26] Curtin, 'The EU Automated State Disassembled', in E. Fisher, J. King, and A. Young (eds), *The Foundations and Future of Public Law: Essays in Honour of Paul Craig* (2020) 233, at 252.

[27] Huysmans, 'What's in an Act: On Security Speech Acts and Little Security Nothings', 42(4–5) *Security Dialogue* (2011) 371.

negotiation between the EU and the US, involving multiple levels and layers of EU decision-making. New institutions like the overseer office might offer creative solutions to address accountability deficits in relation to novel security programmes, but they are also legal hybrids that need further critical attention. How do these new institutions and mechanisms actually work? What kind of accountability documents, devices, and outputs do they entail? What kind of knowledge do they produce, and what remains obfuscated? Do they deliver the key principles of accountability in terms of explanation, justification, and sanction, and if so, how?

As Bovens argues, the social relationships that constitute accountability work through concrete 'mechanism[s] that involve an obligation to explain and justify conduct'.[28] The emphasis on *mechanisms* is relevant here: it directs attention away from accountability as an ideal-typical legal norm towards an examination of how accountability mechanisms work in actual practice (which can then be assessed on a normative basis). Literatures in Science-and-Technology studies (STS) are helpful to grasp such (technological) practices analytically, as they distinguish *accountability* as a political and ethical principle from *account-ability* understood as the material practices that render an order's actions 'observable-reportable'.[29] *Account-ability* in this sense goes beyond an analysis of the mechanisms identified by Bovens to understand accountability as being made up of the concrete, material, sedimented practices through which ideal-typical accountability takes shape. It is made up of everyday activities like 'keeping records, following instructions, justifying actions in relation to guidelines'.[30] It involves choices concerning forms and timing of reporting, technical specifications of what and how to report, priorities in justification, and the specification of appropriate modes of public questioning.

Three key mechanisms of accountability have been identified in the literature. According to the accountability definition of Bovens, the provision of information is the first stage of the accountability process upon which all further stages rest—no accountability without information.[31] The power holder needs 'to inform the forum about his or her conduct'.[32] Providing information changes the allocation of power both for those who take decisions (the power wielders) and those who want to hold them to account for that use of

[28] Bovens (n. 10) 951.

[29] Neyland, 'Bearing Account-able Witness to the Ethical Algorithmic System', 41(1) *Science, Technology, & Human Values* (2016) 55; Marres and Lezaun, 'Materials and Devices of the Public: an Introduction', 40(4) *Economy and Society* (2011) 489.

[30] Neyland (n. 29) 55.

[31] Moser (n. 21) 125.

[32] Bovens (n. 10) 952.

information. Without information, the power wielders cannot have a basis for their decision and its accuracy is otherwise put to account. In this sense information is both an instrument of empowerment and, through withholding it from those outside the enclave, dis-empowerment. At the level of EU databases, the information holder is at the European level and subject to its rules and regulations and the data is transferred/shared with an information recipient that is different to the information provider (the Member State that owns the data). In this information triangle, the common outsider is the individual whose data is at stake. Without information to hold the power wielder to account, the individual cannot hope to attain accountability for the actual decision taken, which may be of a transient nature, for example, exclusion from the territory of a Member State/EU, and in many cases will not lead to a full judicial hearing where the data relied on is scrutinized at the national level.

The second principle of accountability is explanation, which is closely coupled to justification. According to Bovens, the citizen forum 'needs to be able to interrogate the actor' and the actor needs to be able to explain choices and justify courses of action.[33] Again, it is useful to think concretely about how such justifications are performed in practice and how they are rendered materially possible. Boltanski and Thévenot suggest that we examine the concrete 'operations' that are performed in order to link an actor's decisions to general normative principles.[34] How are specific judgments related and explained with reference to the common good? As new and hybrid accountability institutions and practices emerge within EU data-led security, it is imperative to examine critically the concrete operation of justification.

The third and final principle of accountability is the crucial question *for what* an actor can be held to account/sanctioned by an appropriate accountability forum, and whether and how they may 'face consequences'.[35] Is it for the quality or quantity of information provided or for the actual conduct that has been undertaken on the basis of the data accesses by the (national) actor? The power of a forum to sanction for the content of the account is what Philip called a 'contingent condition of accountability'.[36] The obligation to provide information is on this analysis the *necessary* condition of accountability. In the area of police cooperation and shared information in interoperable databases and otherwise, as we shall see, there are a number of characteristics that are

33 Ibid. 953.

34 Boltanski and Thévenot, 'The Reality of Moral Expectations: A Sociology of Situated Judgment', 3 *Philosophical Explorations* (2000) 208.

35 Bovens (n. 10) 952.

36 Moser (n. 21) 125.

quite specific and might lead to the conclusion that one of the fundamental reasons why accountability is inhibited in these enclaves is that the mechanisms of accountability are quite simply 'logged-out' or disconnected from the content and use of the data in question (as opposed to its retention and collection). This customization of existing notions of accountability to interoperable AFSJ databases and agency cooperation may lead to novel conceptualizations of what accountability can mean in this context.

In relation to data-led security, these three principles of accountability are more complex than the literature initially presumed. As we have discussed elsewhere, data-led security can be understood as a chain-like process, where each analytical step in the chain feeds into the next, in bits, bytes, searches, and possible hits. In such chain-like processes, data are captured (often from commercial systems), they are curated into transferable datasets, they are shared across systems or jurisdictions (through techno-juridical arrangements), and they are analysed (with the aid of trained algorithms).[37] Alternatively, in models of interoperability, databases remain decentralized, but can be queried and connected through specific nodal points and techno-juridical arrangements. These chain-like workflows ultimately produce particular security decisions, whereby the outcomes of one link in the chain feed into the next step in the process. Consequently, data-led security decisions are not momentary or hidden inside an algorithmic 'black box', but they are processual and iterative. Security decisions are dispersed across iterative processes of data curation, transfer, and analysis.

Subsequently, we find that questions of accountability in data-led security too often focus on unpacking the inner workings of the algorithm, by seeking to 'open the black box' of the algorithm.[38] Till Straube has argued that the metaphor of opening the algorithmic black box is a seductive fallacy that 'appeals to the researcher's fantasy of bringing the (dark) secrets of an elusive object to light ... [Yet] even if we succeed, what we usually find is more black boxes'.[39] In contrast, if data-led security is understood as a technical-juridical *process*, the

[37] de Goede, 'The Chain of Security', 44 *Review of International Studies* (2018) 24; Bellanova and de Goede, 'The Algorithmic Regulation of Security: An Infrastructural Perspective', *Regulation & Governance* (2022) 16 (1), 102–118; L. Amoore, *Cloud Ethics: Algorithms and the Attributes of Ourselves and Others* (2020).

[38] What M. Ziewitz calls 'the algorithmic drama' in Ziewitz, 'Governing Algorithms', 41(1) *Science, Technology & Human Values* (2020) 3; Koivisto, 'Thinking Inside the Box: The Promise and Boundaries of Transparency in Automated Decision-Making', 1 *EUI Working Paper AEL 2020/01* (2020) https://cadmus.eui.eu/bitstream/handle/1814/67272/AEL_2020_01.pdf? 11; also Koivisto, Chapter 3, this volume.

[39] Straube, 'The Black Box and its Dis/Contents', in E. Bosma, M. de Goede, and P. Pallister-Wilkins (eds), *Secrecy and Methods in Security Research: A Guide to Qualitative Fieldwork* (2020) 175, at 178 and 182.

challenges to accountability are dispersed across the iterative, socio-technical process of data-led sensemaking.

These challenges thoroughly problematize the actor–forum–relation triad that Bovens theorizes. First, it is not always clear who the *actor* to be held to account is. Data-led security involves complex public–private cooperation and the use of mundane, commercial data for security analytics.[40] Actors are not always (national) governments or governmental institutions but can be transnational agencies or public–private collaborations that have been institutionalized with complex data architectures and interlinking databases. Interoperability generates the (partial) connection of different actors and (pre-existing) databases in decentralized and ways. There is almost always a multiplicity of public–private actors involved in data-led security programmes, from the commercial providers who compile and curate databases, to public actors who are able to retrieve hits from interconnected databases that inform their security analysis and actions. The key challenge to accountability is not simply how to hold an actor to account, but how to log into the processual collaboration of multiple actors and databases, to enforce specific moments or processes of public visibility and giving account.

Second, the citizen *forum* to which account must be given is not a national citizenry but a multinational and dispersed public. The public forum, as we know from the work of Marres and Lezaun, is not independent from its material gathering, like, for example, a hearing or a court procedure. An approach informed by STS asks about the 'materials and devices of public participation', instead of defining 'publics and their politics largely in discursive ... or procedural terms'.[41] So this means that we need to be attentive to how accountability fora are able to emerge; where questions can be posed and an investigation can take place. Concretely then, one question for data-led security is how complaints or cases of harm can be heard; how they can be rendered visible and audible to the extent that they become a matter of concern around which a public can assemble?[42]

Third, the *relation* between the actor and the forum in EU data-led security is multilevel and complex. The political science literature that analyses the rise of

[40] L. Amoore, *The Politics of Possibility* (2013); Amoore and de Goede, 'Transactions after 9/11: The Banal Face of the Preemptive Strike', 33(2) *Transactions of the Institute of British Geographers* (2008) 173; Bures and Carrapiço, 'Private Security Beyond Private Military and Security Companies', 67(3) *Crime, Law and Social Change* (2017) 229; Mitsilegas, 'Transatlantic Counterterrorism Cooperation and European Values' in E. Fahey and D. Curtin (eds) *A Transatlantic Community of Law* (2014) 289.

[41] Marres and Lezaun (n. 29) 490.

[42] B. Latour, *What Is the Style of Matters of Concern? Two Lectures in Empirical Philosophy* (2008); Marres, 'Front-Staging Non-Humans: Publicity as a Constraint on the Political Activity of Things', in B. Braun and S. J. Whatmore (eds), *Political Matter: Technoscience, Democracy, and Public Life* (2010).

European administrative networks in general points out that the dispersion of tasks within such networks dilutes political responsibility; and that those networks' weak visibility 'insulates them from public scrutiny'.[43] Yet these issues are exacerbated in the chain-like processes of interoperability in particular. As was mentioned before, the very dataflows and the infrastructure created to enable them involve sensitive information, either because that information concerns personal data or because the purposes for which such data are collected and processed, more specifically security purposes, can often not be reconciled with total transparency to the public at large. Accountability does require that a forum exists to pass judgment on the actions of authorities; yet the secretive and highly technical nature of interoperability makes the accountability fora more exclusive, more remote and therefore in practice limited, not logged-in to the chain-like processes. To a large extent, and where they are provided for at all, the accountability mechanisms of interoperable sharing and automated processing of personal data are designed to be deployed away from the eyes of the public and often away from the eyes of public accountability forums. This may be more a form of shielded accountability to privileged forums or entities rather than any reasonable understanding of public accountability. This will be explored in the following sections, both in terms of mechanism and in actual logging practice.

4. Account-ability in EU Data-led Security: Logged-out Mechanisms and Practices

The remainder of this chapter examines how the concrete mechanisms of account-ability are taking shape in relation to selected EU data-led security programmes. This will allow us to theorize trends and critically analyse the limits to accountability in security database interoperability. The focus, first, is on mapping and analysing the concrete practices through which specific security programmes seek to render their actions account-able. What kind of documents, devices, and offices have been created within these security programmes to offer public information and (a measure of) justification for actions and decisions taken? What are the technical and legal forms of narrative justification that are being designed? In this context, it is equally important to

[43] Mastenbroek and Sindbjerg Martinsen, 'Filling the Gap in the European Administrative Space: The Role of Administrative Networks in EU Implementation and Enforcement', 25(3) *Journal of European Public Policy* (2018) 422, at 429.

map the aspects of such security programmes that remain invisible, and that are not able to be accounted for. As a growing literature points out, silences and obfuscation in international politics can be part of 'strategic ignorance', which distributes responsibility in specific ways.[44] Furthermore, what kind of sanctions or consequences could actors face, if any, in case their accounts are rejected by European publics? Is it possible at all for public fora to be assembled through the mechanisms and devices created within these programmes?

In these empirical sections, we focus on four selected EU data-led security programmes. First, the TFTP is a transatlantic security programme whereby financial transactions data of the financial telecommunications company SWIFT are shared transatlantically with US security authorities in the context of counterterrorism investigations. It is based on a 2010 EU–US specifically negotiated Treaty (the TFTP Treaty).[45] Second, TERREG is a recently adopted EU Regulation for 'Preventing the Dissemination of Terrorist Content Online', which came into force in May 2021.[46] It authorizes social media service providers to police and remove utterances from their platforms, and enables the use of EU-led 'referrals' whereby European police authorities flag suspicious content to providers. Both TERREG and TFTP entail a security practice whereby commercial data are shared and algorithmically analysed in the context of counterterrorism, leading to concrete security decisions to alert security authorities, freeze financial transactions, or take content offline. Third, ETIAS is an automated data-led border control system, specifically to register visitors from countries who do not need a visa to enter the Schengen Zone. ETIAS gathers and analyses personal data (including travel documents and criminal records) and screens against existing watchlists (such as the Europol information system, VIS, Eurodac, SIS II, and the new Entry/Exit System [EES]), with the objective 'to make sure that these people are not a security threat'.[47] The personal data processed through the ETIAS Central System, a new database, is not simply checked against *existing* lists of 'persons of interest', but mined and used to profile prospective travellers based on data that already exists about *other* individuals.[48] ETIAS is expected to become operational in 2022. Finally, 2019

[44] McGoey, 'Strategic Unknowns: Towards a Sociology of Ignorance', 41 *Economy and Society* (2012) 1; McGoey, 'The Logic of Strategic Ignorance', 63 *The British Journal of Sociology* (2012) 533.

[45] Regulation (EU) 2021/784 of the European Parliament and of the Council of 29 April 2021 on addressing the dissemination of terrorist content online, OJ L 172/79.

[46] The European Parliament approved TERREG with a vote in the plenary on 28 May 2021. The Regulation entered into force on 6 June 2021 and will apply as of 7 June 2022.

[47] European Travel Information and Authorisation System (ETIAS), https://www.schengenvisainfo.com/etias/ (last visited 15 December 2021); on the politics of watchlist screening, Sullivan and de Goede (n. 6).

[48] Alegre, Jeandesboz, and Vavoula (n. 16) 24.

saw the adoption of the Regulation establishing ECRIS-TCN, the European Criminal Records Information System that allows the exchange of criminal conviction data concerning third-country nationals.[49] Unlike the previously existing ECRIS system, which basically interconnects the national criminal records on EU nationals, ECRIS-TCN facilitates finding the Member State that holds information on the criminal records of third-country nationals.[50]

Of these four programmes, only one, the TFTP, is relatively well-developed with established practices both of reporting and accounting, while in the other three this is still emerging. TERREG, ETIAS, and ECRIS-TCN have little to no actual practice yet in the form of logging, reporting, and accounting beyond what is prescribed in the foundational instruments and some institutional dialogue prior to and at the time of creation. Yet, all four of these EU security programmes have complex constellations of actors: national and supranational, public and private, as well as complex techno-juridical processes of data transfer and/or database interoperability. They are, however, negotiated by different actors and embedded in different (accountability) structures. Whereas the TFTP belongs in the external relations space (via a specific Treaty of the EU with a third state, the US), the other three programmes are largely internal to the EU. TERREG is the most explicit in the relationship with and imposition of obligations on private actors while the other two, ETIAS and ECRIS-TCN, essentially involve relationships among various types of institutions and agencies at different governance levels. TERREG involves an ongoing relationship with the EU agency Europol, whereas both ETIAS and ECRIS-TCN, exist by virtue of the little-known EU agency, eu-LISA. eu-LISA maintains these databases and is also largely responsible for account giving in the sense of reporting, such as it is, on both large-scale programmes. The relationship of these agencies with other core institutional actors at the EU level is also key in terms of to whom the account giving is made. Beyond the bare words of the founding regulations we extrapolate as to both the future role of and accounting by Europol on TERREG and the future role of and accounting by eu-LISA on ETIAS and ECRIS-TCN from the practice that has already developed by these relatively long-standing EU agencies with regard to other similar programmes/databases (Europol IRU in the case of TERREG and SIS II, VIS and Eurodac in the case of the other two newer databases).

[49] Regulation (EU) 2019/816 of the European Parliament and of the Council of 17 April 2019 establishing a centralised system for the identification of Member States holding conviction information on third-country nationals and stateless persons (ECRIS-TCN) to supplement the European Criminal Records Information System and amending Regulation (EU) 2018/1726 OJ L 135/1.

[50] For an overview of ECRIS-TCN, see Brouwer (n. 12).

In our view, this 'first cut' mapping of emerging accountability practices is not only a useful exercise in and of itself but it also provides pointers to the nature of the accountability arrangements in place for highly data specific programmes that follow their own internal logic and sharing practices that may not be visible at all to the outside world (or even to parts of the inside world) unless windows are opened in a timely and/or strategic fashion to targeted audiences that may evaluate what has happened and reveal no operational details publicly. ETIAS also makes provision for the algorithmic profiling of third country travellers in a sophisticated manner. ETIAS and ECRIS-TCN are two distinct information systems, with many structural similarities in how they are organized, as well as the fact that they are intended for the exchange and processing of information on third country nationals, with the purpose of public security in mind.

The four data-led security programmes are distinctive in terms of set-up, scale, sharing arrangements, and regulatory framework. In terms of commercial data, the TFTP and TERREG most clearly work with data captured and mined from private actors (SWIFT in the case of the TFTP and internet platforms in the case of TERREG). In contrast, both ETIAS and ECRIS-TCN are border management and judicial cooperation programmes (primarily for security purposes) that are basically public databases that share data gathered by various public authorities. In the case of ECRIS-TCN this is relatively straightforward but ETIAS is much more open for example through the European Search Portal in gathering data from public databases through a system of interoperability. Personal data has been gathered for largely specific purposes (e.g. visas, etc.) unrelated to the purposes for which they will be used, and connected though the auspices of the new ETIAS. Part of the cross-checking of ETIAS applications will be against data held by Europol. Europol databases include data gathered from private parties and, under the latest proposal, it will have even more opportunities to gather and share such data.

In all of our cases, we see that EU agencies play a crucial role in developing technical infrastructures, presenting themselves as offering 'merely' technical support. However, it should be clear that the design and operation of technical infrastructures for data sharing entails political choices and consequences for the operation of accountability (or lack thereof).[51] For example, eu-LISA is responsible for the operational management of both ETIAS and ECRIS-TCN. In

[51] Bellanova and de Goede (n. 37); Bellanova and Glouftsios, 'Controlling the Schengen Information System (SIS II): The Infrastructural Politics of Fragility and Maintenance,' 27:1 *Geopolitics* (2022) 160–184.

ETIAS, two other EU agencies play an important role. Frontex will be setting up and running the ETIAS Central Unit, and Europol will be contributing to and reviewing the ETIAS watchlist.[52] This is the main role that these interoperable information systems attribute to eu-LISA, the EU's large-scale information systems agency. eu-LISA is comparatively old, having been established in 2011 and starting its activities in 2012. It was envisaged as a type of management authority entrusted with all the activities necessary to keep large-scale IT systems such as VIS, Schengen etc. alive and took over tasks in the early years from the Commission, in particular DG HOME. Whereas as yet there is no actual reporting in place for ETIAS and ECRIS-TCN we look below by analogy to the reporting by eu-LISA of VIS and other systems to understand the kinds of issues that arise and the approach (that may be) taken. TFTP and TERREG, by comparison, do not work through eu-LISA, but have technical infrastructures that work through Europol. For example, Europol serves as point of contact for TFTP-related leads that are shared to and from the US Treasury in the context of counterterrorism investigations.

All four programmes involve the transnational interoperability of national databases that contain sensitive personal data. Three of them (excluding ECRIS-TCN) involve complex chains of public–private data sharing and collaboration, which challenge and complicate traditional mechanisms of accountability. As discussed in the first part of this chapter, traditional mechanisms of transparency and redress are difficult to operationalize when security decisions are taken across databases, jurisdictions, and across public and private spaces with lack of clear responsibilities for private companies and public actors. In the sections that follow, we map the ways in which practical account-ability processes and mechanisms are taking shape, in order to reflect on the characteristics and limits of what we call 'logged-in accountability' and possible solutions in the future.

A. Information

The availability of information in EU data-led programmes security consists primarily of self-reporting by the various actors involved, whereby crucial

[52] Arts 75 and 77 ETIAS Regulation (EU) 2018/1240; 'EU: Construction of the European Travel Information and Authorisation System (ETIAS): Progress Reports from Frontex and Europol', *Statewatch News* (2019), https://www.statewatch.org/news/2019/may/eu-construction-of-the-european-travel-information-and-authorisation-system-etias-progress-reports-from-frontex-and-europol/ (last visited 16 December 2021).

'strategic unknowns' are generated.[53] To some extent, we see the transfer of reporting obligations away from the public, towards the private sector, or in other cases made in a non-public way to selected public actors. Because actors themselves select what to disclose, important elements remain publicly unknown—this is not simply an omission but the political production of strategic unknowns. This section maps and analyses the practices, documents and procedures for the provision of information that are in place or will soon be in place (or are by analogy in place in other areas) in our four selected data-led security programmes. It shows if and how information about the scope and numbers of personal data, the technical operations of data transfer, and the processes of accessing and retaining personal data, are being presented and made accessible either in a non-public way or publicly.

The extent to which the various data-led security programmes have a body of empirical data that is publicly available as to their various activities, searches, and hits and otherwise, varies considerably across the cases. This has something to do with the timeline involved but also the actors and regulatory structures put in place at varying moments over the course of the past 12 years. TFTP gives an account of itself through two mechanisms. First, as stipulated in Article 10 of the TFTP Treaty, the parties to the Treaty conduct a regular Joint Review, including a 'proportionality assessment of the Provided Data, based on the value of such data for the investigation, prevention, detection, or prosecution of terrorism or its financing'.[54] This regular review has led to five Joint Review reports to date, yet these are not an independent audit or oversight, but conducted by the Treaty parties themselves. For example, the 2019 EU–US TFTP Joint Review teams included two officials from the European Commission, two representatives of European data protection authorities and seven US officials, from the Departments of Justice and the Treasury, and from the Office of the Director of National Intelligence (Civil Liberties Protection Officer).[55] Second, the TFTP is subject to the Europol independent oversight body, the Joint Supervisory Board (JSB) until 2019, and subsequently the EDPS from 2019. The Europol oversight is a full independent oversight structure, yet it applies only to *part of* the TFTP activities, namely Europol's role in Article 4 of the Treaty, which regulates the US data requests that are the basis of the transatlantic data transfer. It does not examine the practices inside the US Treasury and it does not examine the data transfers on the basis of Articles 9 and 10 of the TFTP Treaty. Moreover,

[53] McGoey, 'Strategic Unknowns' (n. 44); McGoey, 'The Logic of Strategic Ignorance' (n. 44).
[54] Art. 10(1) Terrorist Finance Tracking Programme (TFTP) Treaty.
[55] Commission Report 342 final on the TFTP Joint Review (2019), at 21.

the Annexes to the JSB Reports, in which the substantial evaluation of the programme and its data transfers processes is set out, are classified as EU-Secret and therefore not available publicly or for research purposes, even if the short concluding sections of the JSB Reports are available.

At first glance, then, the publicly available *information* on the TFTP is really quite substantial: five Joint Review reports have been released since the start of the TFTP Treaty (2010) and at least two JSB Reports (even if partially classified). At the time of writing, collectively these reports offer over 200 pages of information and evaluation of a relatively secret security programme. The *information* in these so-called Joint Reviews includes details on the process of evaluation (the review process), as well as details on the nature, number, and results of the searches of personal financial data. In line with examining account-ability as a practice, it is useful to know what information is (not) made available through the Joint Review reports, as this reveals something about the ways in which reporting, analysing, numbering, and accounting is done in practice in the name of accountability. Key information that has become available through the Joint Review reports is the number of *searches* conducted monthly in the TFTP database. These searches have to be based on a 'nexus to terrorism or its financing' (Article 5b of the TFTP Treaty). On the basis of a piece of personal data, for example, a name, address, credit card number, wire transfer, or social security number, searches can pull strings of network information from the TFTP database. Figure 6.1 summarizes the number of searches that are detailed in the

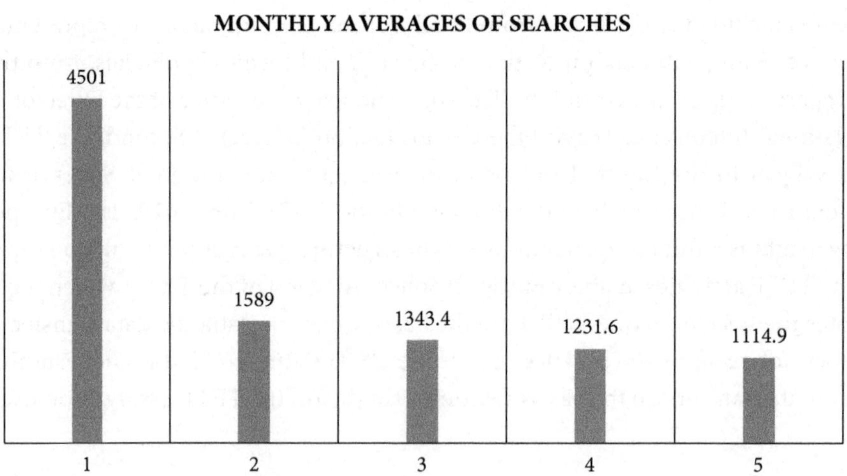

Figure 6.1: Monthly average of searches in the TFTP database per review period. (Data compiled by Asma Balfiqih from Joint Review reports.)

successive review reports between 2010 and 2020. For example, the First Joint Review Report notes that there were 27,000 searches in the first five months of the programme.

Another key piece of information in the Joint Review reports concerns the number of leads shared from the US Treasury with EU Member States and with Europol. There are two ways in which TFTP-derived intelligence can find its way its way back to Europe: first, leads that are voluntarily pushed by the US Treasury/CIA to European counterparts (Article 9). Second, leads that are shared after European requests for information and searches to be done within TFTP (Article 10 requests). The latter was widely criticized as a type of intelligence 'outsourcing', though as we can see in Figure 6.2, this type of request has increased substantially in the most recent review period (2016–2018). The increasingly active use of European intelligence services (via Europol) of the TFTP, is now used as an argument concerning its value and legitimacy.

The TFTP reports are also very useful as they provide indications as to the type of statistical information that is expressly *not* included in the review reports. In the TFTP example, this relates to the data actually requested from SWIFT (the designated provider) and transferred to the US Treasury. We do know that this information is not known, because its existence is addressed and explained in the reports, and its absence constitutes a visible point of contention between the EU and the US. In other words, the size of transatlantic data transfers is no longer a 'deep secret' as it was in the years after 9/11, when

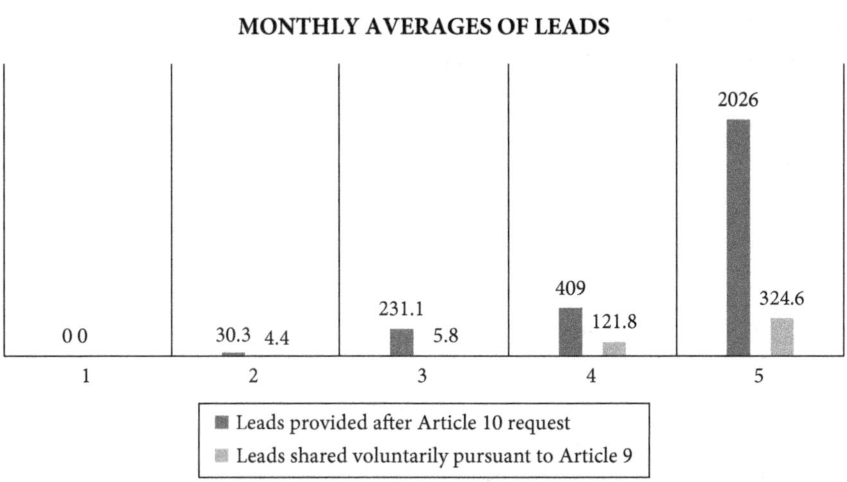

Figure 6.2: Monthly average of leads shared per review period. (Data compiled by Asma Balfiqih from TFTP Joint Review reports.)

it was simply not known that these data transfers took place at all.[56] About this 'overall volume of data provided [by the Designated Provider],' the First Joint Review Report says: 'there is a clear interest from many sides to be informed on this point in order to fully understand the scope of the programme, its possible implications on civil liberties, and thus its proportionality'.[57] However, the US has consistently and explicitly refused to render this information public through the Joint Review process or by other means. This is more than a mere contestation over the publicity of numbers. At the root of the disagreement over the question of whether the scope of data transfers should be public is a deeper disagreement over the nature and definition of 'proportionality' as a data protection measure. The US maintain that the broad scope data transfers are necessary, defined as sets of transactions of a particular message type, within a given timeframe, and to/from particular geographical areas. While the requests detailing these parameters have become ever more substantive (see below), it is not known whether this has led to more tailored and more limited data transfers.

TERREG, by comparison, is wholly within the authority of the EU and it is foreseen that by June 2023 a detailed programme for monitoring the outputs, results, and impacts of TERREG shall be established by the EU Commission.[58] In this sense, the contours of oversight and public reporting are still in the making, even if the Regulation came into force in May 2021. TERREG also stipulates that annual transparency reports by platforms are legally required to record publicly how many pieces of terrorist-related content have been removed. This is important because the deletion and storage of suspect social media content affects the contours of online public space.[59] The definition of what counts as terrorism in social media policing, however, is broad and lacks juridical precision. It can affect broad batches of online user-generated content.[60] Europol IRU—here considered to be a precursor of the impact of TERREG— explicitly advocates the take-down of what it calls 'non-violent terrorist content' including material on terrorist groups' 'alleged utopian aspects',

[56] Abazi (n. 8); de Goede and Wesseling, 'Secrecy and Security in Transatlantic Terrorism Finance Tracking', 39 *Journal of European Integration* (2017) 253.

[57] Commission Report 342 final on the Joint Review of the TFTP (2011), at 7.

[58] Art. 21(2) of TERREG (EU) 2021/784.

[59] S. T. Roberts, *Behind the Screen: Content Moderation in the Shadows of Social Media* (2019); De Gregorio, 'Democratising Online Content Moderation', 36 *Computer Law & Security Review* (2019) 1; Helberger, Pierson, and Poell, 'Governing Online Platforms: From Contested to Cooperative Responsibility', 34 *The Information Society* (2018) 1.

[60] Van Hoboken, 'The Proposed EU Terrorism Content Regulation: Analysis and Recommendations with Respect to Freedom of Expression Implications', *Transatlantic Working Group on Content Moderation Online and Freedom of Expression* (2019) 1.

but also poetry and song lyrics that can be linked to groups like IS.[61] Clearly, such a broad approach to content removal raises questions concerning the scope and application of future TERREG impact.[62]

TERREG stipulates that social media providers publish transparency reports, with information on the measures taken to remove content, the numbers of items removed, the ways in which prevention of re-upload is done ('in particular where automated tools have been used') and the number and outcome of complaints.[63] These transparency reports have to be provided by private platforms, because the decision to remove content ultimately remains a private decision, even if it is steered in content and governed in procedure by public authorities. We may glimpse how such transparency reports will look in practice once TERREG comes into force in June 2022 by examining a similar entity operating under the auspices of Europol, the EU IRU, which also publishes transparency reports. Three have been published to date (2017, 2018, and 2019) and offer valuable information on the number of pieces of 'terrorist content' that are assessed and deleted. On the one hand, we get some quantitative information concerning removals of online content. For example, in the 2018 report, it is noted that: 'A total of 86,076 pieces have been assessed, which triggered 83,871 decisions for referral. The content was detected across 179 online platforms.'[64] On the other hand, the reports do not define how a 'piece of terrorist content' is defined or (algorithmically) recognized. The reports use a lot of jargon concerning the new policies and instruments that are being developed in the context of IRU, discussing for example 'intelligence notification', 'cross-match reports', etc., without explaining and contextualizing what these 'products and services' entail. It may, however, be queried how useful this information is and it seems not to be forwarded to anyone for discussion or debate. Articles 7 and 8 of TERREG prescribe the obligation of annual transparency reports by hosting services and social media platforms, detailing the nature of the information to be included in such reports. Remedies and redress mechanisms are to be designed by the companies themselves, and no mention is made in the Regulation of an independent forum where the transparency

[61] EU IRU, *On the Importance of Taking-Down Non-Violent Terrorist Content*, VoxPol, (2019), https://www.voxpol.eu/on-the-importance-of-taking-down-non-violent-terrorist-content/ (last visited 10 December 2021).

[62] Mandates of the Special Rapporteur on the promotion and protection of the right to freedom of opinion and expression; The Special Rapporteur on the right to privacy and the Special Rapporteur on the promotion and protection of human rights and fundamental freedoms while countering terrorism; Van Hoboken (n. 60).

[63] Section III, Arts 7–8 TERREG (EU) 2021/784.

[64] EU IRU, *Transparency Report 2019* (2020), at 5.

reports are assembled or examined, or where disputes concerning the legitimacy of removal can be taken.

When it comes to ETIAS but also ECRIS-TCN, we move into an assessment of interoperable EU and national information systems that are less obviously connected to private actors in the way the previous two examples are, although ETIAS involves airline companies in pre-boarding checks. The specific nature of the activities of the public authorities involved in interoperable data sharing for security purposes involves the processing of very large amounts of personal data. ETIAS does not process biometric data, but it does process some information on criminal records (also deserving special safeguards). ECRIS-TCN, by contrast, processes both biometric data (fingerprints and potentially facial images) and some information on criminal records (the existence of a criminal record as such).[65]

Both the supervision by the EDPS and the reporting obligations in question require the actors involved in the use, management, and development of ETIAS and ECRIS-TCN—and above all, the concrete mediator, eu-LISA—to continually offer information and explanation about how the two information systems are functioning, and whether they function appropriately in view of data protection and fundamental rights standards.[66] These are undoubtedly practices of account-ability and show how accountability is given concrete shape in these programmes. They require that eu-LISA—and in some instances the European Border and Coast Guard Agency (EBCGA) (in relation to ETIAS and its Central Unit which it houses)—give account of how data is processed and of the lawfulness of their everyday data-sharing practices.

eu-LISA is, in its management and development of both ETIAS and ECRIS-TCN, also subject to a number of accountability practices specifically in this regard. It is, for instance, obliged to regularly report to the Member States and to the Commission on issues it encounters when carrying out quality checks on the data stored in the information systems.[67] It also has to inform the EDPS on measures it takes notably with regards the security of the processing or the lawful use of the data in the systems.[68] This is an important requirement and has analogies in other regulations of large-scale data information schemes such

[65] Arts 67 and 92 ETIAS Regulation (EU) 2018/1240; Arts 29 and 36 ECRIS-TCN Regulation (EU) 2019/816; on the need for supervision, see Quintel, 'Connecting Personal Data of Third Country Nationals: Interoperability of EU Databases in the Light of the CJEU's Case Law on Data Retention', 2 *University of Luxembourg Law Working Paper* (2018) 1; On ETIAS, Michéa and Rousvoal, 'The Criminal Procedure Out of Itself: A Case Study of the Relationship Between EU Law and Criminal Procedure using the ETIAS System', 6(1) *European Papers* (2021) 473.

[66] Art. 67(3) ETIAS Regulation (EU) 2018/1240; Art. 29(3) ECRIS-TCN Regulation (EU) 2019/816.

[67] Art. 11(13) ECRIS-TCN Regulation; Art. 74(5) ETIAS Regulation (EU) 2018/1240.

[68] Art. 59(5) ETIAS Regulation (EU) 2018/1240; Art. 13 ECRIS-TCN Regulation (EU) 2019/861.

as SIS II and VIS.[69] Moreover, whereas the national supervisory authorities ensure that the data transmitted to and from ECRIS-TCN and ETIAS at national level is lawfully processed under data protection law, eu-LISA is specifically subject to the supervision of the EDPS. The latter ensures that an audit is carried out of eu-LISA's personal data processing activities every three years, and that a report on that audit is sent to the European Parliament, the Council, the Commission, eu-LISA, and the supervisory authorities. eu-LISA is specifically required to cooperate with the EDPS by giving him the information she or he requests.[70]

eu-LISA must also report at regular intervals on the operation of the two databases. These reporting duties already start in the development phase of the information systems, and continue afterwards. In fact, Article 36 of ECRIS-TCN Regulation sets out that during its design and development phase, eu-LISA must report to the European Parliament and the Council on the state of development of the information system every six months.[71] The same goes for ETIAS. Article 92 of the Regulation notes that during the development phase, eu-LISA, but also Europol and the European Border and Coast Guard Agency (Frontex) are required to report twice a year on the progress made on the implementation and development of the Regulation.[72] While eu-LISA's reporting focuses among others on the evolution of the Central Unit and the communication infrastructure, the reporting of Frontex and Europol deals essentially with the costs incurred. After the start of ECRIS-TCN and ETIAS operation in 2022, and every two years thereafter, eu-LISA must submit a report on the technical functioning of the systems, including on issues of security, to the Commission.[73]

With regard to the European Commission, the Regulations state that every four years, it will produce a report on the evaluation of the databases.[74] Whereas the evaluation of ECRIS-TCN shall focus on the application of the Regulation, the results achieved, and the impact on fundamental rights, the evaluation of ETIAS also addresses the screening rules and the potential need to modify the mandate. The reports are based on information given to it by eu-LISA and the Member States. It may include recommendations or legislative

[69] Arts 15, 60(3) and 74 SIS II Regulation (EU) 2018/1862 on police and judicial cooperation in criminal matters OJ L 312/56; Arts 45 and 60 SIS II Regulation (EU) 2018/1861 on border checks OJ L 312/14; Art. 16 SIS II Regulation (EU) 2018/1860 on return of illegally staying third-country nationals OJ L 312/1; Arts 29 and 50(3) VIS Regulation (EU) 2021/1133 OJ L 248/1.

[70] Art. 67 ETIAS Regulation (EU) 2918/1240; Art. 29 ECRIS-TCN Regulation (EU) 2019/861.

[71] Art. 36(3) ECRIS-TCN Regulation (EU) 2019/861.

[72] Art. 92(2) ETIAS Regulation (EU) 2018/1240.

[73] Art. 92(4) ETIAS Regulation (EU) 2018/1240; Art. 36(8) ECRIS-TCN Regulation (EU) 2019/861.

[74] Art. 92(5) ETIAS Regulation (EU) 2018/1240; Art. 36(9) ECRIS-TCN Regulation (EU) 2019/861.

proposals to the European Parliament and the Council, and is sent to the European Parliament, the Council, the EDPS, and the FRA. One could say that, indirectly, the Commission's obligations to report to the remaining relevant EU institutions renders eu-LISA accountable to it, as eu-LISA must explain how the databases are functioning, so that the Commission may do the same. As of today, no practice can be found on reporting of these two databases, and it remains thus unclear what the control will look like. By analogy, one can analyse the evaluation reports made by the Commission on the SIS II and VIS.[75] These include statistical reports, studies, questionnaires, and interviews, and followed an assessment of the following criteria—effectiveness, coherence, efficiency, relevance, and added value. Thus, the future evaluation on ECRIS-TCN and ETIAS shall presumably follow the same approach.

ETIAS has a particularity in the sense that the overall framework for the processing of personal data is the responsibility of eu-LISA (as is the case with ECRIS-TCN), but it is for the EBCGA to set up the ETIAS Central Unit. The actual processing of personal data is the responsibility of the national authorities involved. Even if the involvement of the EU agencies in concrete, individual instances of data sharing will remain comparatively limited, the EBCGA and eu-LISA are nevertheless subject to various accountability mechanisms. The ETIAS Central Unit, which is established within the EBCGA, must publish an annual activity report that must include several statistics. The reports include notably the numbers of travel authorizations automatically issued by the ETIAS Central System, the numbers of applications verified by that unit, the numbers of applications manually processed per Member State, as well as the numbers of applications of third country nationals that were refused, along with the grounds for that refusal. In addition to such statistical information, the annual activity report by the ETIAS Central Unit must provide general information on the functioning of the ETIAS Central Unit and the challenges that it faces in exercising its tasks. The report is to be submitted to the European Parliament, the Council, and the Commission for information and possible debate.[76] Finally, ETIAS also devotes more attention to the accountability mechanisms that should apply to eu-LISA. It regularly reports to the Member States, the European Parliament, the Council, and the Commission, but also to ETIAS

[75] For example, European Commission 880 final, Report from the Commission to the European Parliament and the Council on the evaluation of the second-generation SIS II (2016); European Commission 328 final Staff Working Document (2016), Evaluation of the implementation of Regulation (EC) No 767/2008 of the European Parliament and Council concerning the VIS and the exchange of data between Member States on short-stay visas (VIS Regulation) of 14 October 2016.

[76] Art. 7(3) ETIAS Regulation (EU) 2018/1240.

Central Unit, when carrying out quality checks on the data contained in the ETIAS Central System.[77]

We have discussed present and future modes of reporting and public information as they exist within TFTP and IRU, and as they are taking shape in relation to TERREG, ECRIS-TCN, and ETIAS. A tabular summary of this discussion is provided in Table 6.1. Based on this overview, our preliminary conclusions are threefold. (1) Across the board, it seems that the provision of information is done by actors themselves, on their own terms, and using their own terminology and criteria. That terminology is (or may in the future) often be obfuscated and imprecise, and not easy to discern for a wider public. For example, what is a 'piece of terrorist-related content' in TERREG? What does 'transparency' and 'accountability' mean when used by eu-LISA in a telegraphic and self-referential way? (2) The provision of information is post hoc and focused on recounting technical facts (for example, numbers of searches, numbers of hits, numbers of pushes). In the case of ETIAS, ECRIS-TCN, and TERREG there is no actual practice yet of logging and reporting so reliance is placed on how Europol and eu-LISA have performed similar kinds of reporting in other data-driven environments. These deal essentially with the technical aspects of the infrastructure and the system, but also touch upon broader issues of security, data protection, and interoperability. (3) It is not clear to what extent there is an obligation for the institutional actor or accountability forum to debate, write a report on or investigate further through questioning of, for example, the Director of EU agencies (Europol and eu-LISA) after receiving the annual activity report or other less frequent evaluation reports. The role of the EDPS seems to be a limited one in these programmes, as does that of the national data protection authorities. This is not surprising given their limited resources and lack of technical knowledge.[78] The European Ombudsman does not seem to have a role in this context and the fact that already now there is such scarce information on actual supervision in practice of the existing databases feeds the expectation that this trend will continue in the future with the systems now emerging in the pipeline.

The depth of the analysis presented as well as the subsequent accountability trajectory in terms of dialogue will now be examined under the related accountability criteria of 'justification' and sanction and/or consequence imposed by another actor (public accountability forum).

[77] Art. 75(5) ETIAS Regulation (EU) 2018/1240.

[78] Lynskey, 'The Europeanisation of Data Protection Law', 19 *Cambridge Yearbook of European Legal Studies* (2017) 252, at 252–253.

Table 6.1 Information practices in TFTP, TERREG, ETIAS, and ECRIS-TCN.

	Report available and limitations	Who gives the information
TFTP	- Five review reports (Joint Reviews) including details on the process of evaluation, on the nature, number, and results of the searches, number of leads shared, etc. - JBS/EDPS Reports. - Crucial information is not included in the review reports (e.g. number data actually requested from SWIFT). - JSB/EDPS Reports are EU-Classified with the exception of their short concluding parts.	Joint Review Team (EU–US) Europol Oversight bodies.
TERREG	- Annual transparency reports by platforms include how many pieces of terrorist-related content have been removed, overview of complaint procedures, etc. - No definition of 'a piece of terrorist content'.	Report provided by private platforms.
ETIAS	- Reports during the development phase by eu-LISA, Europol, and Frontex, twice per year on the state of development and progress made. - Reports by eu-LISA once ETIAS is in operation on the technical functioning of the system (including security issues). - Audits by the EDPS on eu-LISA and the system. - ETIAS Central Unit, established within the EBCGA, publishes an annual activity report which includes several statistics. - eu-LISA regularly reports to Member States, the Commission, and EDPS on quality checks and security issues. - Report of the Commission on the evaluation of the system.	eu-LISA offers information and explanation on how the information system functions.
ECRIS-TCN	- Reports during the development phase by eu-LISA on the state of development and progress made (twice per year). - Reports by eu-LISA once ECRIS-TCN is in operation on the technical functioning of the system (including security issues). - Audits by the EDPS on eu-LISA and on the system. - eu-LISA regularly reports to Member States, the Commission, and EDPS on quality checks and security issue. - Report from the Commission on the evaluation of the system.	eu-LISA offers information and explanation on how the information system functions. Frontex accounts on how data is processed and the lawfulness of the everyday data-sharing practices.

B. Justification

The second mechanism of accountability is that of justification, which is needed before deliberation by an accountability forum is possible. Which decisions and choices are justified by the actor(s) involved, and how? Which decisions and choices simply remain unknown? Who is in charge of the narrative explanation concerning the actions and decisions made within data-led security programmes? And what are the normative terms of reference that are mobilized to justify a programme or a programme's actions? We find that the self-reporting by security authorities affects the manner in which explanation is structured and limited. As Ida Koivisto argues, algorithmic transparency often works through 'iconophilia', meaning that it focuses on 'illustrations, statistics, reports, memoranda etc.', that may prioritize visibility over explanation and justification.[79]

First, let us examine arguments and examples on effectiveness that are mobilized in relation to the TFTP and that justify it. In this programme, we can observe the emergence of specific narratives of justification that appeal to the effectiveness of the programme in relation to counterterrorism, but that ultimately reveal very little information on how algorithmic security works in the TFTP. It has become widely claimed that the TFTP is effective in its operations, yet public information that demonstrate the effectiveness remains limited. In the First Joint Review Report questions about the 'added value' of the TFTP to terrorist investigations were raised, and the report stated:

> the EU review team is of the opinion that efforts should be made to further substantiate the added value of the program, in particular through more systematic monitoring of the results ... Treasury should seek feedback from the agencies which receive TFTP derived information on a systematic basis in order to verify the added value of the information.[80]

In response to this call, from the Second Joint Review Report onward, the reporting includes case examples where TFTP-derived information ostensibly played an important role. These are important cases, mostly of well-known terrorist plots and suspects, that have been identified and, in some cases, prosecuted. For example, the 2017 Joint Review report mentions several so-called 'value examples' where TFTP information was used in cases of specific named

[79] Koivisto, 'Thinking Inside the Box' (n. 38) 11; also Koivisto, this volume (n. 38).
[80] TFTP First Joint Review Report (n. 57) 6.

terrorist suspects, terrorist perpetrators, and those advocating or recruiting for the conflict in Syria.[81] Yet at the same time, the precise link between these named cases and the algorithmic analysis within TFTP remains unclear.[82] It is not known which information about a case is TFTP-derived, and how such information was shared with national authorities. As such, the information in the case examples of the Joint Reviews cannot be independently verified by observers and researchers, and the question of whether TFTP-derived information was decisive, crucial, tangential, marginal, or irrelevant to a case, remains unanswerable. The generic case examples offered in review reports offer narrative justification that seems to underscore the effectiveness of the programme. However, the narratives are on the actors' own terms and cannot be independently verified. They fall (far) short of 'algorithmic accountability' that could log into the TFTP system to explain how TFTP search terms are linked to particular automated outcomes.

Similar considerations are very likely to apply to the use of algorithms in the context of ETIAS screening. Indeed, it may often be near-impossible to determine the exact causal links between a multitude of different human agents that fed the training data to the algorithm and how that algorithm actually worked later on in practice.[83] Engstrom and Ho aptly capture the nature of the problem at stake here: '[O]n the one hand, the body of law that governs how agencies do their work is premised on transparency, accountability and reason-giving. ... On the other hand, the algorithmic tools that agencies are increasingly using to make and support public decisions are not, by their structure, fully explainable.' The opacity of the algorithms that public agencies deploy inevitably becomes a matter of the opacity and accountability of the agencies themselves.[84]

Second, looking at IRU and TERREG, we ask how the effectiveness of these programmes is elaborated and justified. When it comes to the narrative justification of interventions and removals, the IRU reports offer cryptic formulations and little detail. For example, the 2017 IRU report notes that: 'The EU IRU supported 167 EU MS operations and produced 192 operational products.'[85] As previously mentioned, it remains unclear what 'operations' and 'operational

[81] Commission Report 31 final on the Fourth Joint Review Report of the TFTP (2017) at 41–43.

[82] M. Wesseling, 'The European Fight Against Terrorism Financing' (2013) (PhD dissertation, University of Amsterdam).

[83] Hayes, Van de Poel, and Steen, 'Algorithms and Values in Justice and Security', 35 *AI & Society* (2020) 533.

[84] Freeman Engstrom and Ho, 'Algorithmic Accountability in the Administrative State', 37 *Yale Journal on Regulation* (2020) 19, at 21–22.

[85] EU IRU, *Transparency Report 2017* Report (2018) at 7.

products' are in the context of flagging and removing online content. It remains to be seen how service providers will explain and justify operations and take-downs once TERREG mandated reports are issued. Removals have to be publicly reported and appeal mechanisms for mistakes and incorrect removals have to be designed, but this is to be done *by* the company and *within* the company, not through a broader, independent or publicly managed platform.

When it comes to ETIAS we can only deduce for now from the types of justification that are given on similar kinds of material by other mediating actors such as Europol and eu-LISA in other contexts. For example, when it comes to knowing the access of Europol to SIS II and the numbers of searches and hits then numbers are 'logged' in various reports. It is a matter of patching it together through the reporting by Europol itself as eu-LISA does not cover Europol access when it provides its general report on the operation of SIS II.[86] Not only is justification as such not given nor in any sense the practice by either agency but the amount of explanation given for any key choices is minimal, perhaps even non-existent. For example, a key choice was to install the capability to launch automated batch searches that facilitates more structured cross-checking of large amounts of relevant Europol data against the SIS.[87] It simply says: 'Schengen Information System (SIS) II: the batch search functionality was installed at the end of 2016. The efficiency of the process had a positive impact on the ability of Europol to utilize the system in supporting operations, with searches moving from 630 in 2016 to 21,951 from 1 January until 11 September 2017.'[88] No information on Europol access is included in the eu-LISA general reports.[89] A one word justification in the form of efficiency is all there is. This is paradigmatic for the kind of reporting that takes place in annual activity reports and database specific reporting by eu-LISA, such as on SIS II. The success of SIS II 'lies in its flexibility, vague wording and wide discretion to define the outer limits of who constitutes part of the risk population and be subject to surveillance of movement'.[90] Creating links between alerts may lead to situations where persons who were previously innocent become connected with crime or criminal networks, with adverse effects on their status.[91] Given the size and nature of SIS II this is of concern. When ETIAS comes into

[86] eu-LISA, *SIS II—2020 Statistics* (March 2021) notes that: 'However, the statistics on access to SIS II by the EU agencies are not included within the scope of this document [...]'.
[87] Europol, *Europol Programming Document 2018–2020* (2018) at 35–36.
[88] Europol, *2017 Consolidated Annual Activity Report* (2018), at 20.
[89] eu-LISA (n. 86) 5.
[90] N. Vavoula, *Immigration and Privacy in the Law of the European Union—The Case of Databases* (2019) at 135.
[91] F. Boehm, *Information Sharing and Data Protection in the Area of Freedom, Security and Justice, towards Harmonized Data Protection Principles for Information Exchange at EU-Level* (2012) at 266.

operation, this concern multiplies many times given the nature of the interoperability envisaged. ETIAS promises to deliver a 'justification of the refusal' to rejected applicants, yet it remains to be seen how such justifications are narrated and substantiated, especially as cases concerning lack of explanation in visa rejections have previously been brought before the EU courts.[92] In principle, the justification shall include the reason for the denial, reference to the ETIAS National Unit that refused the application and information on the right to lodge an appeal, but the basis of the decision will remain unknown (Europol data, from an alert, etc.).[93]

When it comes to ECRIS-TCN, not much is said about justification. It is only mentioned once in the Regulation: 'The log of consultations and disclosures shall make it possible to establish the justification of such operation.'[94] Thus, justification as such is not given in any sense; however, it shall be made possible at a later stage.

With regard to eu-LISA and its key mediating role creating and managing large-scale databases including both SIS II, VIS, and ETIAS and ECRIS-TCN its practice is to produce periodic reports as to their operation. Yet if one studies the reports that have been made for the other databases that will be interoperable with ETIAS and ECRIS-TCN once it comes into operation, there is a practice and technique of logging what are effectively the bits and bytes of data, the searches that have been made (and if applicable, the hits). There is certainly no justification given for why operations were carried out (even in procedural terms or according to substantive criteria in a way that are not individually operationally specific) and this will make the work of accountability fora such as the data protection authorities and the EDPS very difficult indeed. Such reports are then sent to certain core EU institutions for information. Only when the Commission has to do a four yearly evaluation may it engage in a more pro-active way with eu-LISA in terms of the information it requires. Similar evaluations were conducted on SIS II and VIS, in which the Commission assessed the relevance, effectiveness, efficiency, coherence, and added value of the system.[95] To do so, the Commission based itself on evidence and opinions from national authorities, Europol, the EDPS, and eu-LISA, as

[92] ETIAS, 'The ETIAS Application Process: How it works?' (2021), https://www.etiasvisa.com/etias-news/etias-application-how-it-works (last visited 16 December 2021).

[93] ETIAS, 'Why an ETIAS Application Could Be Denied' (2020), https://www.etiasvisa.com/etias-news/can-etias-be-refused (last visited 16 December 2021).

[94] Art. 31(3) ECRIS-TCN Regulation (EU) 2019/861.

[95] Commission report 880 final on the evaluation of the second generation SIS II (2016); Commission Staff Working Document 328 final, Evaluation of the implementation of Regulation (EC) No 767/2008 of the European Parliament and Council concerning the VIS and the exchange of data between Member States on short-stay visas (VIS Regulation) (2016).

well as questionnaires, surveys, and interviews, notably with eu-LISA's staff. The EDPS, in conducting its audits, has access to all the documents and the premises from eu-LISA.[96] The audits include the verification of on-the-spot compliance and the checking of the security and operational management of the databases. eu-LISA has in this regard a real obligation to assist EDPS inspectors.

When it comes to the European Parliament, its ability to engage substantively and to deliberate on the basis of the information provided by eu-LISA is limited by a number of factors. First the Parliament is a generalist institution that does not possess the kind of specialized knowledge needed to deliberate on the necessity and efficiency of complex data-driven operations and the procedures in place in that regard (or only to a very limited extent). Second, its powers of active investigation are limited and can only be triggered at present in a non-autonomous fashion and most likely only if information is leaked or there is a whistle-blower.[97] Third, much of the information it may hypothetically require access to will have been classified and there are no arrangements in place, as in other areas, for example, Customs Freight Simplified Procedures (CFSP), for it to obtain privileged access in a non-public and controlled fashion even if eu-LISA was willing to engage in this manner. The latter is not likely given its own rhetoric and justification for its mediating role and the fact that it merely facilitates and manages the technical sides of large-scale infrastructures.

Table 6.2 summarizes the justification practices of the four programmes discussed in this section. Secrecy is the elephant in the room. It looms large in this area of data-led security programmes. The argument is always that, for reasons of security and also for efficiency and operational reasons, no access can be given to data other than the logging that is reported in various activity reports by a number of actors. But actually, the secrecy system is deeper than this. One of the areas where there is some public visibility (through the website and various documents included) are the security rules and the rules on classifying documents.[98] There are two points to note. First, the rules are factual, largely aligned with EU-wide rules and offer little if any 'justification'. Second, a system is put in place as is usual in systems of classified information where there is only a small cohort of officials internal to the agencies in question who

[96] Art. 67(3) ETIAS Regulation (EU) 2018/1240; Art. 29(3) ECRIS-TCN Regulation (EU) 2019/816.

[97] See, for example, with regards to Frontex, ECRE, 'Frontex: One Investigation Closes as Another Begins and the Agency's Role in Return and Ability to Purchase Firearms under Scrutiny' (2021), https://ecre.org/frontex-one-investigation-closes-as-another-begins-and-the-agencys-role-in-return-and-ability-to-purchase-firearms-under-scrutiny/ (last visited 16 December 2021).

[98] See, for example, for eu-LISA, Decision of the Management Board on the Security Rules for Protection EU Classified Information in eu-LISA (2019) 273.

Table 6.2 Justification practices in TFTP, TERREG, ETIAS, and ECRIS-TCN

TFTP	- Emergence of specific narrative of justification that appeal to the effectiveness of the programme. - Case examples included in the reports where TFTP info was used BUT very little information on how algorithmic analysis and algorithmic security works, and how links are made.
TERREG	- Overview of numbers of removals and referrals. BUT little detail and cryptic formulations, lack of meaningful narrative justification
ETIAS	- Promise to deliver a 'justification of the refusal' that includes reason for denial, reference to ETIAS National Unit that refused the application and information on the right to lodge an appeal. BUT it is unclear how such justification is narrated and substantiated. The basis of the decision will remain unclear (alert, Europol data . . .).
ECRIS-TCN	- Possibility to establish the justification. BUT unclear how the justification is narrated and substantiated.

have access to (all) information above a certain level. It is not clear what the connection is in this regard between similarly situated officials in one institution or agency and other similarly situated officials in other institutions and agencies. There is no information available on this, perhaps unsurprisingly. It follows from the highly classified systems in place that information on data in terms of justification will almost never be available, other than certain raw components. Where visibility does exist—for example, in relation to number of searches (in TFTP), number of rejections (of visa applications in ETIAS), and number of removals (of online content pursuant to TERREG)—there is the question of whether numerical visibility constitutes meaningful justification, especially if the reports cannot themselves be independently verified and/or questioned and scrutinized in the European Parliament. As Koivisto puts it, 'transparency is not enough to guarantee understandability'.[99]

C. Sanction/Public Fora

The third mechanism of accountability is that of consequences. Questions here are not just about the consequences for actors, like penalties, disruptions, or fines that they may face in case their explanations are rejected by the public. Questions can also be raised about the concrete ways in which cases may be

[99] Koivisto, 'Thinking Inside the Box' (n. 38) 11.

heard and public fora may be assembled to address mistakes, bias, or abuse *in the first place*. Is it possible at all for cases of harm or wrongdoing in our selected security programmes to appear before a public accountability forum, and if so how?

First, the TFTP is a multi-actor system, in which a private company (SWIFT as the designated provider) works with public authorities on both sides of the Atlantic to generate data analytics and policing leads. As such, it demonstrates the challenges that algorithmic security poses to traditional models and mechanisms of accountability, for there is not one territorially-based actor that can be sanctioned or penalized in case of accountability breaches. Yet, the TFTP does show how multi-jurisdictional models of accountability could work. Under the conditions of the Treaty, it is possible for overseers to interrupt and even cancel TFTP searches when the scope conditions of the Treaty are not fulfilled. However, in all years of its existence, TFTP searches have never been stopped periodically, even during the time that strong transatlantic controversy over the programme's legitimacy took place. In the current, Treaty-based regulation of TFTP accountability, it does however happen that individual searches are blocked and delayed, when additional information is requested by the TFTP overseer(s). Most often, additional information is requested post hoc, thus without interrupting the searches.[100] However, search interruptions do take place within the TFTP: for example, the Fourth Review Report (covering the period 2014–2015) notes that 45 searches were blocked by the overseers (out of a total of 27,095 searches), because 'the search terms ... were considered to be too broad'.[101] By comparison, during the period of the Fifth Review Report (2016–2018), 53 searches (out of 39,000) were blocked for the same reason, and 645 searches were queried by the overseers.[102]

Yet, beyond the interruption of searches, there is very little by way of sanctions when TFTP operations breach accountability or operate unfairly, for example, by engaging in discrimination of certain groups. Arguably, the TFTP is discriminatory in nature, because its data requests are always directed at transfers to and from particular geographic regions and countries. However, the lack of algorithmic accountability in the programme means that neither the public nor even the relevant security authorities are aware whether and how particular police leads, interventions, or raids are TFTP-derived. Operators who receive intelligence do not know that these leads are TFTP-derived. This

[100] Commission Staff Working Document 301 final on the Fifth Joint Review of the TFTP (2019) 27.
[101] Commission Staff Working Document 17 final on the Fourth Joint Review of the TFTP (2017) 14.
[102] Commission Staff Working Document Fifth Joint Review TFTP (n. 100) 12.

means that sanctions in case of unfair or disproportional targeting and discrimination cannot be effected.

Furthermore, although the TFTP formally offers the possibility for data subject rectification and redress, it is practically impossible for cases of concern regarding TFTP to be heard publicly. If a citizen sends a request to access and verify their personal data held in the system, they will be told that *either* the question cannot be addressed because data cannot be extracted from the black boxed database because there is no known 'nexus' to terrorism *or* the question cannot be addressed because personal data have been extracted from the black boxed database, in which case the subject is considered suspect and not entitled to further information. In addition, security authorities who receive TFTP-derived information or leads typically do not know about the information's origin.[103] Consequently, it is impossible in practice to bring cases of harm, mistakes, or abuse to a public forum. In terms of formal oversight, the EDPS—as supervisory body of Europol—does have a mandate in relation to TFTP, but only as it concerns Article 4 of the Treaty, which sets out the procedure for US data request that 'shall be tailored as narrowly as possible'.[104] In this regard, the 2019 EDPS Report concludes, inter alia, that: 'Europol only relies on the US claims that such assessment has been conducted without actually having access to this analysis.'[105]

When it comes to TERREG, it is crucial to understand that it seeks to shape and govern the *private accountability mechanisms* of platforms and service providers. In TERREG, the 'duty of care' is a key concept that intends to strengthen and harmonize platforms' efforts in counterterrorism-related removal and to help shape the private reporting on removal actions.[106] Section III of TERREG sets out 'safeguards and accountability': these are aimed at guiding the formulation of private Terms-of-Service Regulations. Concerning redress, for example, Article 10 TERREG stipulates that: 'service providers shall establish effective and accessible mechanisms allowing content providers whose content has been removed ... to submit a complaint against the action of the hosting service provider'. How this will be shaped in practice remains unclear: currently, platforms do not habitually have complaint or redress procedures for users whose contents is removed. Article 18.4 of TERREG foresees penalties

[103] Commission TFTP First Joint Review Report (n. 57) 12.
[104] Art. 4(2) of the TFTP Treaty.
[105] EDPS case number 2018-0683, TFTP Inspection Report, The Hague, (2019) at 2.
[106] Bellanova and de Goede (n. 37); Bellanova and de Goede, 'Co-producing Security: Platform Content Moderation and European Security Integration', *Journal of Common Market Studies* (2021).

for online service providers who fail to comply with its obligations of 'up to 4% of the hosting service provider's global turnover of the last business year'.

Ultimately, TERREG (in the future) and IRU (currently) place any sanctions for incorrect removals on private platforms and services. Concretely, Europol IRU does not actually remove online content, but focuses its work on producing *referrals* for private companies to take action under their own Terms-of-Service Regulations. These referrals are perhaps even more important for smaller platforms than they are for larger ones, because small platforms lack the means and resources for continuous, real-time monitoring of their content. Any removal decision is ultimately a private, platform decision, for which platforms are responsible and accountable. In terms of logged-out accountability, the TERREG case shows how accountability is a complex practice of public–private coproduction, whereby the EU is seeking to shape the removal actions and Term-of-Service regulations of private providers. For citizens affected by removal decisions, however, the landscape of redress is complex and privatized, and full algorithmic accountability of how online content is assessed and classified remains lacking.

The ETIAS Regulation establishes an independent ETIAS Fundamental Rights Guidance Board, which is composed of the Fundamental Rights Officer of EBCGA and of representatives of the EDPS, of the European Data Protection Board, and of the European Union Agency for Fundamental Rights. Initially, the European Parliament required the Board to perform audit duties, but this was not accepted in light of the EDPS role.[107] The ETIAS Fundamental Rights Guidance Board must produce an annual report on the observance of fundamental rights in ETIAS. The fact that the ETIAS Regulation specifically requires that reports be public suggests that they must be accessible and comprehensible to citizens at large.[108] It is highly likely that in these reports justifications will be given one way or another for the conclusions that are reached so that a deliberation can be made and, if appropriate, consequences imposed. ECRIS-TCN does not establish such an independent board, but the EDPS and Commission play a key role in the monitoring of the processing activities.

The EDPS, moreover, fulfils an important role in monitoring the personal data processing activities of eu-LISA, Europol, and the European Border and Coast Guard Agency related to ETIAS. The EDPS ensures that an audit of eu-LISA's and the ETIAS Central Unit's personal data processing activities is carried out in accordance with relevant international auditing standards at least

[107] K. Gál (European Parliament rapporteur), *Report on the proposal for ETIAS Regulation* (2017).
[108] Arts 10(1) and (5) ETIAS Regulation (EU) 2018/1240.

every three years. Based on the information resulting from that audit, the EDPS must draft a report, in which it offers recommendations in order to ensure, for example, higher data protection and security of the system. The EDPS shall submit the report to the European Parliament, to the Council, to the Commission, to eu-LISA, and to the supervisory authorities.[109] eu-LISA and Frontex can comment on the report. The same applies to ECRIS-TCN, with the exception of the role of the Central Unit and consequently Frontex's role in it. None of the audits on eu-LISA, Europol, or Frontex are publicly available.

The specific accountability mechanisms that apply within ETIAS and ECRIS-TCN are in addition to those that already exist in the general legal framework of eu-LISA. eu-LISA—along with the ETIAS Central Unit for ETIAS—must provide the Commission with all the information it requires, so that it may evaluate ETIAS and ECRIS-TCN every four years and submit a report on that evaluation to the European Parliament, the Council, the EDPS, and the European Agency for Fundamental Rights. That evaluation includes, for instance, the results, impact, effectiveness, and efficiency of ETIAS' performance, along with an assessment of its security and its impact on fundamental rights.[110] The Commission thus has the opportunity every four years to examine if eu-LISA is fulfilling its role effectively and in compliance with its founding Regulation. The findings of the Commission in this respect may lead it to propose legislation changing eu-LISA's mandate or even to suggest abolishing the agency altogether. This would obviously be the most severe judgment possible on the performance and indeed necessity of eu-LISA and clearly represents a tool of accountability that seems reserved for use in only extreme circumstances of mismanagement, maladministration, or incompetence.[111] Less stringent recommendations may include changes at the management and organizational level, such as changing the rules of procedures. Interim reports are required every year to evaluate the progress made in the implementation of the planned activities.

This section has mapped the possible consequences and sanctions built into the accountability mechanisms of our four selected data-led security programmes, as summarized in Table 6.3. We have also asked how public fora may

[109] Art. 67 ETIAS Regulation (EU) 2018/1240.

[110] Arts 92(5) and (7) ETIAS Regulation (EU) 2018/1240.

[111] See, for example, on Frontex's mismanagement, the reaction of the European Commission that asked for clarifications and supported the European Parliament's investigations, Liboreiro and McCaffrey, 'EU Migration Chief Urges Frontex to Clarify Pushbacks Allegations', *Euronews* (2021), https://www.euronews.com/2021/01/20/eu-migration-chief-urges-frontex-to-clarify-pushback-allegations (last visited 16 December 2021).

Table 6.3 Sanctions practices in TFTP, TERREG, ETIAS, and ECRIS-TCN

TFTP	- Multi-actor system and multi-jurisdiction models of accountability. - The overseer(s) can interrupt and cancel TFTP searches. - Individual searches can be blocked and additional info requested, and it is possibility for data subject to ask for rectification and redress. However, **impossible** to be hear publicly. - Formal oversight from the EDPS remains limited.
TERREG	- Shapes and governs private accountability mechanisms of platforms and service providers. - Redress possible: submit a complaint against the actions of the hosting service provides (practice is unclear). - Removal and redress remain *private* mechanisms and decision which leads to complex public–private coproduction.
ETIAS	- ETIAS FRA Guidance Board publishes a public report and may impose consequences. - EDPS monitors eu-LISA, Europol, and Frontex's processing of personal data (with recommendations). - Commission's evaluation can recommend changes at management and organizational level, legislative changes, or the abolishment of the agency.
ECRIS-TCN	- EDPS monitors eu-LISA and offers recommendations. - Commission's evaluation can recommend changes at management and organizational level, legislative changes, or the abolishment of the agency.

assemble to address questions of accountability in data-led security. We draw the following overall conclusions. First, there are examples of (possible) sanction within these programmes, from the interruption of searches in TFTP to the discontinuation of the eu-LISA agency (in theory). However, and this is our second conclusion, in data-led security, the actor and the forum to which an account is to be offered are profoundly disconnected. There is a lack of concrete mechanisms through which cases can be heard before a forum. Indeed, it is often difficult, if not impossible, for citizens to know whether and how their data were captured and analysed, and how algorithmic analytics led to certain outcomes (like visa rejections or criminal prosecutions). This is due not just to the classification or secrecy of the processes of data analytics; it is also because algorithmic logic generally affects the relation between cause and effect, in order to govern through anomaly.[112] Machine learning programmes do not necessarily operate with a predefined notion of deviance to be identified, but

[112] Aradau and Blanke, 'Governing Others: Anomaly and the Algorithmic Subject of Security', 3 *European Journal of International Security* (2018) 1; Amoore, 'Machine Learning Political Orders', *Review of International Studies* (2022) 1.

instead let 'anomaly' be found and defined through the data analytics themselves. The behaviour or transaction that is anomalous is not a predefined wrong or harm, but an outcome generated through the analytic process itself, and determinable only in relation to seemingly normal patterns of behaviour. Such 'machine learning political order' affects the sequence between cause and effect, and obfuscates the relation between personal data and security outcomes.[113] The very invisibility of the information-sharing process means that citizens have real challenges in obtaining access to legal remedies, for example, for a breach of the purpose limitation principle which foresees that personal data should not be used for purposes other than those originally foreseen, one of the most core principles of data protection in Europe.[114]

5. In Search of Logged-in EU Security Oversight

In this chapter, we have mapped the concrete mechanisms and practices of 'giving account' that are in operation and in design in four data-led security programmes. We have shown how these remain largely 'logged-out' of the algorithmic processes—overall, they rely on industry self-reporting, they prioritize visibility over explanation,[115] and explanability is severely limited by the secrecy and obfuscation that accompanies security programmes more generally. In all of our cases, it is not clear how public accountability forums can be assembled to foster genuine public deliberation concerning the (far-reaching) security decisions taken within these programmes. In some of our cases, new laws and oversight mechanisms are still being developed and it remains to be seen how these will function in practice. By focusing on the precursors of new programmes (IRU in the case of TERREG; SIS II in the case of ETIAS), we have been able to make a preliminary assessment. Thus, we have shown how information, justification, and sanction are taking shape in practice in new EU data-led security programmes. These emerging practices are only partially able to give a meaningful account of security decisions that can have major impacts on people's lives (including the denial of visas, or the sharing of their financial transaction information).

[113] Amoore (n. 112).

[114] Brouwer, 'Legality and Data Protection Law: The Forgotten Purpose of Purpose Limitation', in L. F. M. Besselink, S. Prechal, and F. Pennings (eds), *The Eclipse of the Legality Principle in the European Union* (2011) 273; Vavoula (n. 25).

[115] Koivisto, this volume (n. 38).

In this conclusion, we ask what a 'logged-in' accountability might look like, and what the conditions are for meaningful oversight of EU data-led security practices. This fits into a broader question concerning 'data justice', which asks how to 'determine ethical paths in a datafying world'.[116] The involvement of the EDPS, and indeed of other, national, data protection supervisors, represents a relatively obvious feature of accountability in interoperable information sharing. In the past, some scholars have noted how information systems generate serious problems from the point of view of judicial protection, given that there is generally 'no remedy against the use and computation of information once it has entered administrative networks, as long as this information does not lead to a final decision either on the European or the Member State level'.[117] Besides that issue, which results from the EU judicial system's focus on the review of legal acts, adopted in the exercise of decision-making powers, the very multitude of authorities linked through interoperable databases also makes it hard to determine which would be the competent jurisdiction to initiate judicial proceedings.

The difficulties in using other common accountability tools—such as independent judicial review—justifies the development of others, that may also prove more appropriate in light of the specific nature of the activities of the authorities involved in interoperable data-sharing for security purposes. Since those activities involve the processing of very large amounts of personal data, much of which is sensitive biometric data, and since the relatively novel character of interoperability requires continual improvement and scrutiny, it is logical that ETIAS and ECRIS-TCN emphasize in particular two types of accountability mechanisms: first, supervision by data protection watchdogs (the EDPS more specifically) and, second, reporting obligations to expert bodies (such as again the EDPS and the EU FRA) and institutional actors (such as the European Parliament, the Council, and the Commission), which would be involved in any political process leading to legislative reform of either ETIAS or ECRIS-TCN.[118]

[116] Taylor (n. 5) 2.

[117] Hofmann, 'Composite Decision Making Procedures in EU Administrative Law', in H. C.H. Hofmann and A. H. Türk, *Legal Challenges in EU Administrative Law* (2009) 136, at 161; Hofmann, 'Legal Protection and Liability in the European Composite Administration', in O. Jansen and B. Schöndorf-Haubold (eds), *The European Composite Administration* (2011) 441.

[118] Arts 67 and 92 ETIAS Regulation (EU) 2018/1240; Arts 29 and 36 ECRIS-TCN Regulation (EU) 2019/816; on the need for supervision, see Quintel, 'Connecting Personal Data of Third Country Nationals: Interoperability of EU Databases in the Light of the CJEU's Case Law on Data Retention', 2 *University of Luxembourg Law Working Paper* (2018) 1; On ETIAS, Michéa and Rousvoal, 'The Criminal Procedure Out of Itself: A Case Study of the Relationship Between EU Law and Criminal Procedure using the ETIAS System', 6(1) *European Papers* (2021) 473.

Both the supervision by the EDPS and the reporting obligations in question require the actors involved in the use, management, and development of ETIAS and ECRIS-TCN—and above all, eu-LISA—to continually offer information and explanation as to how the two information systems are functioning, and as to whether they function appropriately in view of data protection and fundamental rights standards. These are undoubtedly instruments of accountability: they require that eu-LISA—and in some instances the EBCGA—give account of how data is processed and of the lawfulness of their everyday data-sharing practices.

But this description and the investigation carried out more generally in this chapter of all four programmes shows the limits of this approach, with bits of accountability not keeping pace with the bytes, searches, and hits in the real world of security practice, which are then potentially shared with a variety of actors at different governance levels. The panoply of institutions or forums that are presented with what are essentially logging reports (except when less frequent periodic evaluations are made publicly available) are not able to deliberate in substance on the raw information they receive. It seems to be more of a box ticking exercise than anything else. This does not mean that other accountability forums might not get involved on their own initiative (perhaps subsequent to leaking or whistleblowing). For example, the European Ombudsman has opened an investigation with regard to Frontex, and her powers enable her to actively investigate and question and request and receive detailed and targeted information in a way that other accountability forums that are provided with logging reports cannot. Another example is that of the Court of Auditors which recently, on its own initiative and outside of its normal auditing function of approving the annual accounts of each of the EU agencies (including those which house significant databases), prepared a report on general large-scale information systems.[119] The conclusions are on the nature of the data collected and the need for more focused and timely data. The exercise mainly involved an evaluation and assessment of border data from the point of view of efficiency and entailed detailed consideration of the information systems in question. The investigations of both the European Ombudsman and the European Court of Auditors involved post hoc examinations with, at best, some recommendations for the future that may or may not be implemented.

What the EU system lacks is one or more EU overseers specifically for data-driven accountability programmes. A broad analogy could be made with the

[119] European Court of Auditors Special Report No. 20/2019 on EU information systems supporting border control—a strong tool, but more focus needed on timely and complete data.

idea of having an information commissioner in pre-digital times, pre-large-scale information systems that are interoperable in nature and practice. The focus of a 'data-led security overseer office' would be specifically on real-time data infrastructures inside specific agencies, examining how data are requested, searched, accessed, and shared. As the name implies, data-led security programmes would need an external insider 'overseeing' what is happening and why, with the power to stop searches or require further more targeted justification. In this sense, the EU TFTP overseer is a unique and promising model, with the ability to examine and block algorithmic searches in real time, yet it is a model that currently still has profound shortcomings, especially the secrecy of the overseers' names and reports, and the lack of public information on the size and scope of data transfers.

What we call 'data-led security overseers' would be logged-into the algorithmic processes of analysis and intervention. They could be subject to not only reporting requirements but also the obligation to go before a general accountability forum (e.g. the European Parliament), answer questions, and engage, within limits, in a dialogue. An EU data-led security overseer can be conceptualized as a type of internal ombudsman, but one who is an expert in the technical data-driven nature of the programmes and with experience of relationships of accountability and the need for some public justification on the procedures in place, at the very least. An EU data-led security overseer would supervise adequate and practicable redress mechanisms and their public visibility. With the power to stop searches, interrupt programmes, and document rights infringements across programmes, an EU data-led security overseer office could be a genuine counterbalancing power to the proliferation and sometimes hasty and ad hoc design of European data-led security powers.

Afterword

Niovi Vavoula

Drafting the afterword of an edited collection that follows chapters by distinguished experts in the fields of EU data protection and administrative law is certainly a daunting exercise for a junior scholar. This afterword has the modest aim of bringing together some of the most intriguing ideas put forward by the authors and hopefully will provide additional insights—certainly not solutions—into the complex legal questions that were problematized.

During the past few decades, societies have become progressively datafied,[1] whereby growing amounts of personal data on everyday activities are collected and translated into manageable information that becomes available for analysis processes. The increased value of data as an essential resource for economic growth, competitiveness, innovation, job creation, and societal progress in general has signified intense legislative activity. Particularly, in the past few years, the rate of legislative production has increased significantly, exemplified by the release of Commission proposals for an AI Act (AI Act),[2] a Digital Services Act (DSA),[3] a Digital Markets Act,[4] a Data Governance Act[5] in the internal market field, along with a number of initiatives to promote digitalization of police and judicial cooperation[6] or of immigration control.[7] These

[1] On datafication of society see V. Mayer-Schönberger and K. Cukier, *Big Data: A Revolution that Will Transform How We Live, Work, and Think* (2013).

[2] Commission, 'Proposal for a Regulation of the European Parliament and of the Council laying down harmonised rules on Artificial Intelligence (Artificial Intelligence Act) and amending certain Union legislative acts', COM(2021) 206 final.

[3] Commission, 'Proposal for a Regulation of the European Parliament and of the Council on a Single Market For Digital Services (Digital Services Act) and amending Directive 2000/31/EC', COM(2020) 825 final.

[4] Commission, 'Proposal for a Regulation of the European Parliament and of the Council on contestable and fair markets in the digital sector (Digital Markets Act)', COM(2020) 842 final.

[5] Commission, 'Proposal for a Regulation of the European Parliament and of the Council on European data governance, COM(2020) 767 final, recently adopted as Regulation (EU) 868/2022 of the European Parliament and of the Council of 30 May 2022 on European data governance and amending Regulation (EU) 2018/1724 (Data Governance Act).

[6] See V. Mitsilegas and N. Vavoula, 'Databases', in V. Mitsilegas, *EU Criminal Law* (2nd ed., 2022).

[7] N. Vavoula, *Immigration and Privacy in the Law of the EU: The Case of Information Systems* (2022); M. McAulifee and R. Wilson, *Research Handbook on International Migration and Digital Technology* (2021).

Niovi Vavoula, *Afterword* In: *Data at the Boundaries of European Law*. Edited by: Deirdre Curtin and Mariavittoria Catanzariti, Oxford University Press. © Niovi Vavoula 2023.
DOI: 10.1093/oso/9780198874195.003.0007

developments are undoubtedly matched by an even faster pace of development in digital technologies and their applications. Regulating the digital data society presents a number of challenges, not least because of the need to reflect creatively on technical matters that have significant fundamental rights implications, some of which are not easily discernible at the time of their inception, and the need for forward-thinking provisions so that the legislation is future-proofed. The authors in this edited volume have grappled with some of the most pressing questions, highlighting legal gaps and demonstrating how the traditional content of certain concepts either remains illusive or may prove to be insufficient on its own to address the challenges in the digital era.

In his contribution, De Hert rightly criticizes the mimetic approach of a series of post-GDPR laws that concern data protection. Mimesis is uninspiring, often inappropriate, and fraught with superficial references and varied terminology, leading to significant regulatory gaps or unaddressed overlaps. A similar scoping exercise has been conducted by Codagnone, Liva and Rodriguez de las Heras Barrell[8] in their analysis of the AI Act, who similarly identified grey areas in the interplay between the AI Act as the core component of the AI regulatory framework and other legal acts, such as the proposal for a DSA. Certainly, the 'Brussels effect' has been at the forefront of EU efforts in the field of data protection;[9] particularly, in the case of the AI Act, the fact that the EU is considered to be lagging behind the United States and China, a mimetic approach of the 'success story' of the GDPR has been viewed as a shortcut to catching up and achieving similar effects in the AI world. However, as De Hert contends, mimesis is essentially 'a bad thing' as, among other flaws, it is symptomatic of a lack of creativity. Legislating cannot be reduced to a checklist exercise and a relatively successful approach in a specific context cannot be transplanted to similar contexts. The interplay between the AI Act and the GDPR is multi-faceted and conspicuous. For example, the AI Act acknowledges that its provisions are without prejudice to any other EU legal acts and that the operators of AI systems must abide by the data protection regime.[10] The AI Act further stresses that it should not be interpreted as providing the legal ground for processing of personal data. However, such a generic statement of compatibility between the AI Act and the personal data protection regime may not be sufficient to cover all possible uses of data by AI systems. Therefore, more clarity

[8] C. Codagnone, G. Liva, and T. Rodriguez de las Heras Barrell, 'Identification and assessment of existing and draft EU legislation in the digital field' (Study for the AIDA Special Committee of the European Parliament 2022).

[9] A. Bradford, *The Brussels Effect: How the European Union Rules the World* (2020).

[10] Recital 41.

in the AI Act regarding the processing of personal data is needed. De Hert also suggests as a potential solution 'adding provisions to the GDPR, hardening certain rules and ensuring explicit cross references to other post-GDPR laws'. I am not so sure that a legislative intervention to the GDPR is the right way forward at this particular moment. To be fair, the GDPR is far from perfect. For example, in her contribution Koivisto briefly discusses the debate surrounding the potential need for a separate 'right to explanation' distinct from a 'right to information' in relation to automated decision-making (ADM). However, tempting it may be for the EU legislature to amend the GDPR in a manner that would downgrade important safeguards, it could open up Pandora's box.[11] Thus, the reverse exercise of spelling out in detail the interactions of provisions with the GDPR may be less problematic.

Grasping the implications of the progressive move towards the use of AI-based systems, such as natural language processing (NLP) in the context of the administration of justice through prediction of judgments (PoJ) and ADM, is at the heart of the contributions by Hildebrandt and Koivisto. The former focuses on data-driven 'law' enabled by predictive technologies based on machine learning and unearths the significant implications for individuals if these kinds of technologies are to be adopted, potentially 'disrespecting the boundary between a law that addresses people as human agents and a law that treats them as subject to a statistical, machinic logic'. As machine learning merely scales past decision-making, predictive technologies are destined to replicate past biases and may significantly impact on the fundamental rights of individuals involved in a legal dispute, thus they rightly have been categorized as high risk systems in the AI Act.[12] Hildebrandt calls for legal protection by design (LPbD), whereby controllers must design their systems in ways that minimize infringements of fundamental rights while integrating the checks and balances that are inherent in the rule of law. She rightly suggests limits to the use of PoJ: for decision support and subject to a series of conditions that ensure that past injustices are not replicated and that administrative convenience and streamlining does not come at the expense of the remedies afforded to individuals.

Koivisto in turn delves into the core of transparency as a solution to the so-called 'black box' problem of algorithms. Transparency, she argues, is 'a more complex ideal than is portrayed in mainstream narratives'. Transparency is

[11] Such proposals have been particularly voiced by Axel Voss, the Rapporteur of the AIDA Subcommittee. See A. Voss, *Fixing the GDPR: Towards Version 2.0* (2021).

[12] Annex III categorizes 'AI systems intended to assist a judicial authority in researching and interpreting facts and the law and in applying the law to a concrete set of facts' as high risk.

performative in nature, meaning that it can merely describe and explain how the black box actually operates regardless of whether we understood the process, and is thus constrained by a logic of discovery. Consequently, despite the very strong emphasis on transparency as a key principle underpinning the GDPR along with fairness and lawfulness and its undeniable importance, it cannot deliver its promise of clear visibility and is destined not to guarantee understanding by laymen of how algorithms actually work. Thus, transparency must be complemented by other concepts such as understandability or explicability, which necessarily require human intervention. Her findings are crucial in comprehending both the limits of transparency—revealing the algorithm, though procedurally fulfilling the transparency requirement, would not mean that its logic is understood nor ADM would become any more trustworthy[13]—and the ultimate dystopian realization that dismantling the black boxes in ADM cannot be achieved. The author also reveals some of the limits of the GDPR in relation to the right to information in respect of ADM and Article 22. The latter is certainly insufficient on its own to regulate ADM. Its complex architecture, ambiguous status (is it a general prohibition on ADM or a right to object to ADM?[14]), and lack of clarity makes it difficult to apply. Perhaps these findings will be particularly useful to the Council of Europe Committee on Artificial Intelligence which has commenced its deliberations on drafting a transversal legal instrument to regulate the design, development, and use of artificial intelligence systems.

The interoperability of information systems for third-country nationals, and its implications, is one of the technical and legal concepts that will continue to preoccupy legal scholars in the coming years. Harvesting the possibilities offered by technological evolution and under the pressure of achieving a 'security union' in the aftermath of various terrorist incidents in the EU since 2015, the Interoperability Regulations aim to improve security, allow for more efficient identity checks, improve detection of individuals on the move who hold multiple identities, and assist in the fight against irregular migration. Interoperability brings together the content of both the existing and forthcoming information systems by creating four interoperability components.

[13] For a slightly more optimistic understanding of transparencey see Grimmelikhuijsen, 'Explaining why the computer says no: algorithmic transparency affects the perceived trustworthiness of automated decision-making', *Public Administration Review* (2022) 1.

[14] Most of the legal literature sees it as a prohibition, including the European Data Protection Board (former Article 29 Working Party). See Article 29 Working Party, 'Guidelines on Automated Individual Decision-Making and Profiling for the Purposes of Regulation 2016/679' (2018); Malgieri, 'Automated Decision-Making in the EU Member States: The Right to Explanation and Other "Suitable Safeguards" in the National Legislations', 35 *Computer Law & Security Review* (2019) 13.

This will lead to varied interaction of records and files present in one information system with those in other systems. Whereas Catanzariti and Curtin rightly mention that no overarching database will be created, the common identity repository is not very far from that as it will encompass a series of personal data stemming from almost all information systems for third-country nationals (the Schengen Information System is excluded for technical reasons). The case of the Multiple Identity Detector (MID) is also particularly interesting as it prominently shows how interoperability fosters the re-use of data, as this component not only brings together personal data from the underlying databases, but will generate new data in the form of links. The authors' analysis regarding the ownership of data in centralized databases clearly shows how the complexity of interoperability, framed as a technical matter, challenges traditional notions of data protection law with significant repercussions for the protection of fundamental rights. Importantly, it shines a light on another important realization: that storage of personal data in interoperable centralized databases does not only signify that individuals whose personal data are collected and stored in systems, but also the the specific bodies or actors that make the data available for interoperable use, may also lose control over the use of the data. To some extent, EU information systems themselves strain the principle of originator control—certain limitations on use exist, through the hit/no hit system or in the case of transfers, whereas some activities require no additional permission and notification. However, interoperability sidelines the principle to the extent that personal data acquire a different shared EU status that is irrevocable by data originators. Calling for a recognition of the concept of data originalism presents certain advantages as it can delimit sharing and prevent misuse. From this perspective it may work together with the purpose limitation principle, the meaning of which has been somewhat lost. Catanzariti and Curtin rightly point out how the complexity of the architecture affects the application of the principle, but additional questions will emerge in the future when the structure of interoperable systems will become even more complex in cases of interconnecting decentralized systems that contain data collected and shared completely under national law. As Wallwork and Baptista suggest, interoperability is 'an umbrella beneath which may exist many disparate yet complementary definitions, according to a given perspective or layer of abstraction'.[15] This broad understanding of interoperability is crucial in defining its limits. The Interoperability Regulations are merely a stepping stone towards

[15] A. Wallwork and J. Baptista, 'Undertaking interoperability, in structured account of approaches to interoperability' (Future of identity in the information society FIDIS, Report D4.1, 2005).

an emerging architecture of total information awareness in an omniscient EU, whereby decentralized structures will also be interconnected. It will not be surprising if new proposals emerge in the near future linking systems established under the Prüm framework,[16] the Passenger Name Record (PNR) Directive,[17] or the Advance Passenger Information (API) Directive[18] with one or more of the interoperability components. This was already mentioned by the High Level Expert Group (HLEG) on information systems and interoperability in its final report[19] and explicitly stated by the Commission in its proposals.[20] Interoperability between security and border management and customs systems will follow, with the discussions currently progressing even though interoperability is still unfolding.[21] These efforts will confirm the longstanding view that modern technological advents, particularly the most controversial ones, are first 'tested' on third-country nationals before EU nationals are subjected to them.[22] The interoperability apparatus will thus be used to survey and manage the very subjects whose security it is meant to ensure.

Questions of transparency go hand in hand with debates on promoting accountability mechanisms and therefore the last chapter maps the different avenues for accountability in respect of four data-led security instruments, focusing in particular on the Terrorist Finance Tracking Program (TFTP), regarding the monitoring of financial transactions data jointly with the US,[23] online content regulation in accordance with Regulation (EU) 2021/784 (TERREG),[24]

[16] Council Decision 2008/615/JHA of 23 June 2008, OJ L210/1, on the stepping up of cross-border cooperation, particularly in combatting terrorism and cross-border crime.

[17] Directive (EU) 2016/681, OJ L119/132, of the European Parliament and of the Council of 27 April 2016 on the use of passenger name record (PNR) data for the prevention, detection, investigation and prosecution of terrorist offences and serious crime. This fits within the emergence of a Travel Intelligence Architecture. See 'Europol foresees key role in "the EU travel intelligence architecture"' (*Statewatch*, 5 November 2018), www.statewatch.org/news/2018/nov/eu-pnr-iwg-update.htm (last visited 25 April 2022).

[18] Directive 2004/82/EC of 29 April 2004, OJ L261/24, on the obligation of carriers to communicate passenger data.

[19] HLEG, 'Final Report' (2017) 38–40.

[20] Commission, 'Proposal for a Regulation of the European Parliament and of the Council on establishing a framework for interoperability between EU information systems (borders and visa) and amending Council Decision 2004/512/EC, Regulation (EC) No 767/2008, Council Decision 2008/633/JHA, Regulation (EU) 2016/399 and Regulation (EU) 2017/2226', COM(2017) 793 final; 'Proposal for a Regulation of the European Parliament and of the Council on establishing a framework for interoperability between EU information systems (police and judicial cooperation, asylum and migration)', COM(2017) 794 final (collectively Interoperability proposals) 5.

[21] For example see Council, Document 5574/19 (29 January 2019).

[22] B. Hayes, 'NeoConOpticon: The EU security-industrial complex' (2009) 35.

[23] Agreement OJ L8/11 between the European Union and the United States of America on the processing and transfer of Financial Messaging Data from the European Union to the United States for purposes of the Terrorist Finance Tracking Program.

[24] Regulation (EU) 2021/784, OJ L172/79, of the European Parliament and of the Council of 29 April 2021 on addressing the dissemination of terrorist content online.

ETIAS,[25] and ECRIS-TCN.[26] Curtin and de Goede demonstrate that accountability mechanisms, such as self-reporting duties to provide information on the activities entailed or external supervision, are fraught with flaws and omissions. Elsewhere in the book, Catanzariti and Curtin assert that logs on data processing activities are rightly found to be an inadequate safeguard that 'is not a transparent form of governance', as logs provide an incomplete picture of a data transaction that does not enable full supervision. Arguably, supervision authorities, such as the European Data Protection Supervisor (EDPS) or national data protection authorities lack the resources to fully perform their duties in an increasing digital arena. The EDPS has expressed its determination to step up its game in line with its supervision powers.[27] However, in an era where the fundamental rights implications of data processing activities, for example online content moderation, which heavily affects freedom of expression, or AI tools, essentially algorithmic profiling, such as those envisaged in ETIAS and VIS, present challenges for the principle of non-discrimination, data protection authorities and the EDPS may prove insufficient to foster accountability. Therefore, additional avenues may also be considered, for example, fundamental rights officers or boards with holistic expertise on the matters beyond the contours of data protection law and with binding powers, resources, and a sole focus on supervising the implementation of legal instruments. Assignation of sufficient human personnel, time, and monetary resources is essential as a recognition of the omnipresence of processing of personal data, particularly for security-related purposes and to ensure that any accountability mechanisms are not of a merely symbolic nature. In connection to migration-related data processing tools, the European Court of Auditors has conducted its own work condensed in a short report that aims to bring together findings relating to passenger name records, Eurosur, and the operational information systems, SIS, Visa Information System, and Eurodac.[28] This is notwithstanding the fact that the intricacies of each of these systems justifies separate analysis.

[25] Regulation (EU) 2018/1240, OJ L236/1, of the European Parliament and of the Council of 12 September 2018 establishing a European Travel Information and Authorisation System (ETIAS) and amending Regulations (EU) No 1077/2011, (EU) No 515/2014, (EU) 2016/399, (EU) 2016/1624 and (EU) 2017/2226.

[26] Regulation (EU) 2019/816, OJ L135/1, of the European Parliament and of the Council of 17 April 2019 establishing a centralised system for the identification of Member States holding conviction information on third-country nationals and stateless persons (ECRIS-TCN) to supplement the European Criminal Records Information System and amending Regulation (EU) 2018/1726.

[27] As indicated by the Cabinet of the EDPS in the GIG-ARTS Conference 'Global Internet Governance and International Human Rights Whose Rights, Whose Interpretations?' that took place on 12–13 April 2022.

[28] European Court of Auditors, 'EU information systems supporting border control - a strong tool, but more focus needed on timely and complete data' (2019).

Curtin and de Goede are also intrigued by the concept of EU overseers that has been employed in the context of the TFTP, criticizing its limitations and flaws in its configuration—an EU overseer may have been preferred due to the cross-border nature of the TFTP requirements. However, EU overseers may be a promising model more broadly, provided that such overseers could have full independence in their role, transparency in their work, and adequate resources. Finally, EU agencies have data protection officers, whose role could be significantly enhanced, so that their input is fully respected at all times, including for example when new data processing rules are being internally created.

Ultimately, this book deals with different boundaries that shape lawmaking. There are the shifting boundaries between personal data as snippets of the identities of known individuals and as collectively used to form algorithms that predict, score, and foresee personalities and future conduct. The blurring boundaries of the technical and the legal leave scholarship on its own to struggle to keep up with technological evolution and make sure that processing of data remains within the boundaries of the law. Thus, as Hildebrandt contends, lawyers—but also legislators—should regroup, before technology developers take over and transform the law, by working together with scientists to understand the underlying technology and get more creative, as De Hert claims, in designing provisions to protect fundamental rights. No matter how tempting harvesting data may be, ultimately convenience and automaticity should not be at the expense of core EU values.

Index

For the benefit of digital users, indexed terms that span two pages (e.g., 52–53) may, on occasion, appear on only one of those pages.